A Great and Grateful Nation:

From Grievance to Gratitude

Jane Hampton Cook

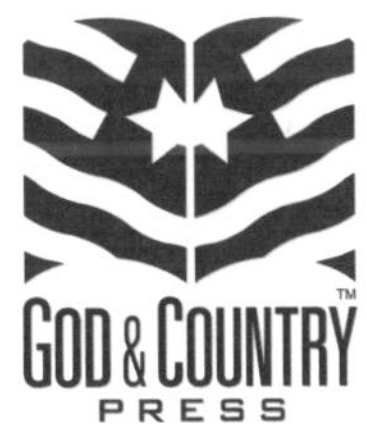

A Great and Grateful Nation: from Grievance to Gratitude

Published by AMG Publishers, Chattanooga, TN

ISBN 13: 978-1-61715-678-6

Printed in Canada

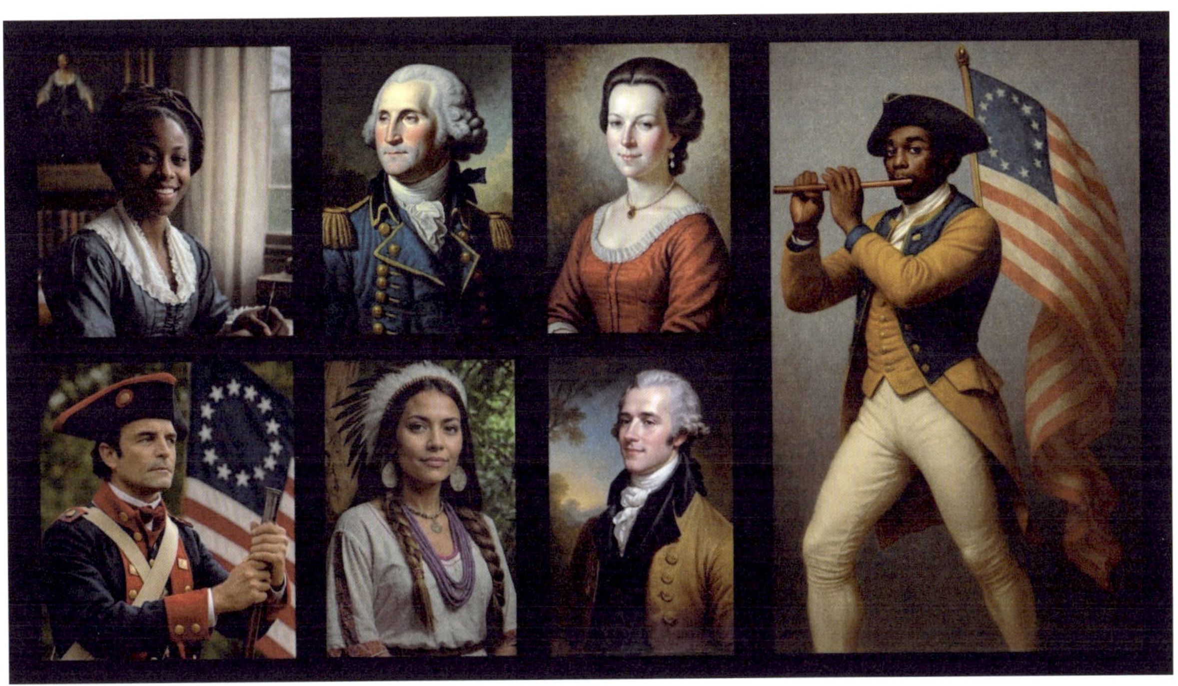

Top row from left to right: Phillis Wheatley, George Washington, Martha Washington, a black fifer (full length). On the bottom row, a soldier from the American Revolution, a Wampanoag female, and Alexander Hamilton.

A word about this book's images. This book features both historical public domain paintings and modern renditions. The modern images generated by AI technology are usually based on faces from original public domain paintings. For example, the above picture of the lady in the red dress is Martha Washington, derived from her face depicted in historical paintings. Why are the originals not used? Often these paintings are not available at a high enough resolution for printing. Jane's goal for this book is to inspire readers through beautiful images and true stories about America's Revolution for America's 250th anniversary.

What Others Are Saying about A Great and Grateful Nation:

"Jane Hampton Cook is one of my favorite contemporary historians. She combines strong research skills and captivating storytelling with a biblical worldview and uplifting, clear-eyed patriotism. From beginning to satisfying ending, Jane holds the reader's attention. Her narratives not only relate accounts from America's storied past but how they relate to the living of these days. This is especially true of her latest book, Great and Grateful Nation. Featuring stunning artwork that makes our Founders instantly relatable to modern readers, the book weaves stories of people and events who helped create and sustain a grateful nation. I strongly suggest this highly readable and enchanting book for readers of all ages. Jane Hampton Cook is making American history great again."

~ Dr. Rebecca Price Janney, Historian and Award-winning author of *East of the Sun* and *The Easton Series*

"America's 250th birthday is around the corner. The true story of American independence reads like a fairy tale. A group of patriots with a love for freedom and trust in God managed to successfully take on the strongest army and navy in the world at that time. Historian Jane Cook has put together a wonderful book on this theme. She reminds us how faith in God was a key factor in how we ever became a new nation. It's not surprising then that America has an annual holiday of Thanksgiving. They were thankful to God then. We should be thankful to God now. The images in this book, many created from AI based on earlier portraits, are truly remarkable. Jane Hampton Cook does great work---as seen in her new book, which I recommend highly."

~Jerry Newcombe, D.Min., executive director of Providence Forum (of Coral Ridge Ministries) and author/co-author of 33 books, including many on America's spiritual roots.

DEDICATION

To my Dad, Larry Hampton, a man who loves his family and taught his children to love their country.

ACKNOWLEDGMENTS

Many thanks to Rebecca Price Janney for her editorial prowess and patriotism. Thanks also belongs to Austin Cook, a sharp-eyed art editor.

CONTENTS

PART I: INTRODUCTION

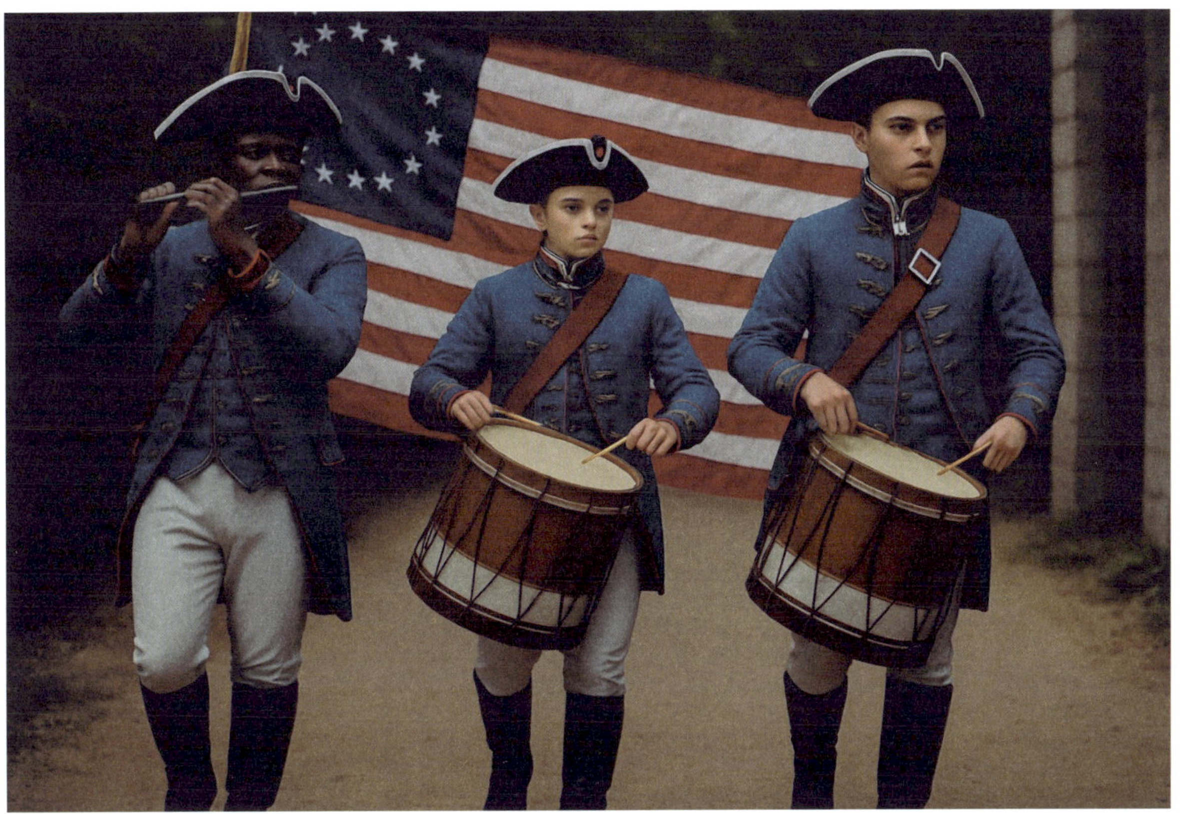

For America's 250th anniversary: A modern rendering of the public domain painting, *The Spirit of 1776*, by Archibald Willard for America's Centennial in 1876.

Jerib Tools and James Sperry were drummers in the First Connecticut Regiment. Barzilai Lew of Massachusetts was a black fifer who played battle commands and *Yankee Doodle* at the Battle of Bunker Hill.

IS AMERICA BECOMING AN UNGRATEFUL NATION?

Is the spirit of 1776 alive as Americans celebrate the nation's 250th birthday? Or is the spirit of liberty on life support? Award-winning scholar Victor Davis Hanson wrote an editorial called *The Ungracious and their Demonization of the Past* in January 2021. He reflected on the decades-long culture war attacking prior generations of U.S. history.[1]

"Critics assume their own judgmental generation is morally superior to those of the past. So, they use their own standards to condemn the mute dead who supposedly do not measure up to them," Hanson explained. "Yet 21st-century critics rarely acknowledge their own present affluence and leisure owe much to history's prior generations whose toil helped create their current comfort."

Hanson identified several modern atrocities that characterize the 2020s, such as rising murder rates, trillions in national debt, and dismal standardized test scores. He asked key questions: "Was it actually moral to discard the 'content of our character' and 'equal opportunity' principles of the prior Civil Rights movement of 60 years ago?"

"Do we ever pause to consider that we enjoy our modern standard of living and security because we were once a meritocracy that quit judging our workforce by tribal affinities and ancient prejudices?"

Hanson pointed out that this trend results in a lack of gratitude, an unhealthy perspective. "Never in history has such a mediocre, but self-important and ungracious generation owed so much, and yet expressed so little gratitude, to its now dead forebears."

"If prior generations were so toxic, why do we continue to take for granted the moral and material world they bequeathed to us, from the Constitution and the Bill of Rights to our airports, freeways, and power plants? Did we ever defeat anything comparable to the Axis powers or Soviet communism?"

He observed that if America is so flawed and racist, then why have the masses sought to settle in the United States? "Shouldn't immigrants at least respect those of the past who created the very country they now so eagerly desire, and died in awful places from Valley Forge to Bastogne to preserve?"

Hanson explained that the symptoms of today's cultural epidemic include demonizing the past, toppling statues, renaming schools, and failing to hold woke modern heroes to the same sinless standards. Today's historical revisions are more of a response to the mob than the result of democratic discussions.

Other symptoms include an absence of patriotic and American history content in education, entertainment, media, books, and products. When was the last time Hollywood funded a feature film about the American Revolution? Twenty years have passed since Mel Gibson ran across the battlefield wielding a giant American flag as a symbol of hope in the Revolutionary War-era feature film, THE PATRIOT.

Over the years, this book's author has been told by a Christian publisher that patriotism doesn't sell. Editors at one of the Smithsonian's institutions asked her to label women's voting rights advocate Susan B. Anthony a racist in an article even though Anthony was an abolitionist who organized petitions calling for the end of slavery during the Civil War.

President Donald Trump described this cultural problem at Mount Rushmore on July 3, 2020: "The radical view of American history is a web of lies – all perspective is removed, every virtue is obscured, every motive is twisted, every fact is distorted, and every flaw is magnified until the history is purged and the record is disfigured beyond recognition."[2] Demonizing America's past leads to the absence of gratitude for the good in America's history. In today's culture, gratitude is a disappearing virtue.

This gift book uses pictures and short essays to show the story of the United States of America's founding. From the nation's beginning, Americans have given thanks to God, especially for their survival and for great, miraculous moments. The people who risked their lives and sacred honor to establish the USA also valued the virtue of gratitude. Likewise, thanksgiving is a shared value that transcends generations and ethnicities.

"Although expressed in many different ways, gratitude practices are deeply embedded in virtually every human society across time and space,"[3] Richard Pickering, deputy director of Plimoth Patuxet Museums, wrote in 2021, which was the 400th anniversary of the historic 1621 Pilgrims-Wampanoag thanksgiving feast that inspired New England's tradition and the national holiday of Thanksgiving.

CAN GRATITUDE UNITE AMERICANS TODAY?

Even though Americans are more diverse than ever, they don't have to be divided. Gratitude helps to bridge the cultural gap between new and long-standing Americans. "After I got here in America, my life completely changed as a free person. Before in North Korea I would probably have died of starvation, but now I'm a college student and have a dream. ... So, I feel very grateful and thankful to America to grant us freedom,"[4] North Korean defector Grace Jo reflected after participating in the White House for Victims of Communism Day in 2019. Through these words, Jo showed that gratitude surpasses ethnicity, race, gender, religion, and other divisions.

Gratitude can unite Americans today through a renewed, healthy perspective. "The only path to unity is to rebuild a shared national identity focused on common American values and virtues of which we have plenty,"[5] President Donald Trump declared in 2020. He also described the American Revolution and subsequent accomplishments in December 2021. "Our miraculous founding, overcoming Civil War, abolishing slavery, defeating communism and fascism, reaching boundless heights of science and discovering so many incredible things ... [show] the United States ultimately becoming a truly great nation."[6]

A Great & Grateful Nation—From Grievance to Gratitude reveals how America became a great nation because Americans were grateful along the way. Through thankfulness, this book shows how previous generations showed grit and gratitude despite their grievances. Gratitude for the great in the nation's past and forgiveness and wisdom from past wrongs are essential for uniting Americans today.

PART II: THE HISTORY OF AMERICA'S FOUNDING

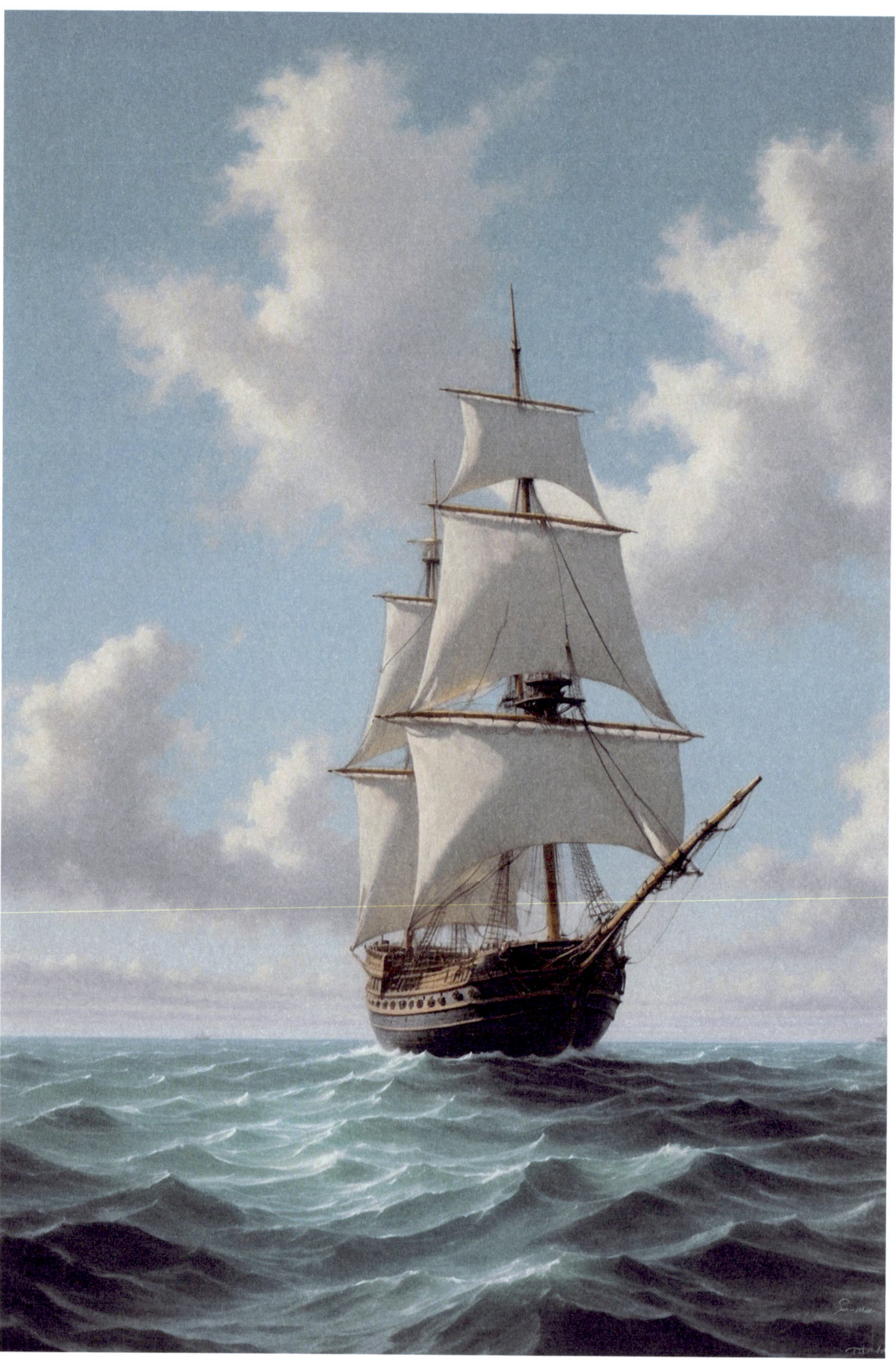

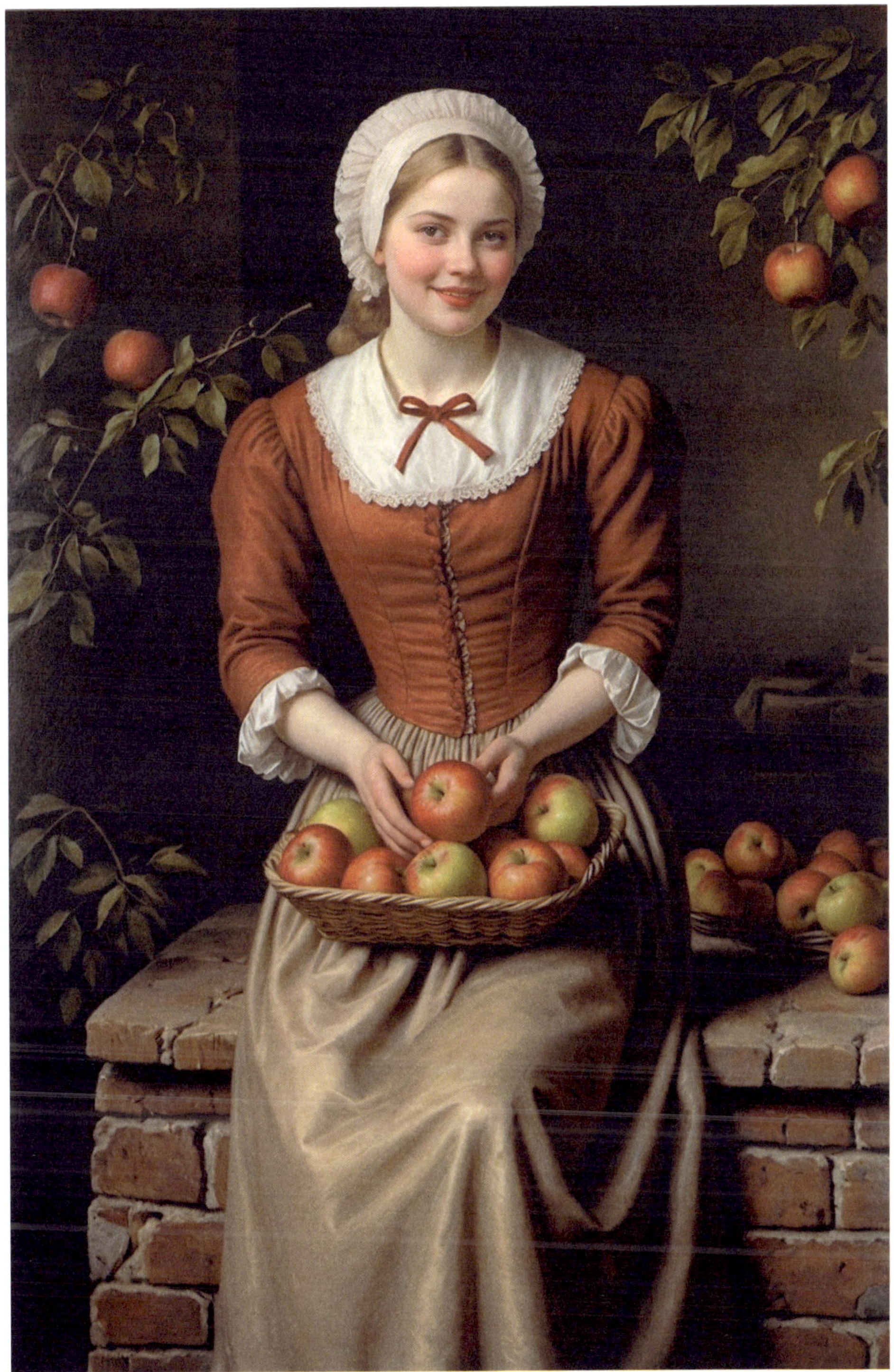

Modern rendition adapted from *A Fair Puritan* by Edward Percy Moran

~5~

CANCELING THANKSGIVING?

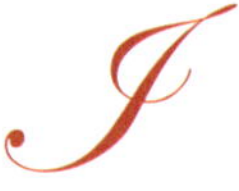n recent years, some extremists have tried to cancel and smear the national holiday of Thanksgiving, which occurs every year on a Thursday in late November. “Thanksgiving canceled?”[7] ran a headline in November 2021.

“Liberal pundits and news outlets across the country are using Thanksgiving week to disparage the holiday and label it a function of white supremacy and genocide,” a news report declared.

In truth, the history of Thanksgiving reveals that giving thanks is a shared value that crosses ethnicities and brings people together through what they have in common.

“Gratitude, one of the most universal of human emotions, runs through all of the traditions surrounding the development of the American Thanksgiving holiday,”[8] Richard Pickering wrote in 2021 in *The Thanksgiving Edition* of the magazine, *Plimoth Patuxet Life*. The year 2021 was the 400th anniversary of the 1621 Thanksgiving in Massachusetts shared by 90 members of the Wampanoag tribe of Pokanoket and 53 members of the *Mayflower* pilgrims of Plymouth. Pickering noted that both the lives of the Plymouth colonists and Pokanoket families were “built around giving thanks.” Both groups “lived with expressions of gratitude for gifts and mercies.”

Before the pilgrims arrived in Massachusetts, giving thanks to the Creator had long been a ceremonial practice of the indigenous people of North and South America. “Great Spirit, thank you for all that is, for all we take, we will give at least our acknowledgment,” Smiling Dove wrote in a poem published by *Plimoth Patuxet*. Indigenous tribes observed the thirteen moons, which included multiple thanksgivings to the Creator for the spawning of herring in spring, the harvesting of strawberries in summer, the reaping of corn in the fall, and the hunting of game in winter.

THE FIRST THANKSGIVING IN NORTH AMERICA?

MASSACHUSETTS 1621

For years, New Englanders cited the 1621 Thanksgiving as the first celebration in America.

“This was the first Thanksgiving in Massachusetts,”[9] the *Salem Gazette* reported on November 25, 1813 about the 1621 event. “Our annual Thanksgivings have been observed from the first settlement of the country. May this institution be ever held sacred.”

Of the 102 *Mayflower* passengers who arrived in December 1620, nearly half died in the winter of 1621. At its worst point, the death rate was two to three a day. Likewise, the Pokanoket had also lost many to an epidemic a few years earlier. Despite their losses, they came together to give thanks. Pilgrim Edward Winslow documented this Thanksgiving in a letter he wrote to a friend in England in 1621:

”Our harvest being gotten in, our governor sent four men on fowling, that so we might after a special manner rejoice together after we had gathered the fruit of our labors,”[10] Winslow wrote of their efforts to hunt wild game, such as turkeys. The Mayflower survivors killed enough birds to serve everyone food for a week. They shared their bounty with the native tribes they had befriended.

"At which time, among other recreations, we exercised our arms, many of the Indians coming amongst us, and among the rest their greatest king Massasoit, with some ninety men, whom for three days we entertained and feasted, and they went out and killed five deer, which they brought to the plantation and bestowed upon our governor, and upon the captain, and others," Winslow explained. This first Thanksgiving included more native tribesmen than pilgrims. He ended this letter with a reflection of gratitude to God for their survival.

"And although it be not always so plentiful as it was at this time with us, yet by the goodness of God, we are so far from want that we often wish you partakers of our plenty."

Governor William Bradford also observed that "besides waterfowl there was great store of wild turkeys of which they took many." Bradford's account indicated that turkey was on the menu for that Thanksgiving. Winslow's letter and Bradford's papers were published together in an 1841 book called *Chronicles of the Pilgrim Fathers*. "This was the first Thanksgiving in America, the harvest festival of New England," the editor of *Chronicles of the Pilgrim Fathers* proclaimed. Branding the 1621 Thanksgiving as the first, this book also sparked interest in the pilgrims that lasted for many years.

Though Thanksgiving was not a national holiday in 1841 or celebrated everywhere, it was observed publicly in Massachusetts, New Hampshire, Rhode Island, Connecticut, Pennsylvania, and New York. The Thanksgiving tradition meant so much to New Englanders, that they took their tradition with them when they moved to other states. One proud New Englander was Sarah Josepha Hale, who published an annual letter in *Godey's Lady's Book* from 1847 to 1863. She called for Thanksgiving to become a national holiday, and President Abraham Lincoln listened to her idea.

In 1863, the same year that the Emancipation Proclamation freed thousands of slaves, and the Battle of Gettysburg, in which thousands died or were injured, President Abraham Lincoln declared Thanksgiving to be an annual national observance on the last Thursday in November. Establishing the national holiday following the emancipation of slaves was a fitting new beginning for America. That year, New York's *Jewish Messenger* published a Thanksgiving prayer on November 20. This Jewish prayer showed the healing power of giving thanks during divisive times and war.

"To him, enthroned on high, be the glory, the praise, the Thanksgiving! In humility and sincerity we bow ... and offer him a hymn of thankfulness, that the nation has not been prostrated ... but that it is emerging from the ordeal stronger and better than ever."[11]

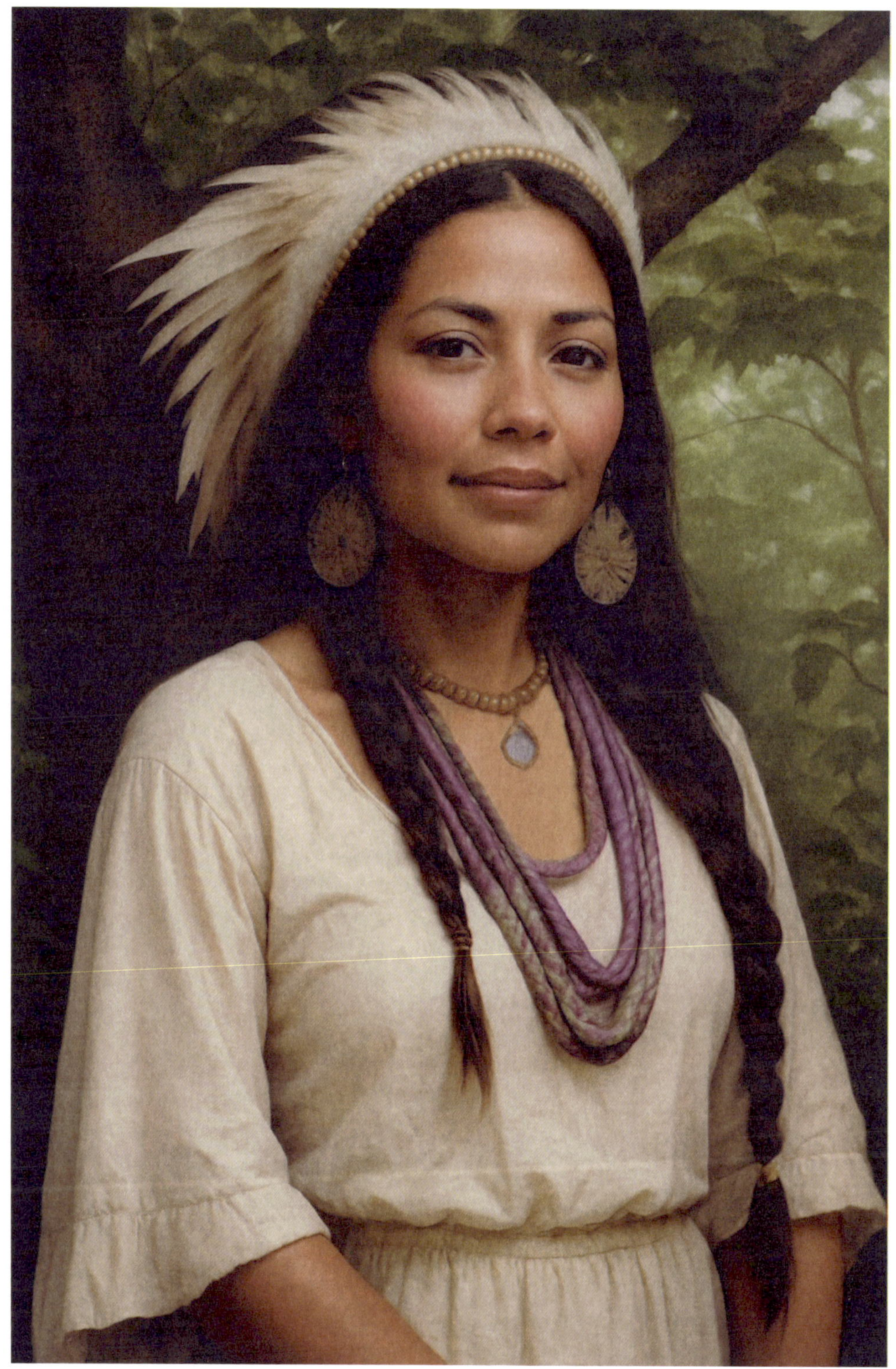

A modern rendering of a Pokanoket woman.

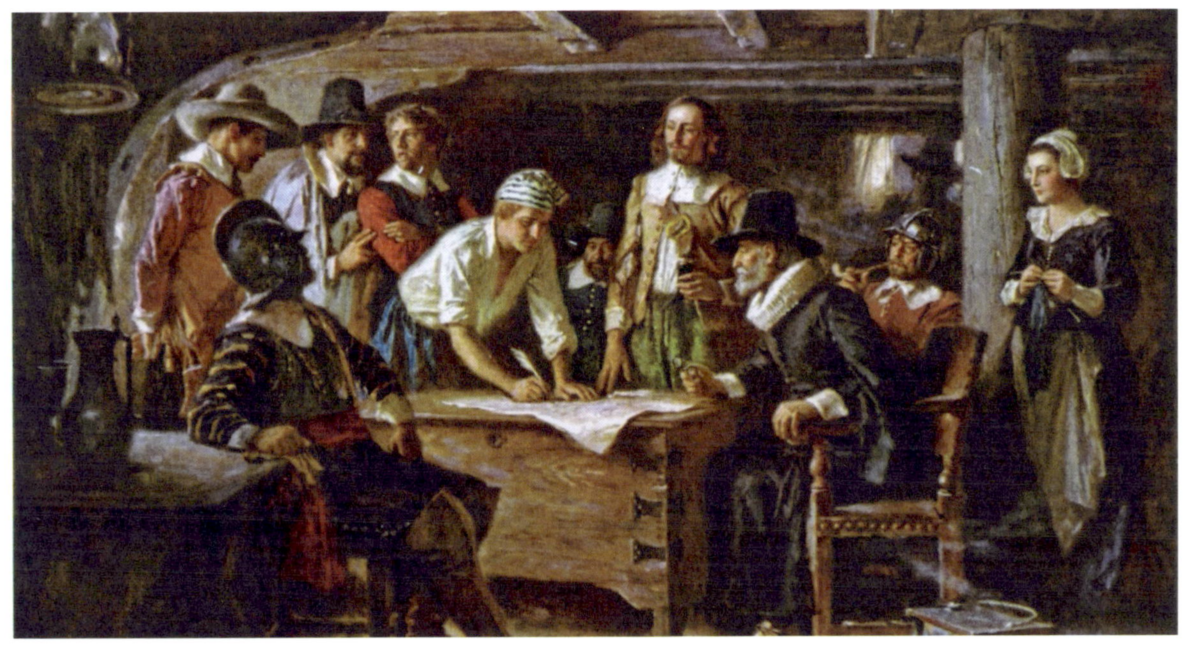

"The Mayflower Compact" by Edward Percy Moran, public domain

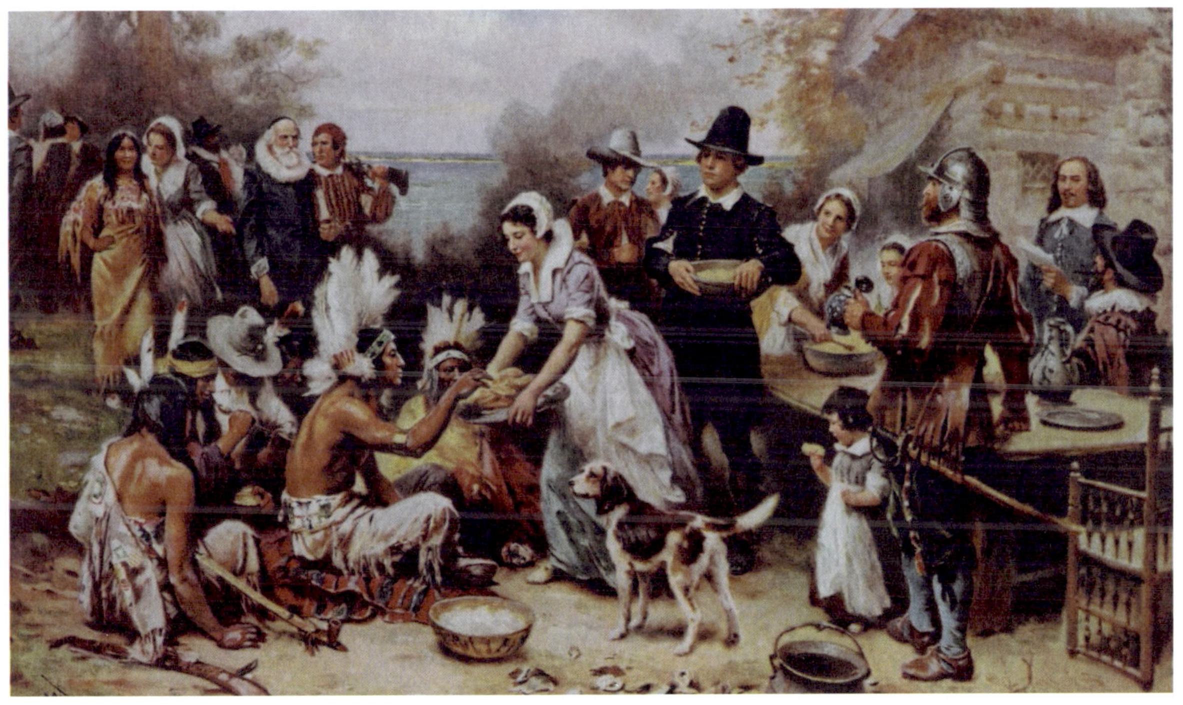

"The First Thanksgiving" (1915) by Jean Louis Gerome Ferris, public domain, Library of Congress

OTHER "FIRST" THANKSGIVINGS

Other states have claimed to be the location of the first European Thanksgiving in America through historic events that predate the Plymouth Thanksgiving.

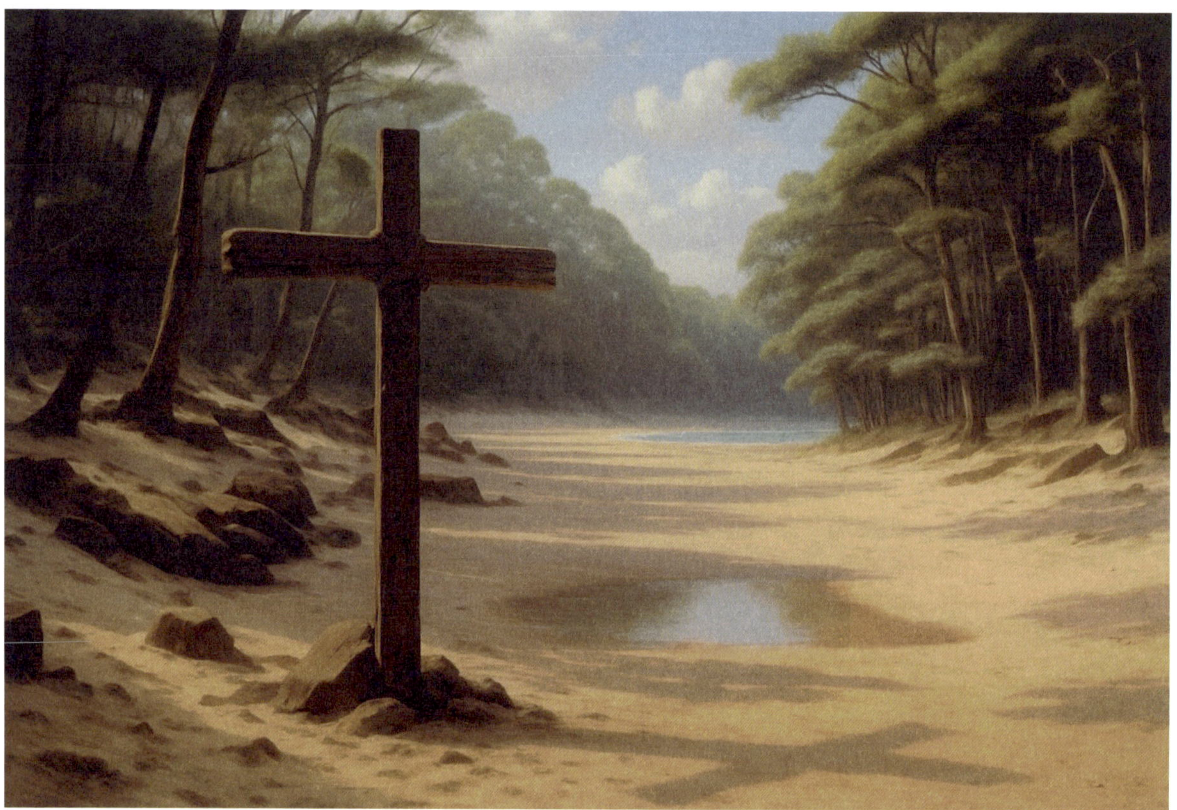

VIRGINIA 1607 AND 1619

The first Europeans to arrive in Virginia gave thanks for surviving their ocean voyage. In the early morning on April 26, 1607, the first permanent settlers of Virginia arrived along the coast. Chaplain Reverend Robert Hunt led these colonists in giving thanks to God for their safe voyage and arrival in a land of fair meadows and tall trees.

On April 29, they symbolized their gratitude by erecting a wooden cross on shore and naming the location Cape Henry, after Henry, the Prince of Wales. They declared:

> *"We do hereby dedicate this land, and ourselves, to reach the people within these shores with the gospel of Jesus Christ, and to raise up godly generations after us, and with these generations take the kingdom of God to all the earth. May this covenant of dedication remain to all generations, as long as this earth*

remains, and may this land, along with England, be evangelist to the world. May all who see this cross, remember what we have done here, and may those who come here to inhabit join us in this covenant and in this most noble work that the holy scriptures may be fulfilled."[12]

This event is called the First Landing. A few years later, another group came to Virginia with the intention of making Thanksgiving an annual observance.

"First Thanksgiving in America Was Decreed for Town of Berkley on James [River],"[13] declared a headline in the *Richmond News Leader* on April 3, 1931. This news explained that newly-discovered papers documenting the 1619 thanksgiving predated Plymouth's thanksgiving by two years.

"We ordain that this day of our ship's arrival ... in the land of Virginia, shall be yearly and perpetually kept holy as a day of Thanksgiving to Almighty God," Captain John Woodlief prayed in a worship service. He led 38 Britons as they landed in Virginia on December 4, 1619. Despite their plans, this Thanksgiving did not become a regular or annual tradition.

FLORIDA 1664-65

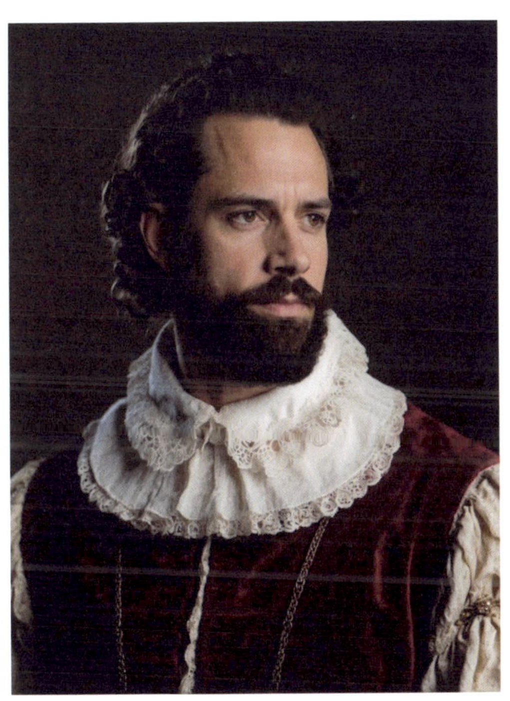

Rene Goulaine de Laudonnière

Virginia was not alone in claiming the first Thanksgiving. Fervent Floridians made an archival argument. Surely the French-speaking Protestants, called French Huguenots, or the Spanish-speaking Catholic Spaniards who arrived in Florida in the 1500s also held a Thanksgiving observance for their arrival and survival? They were correct.

"We sang a psalm of Thanksgiving unto God, beseeching him that it would please his Grace to continue his accustomed goodness toward us,"[14] French Huguenot (Protestant) Rene Goulaine de Laudonnière wrote about a thanksgiving service held in June 1564 to celebrate a new fort, Fort Caroline, in Florida. Tapping their shared value of gratitude, Laudonnière and the French Protestants feasted with the Timucuans to give thanks. A year later, Pedro Menéndez de Avilés led 800 Spaniards onto the shores of St. Augustine, Florida. They held a thanksgiving mass.

TEXAS 1541

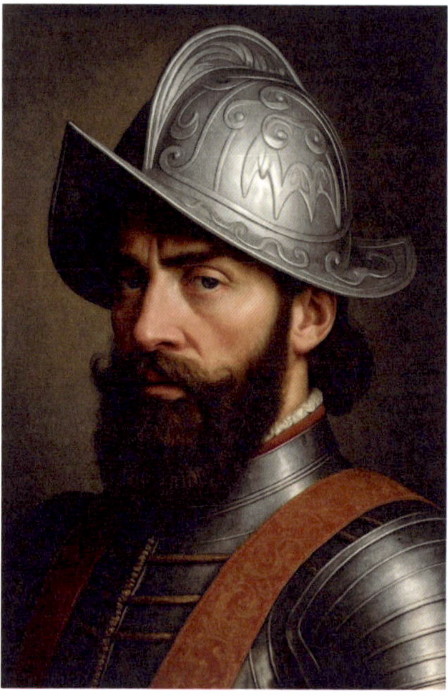
Francisco Vázquez de Coronado

Not to be outdone by Floridians, Texans have also claimed Thanksgiving fame. "On May 29, 1541 with supplies depleted, Coronado entered Palo Duro Canyon,"[15] a 1973 Texas historical marker declared about the expedition of Francisco Vázquez de Coronado. Searching for the golden Seven Cities of Cíbola, this Spaniard and his entourage of 300 Spaniards and 1,000 indigenous people arrived at near present-day Amarillo, Texas after traveling from Mexico.

By the time Coronado came to the land of the friendly Tejas, they were desperate to survive, especially after a hail storm had damaged their supplies and horses. Needing to regroup and reprioritize, Coronado called for a spiritual act of giving thanks, despite not finding the city of gold.

"According to legend, Fray Juan De Padilla conducted a feast of Thanksgiving for the group while in Palo Duro Canyon," the Texas historical marker explained of the ascension mass. Likewise, Captain Pedro Reyes Castañeda, who admired the Tejas' hunting skills, observed that "they killed 500 bulls" and prepared "jerked beef to take with them"[16] Hence, the first European-Indigenous Thanksgiving in America was not over turkey or seafood but over barbecue.

PERSPECTIVE TAKING

The larger point is not which Thanksgiving was first. That claim belongs to the indigenous tribes who for centuries gave thanks thirteen times a year to the Creator in rituals. The point is that giving thanks to God was common to all cultures in some form. Do these multiple *first* thanksgivings mean that all these groups, both European and indigenous, were saints to be celebrated for their lifelong innocence and sinless lives? No. That line of thinking reflects the ridiculous logic of today's history revisionists who seek to destroy Thanksgiving as a holiday.

Intense conflict and fighting existed between Protestants and Catholics in Europe that spilled over into the groups who took refuge in America. Sometimes animosity between the native tribes and colonists led to atrocities from both sides. For example, the Virginia Thanksgiving ended in 1622 after some members of the Powhatan nation massacred 300 of 1,000 Virginia colonists. The author of this book's ancestors, William and Joanna Hampton, survived this attack.

In recent years, some have tried to blame the pilgrims of Plymouth for the sins of others in different colonies and in later generations by calling for mourning on Thanksgiving Day. This is unfair and detracts from the positive message of the joint 1621 Thanksgiving between the pilgrims and the Pokanoket. It also detracts from the long-lasting alliance that held between the two groups for more than 50 years.

"Yet if we resist the temptation to judge the event based on what came after it and reexamine it in its historical moment, the three days of feasting and pastimes become a remarkable meeting between new allies who needed one another," Kate LaPrad managing editor of *Plimoth Patuxet Life* reflected. "The nation's Thanksgiving tradition was born of a particular moment in the 17th century New England. Two fragile communities with recent experiences of tragedy—the Pokanoket and the Pilgrims—found themselves on the same landscape at precisely the same moment in the fall of 1621."[17]

These first thanksgivings show that despite their different theologies, giving thanks to God was a shared spiritual value between the colonists and native people. Regardless of humanity's flawed state, these thanksgivings reveal that giving thanks crossed language barriers. Regardless of whether they spoke English, Spanish, French or a native language, they paused and took time to give thanks to God for specific experiences.

Today, gratitude allows us to appreciate the accomplishments of those who went before us. It also enables us to show forgiveness for the sins of others in the past and look forward to the future with hope. Now it's time to discover the story of independence in America as part of America's 250th anniversary.

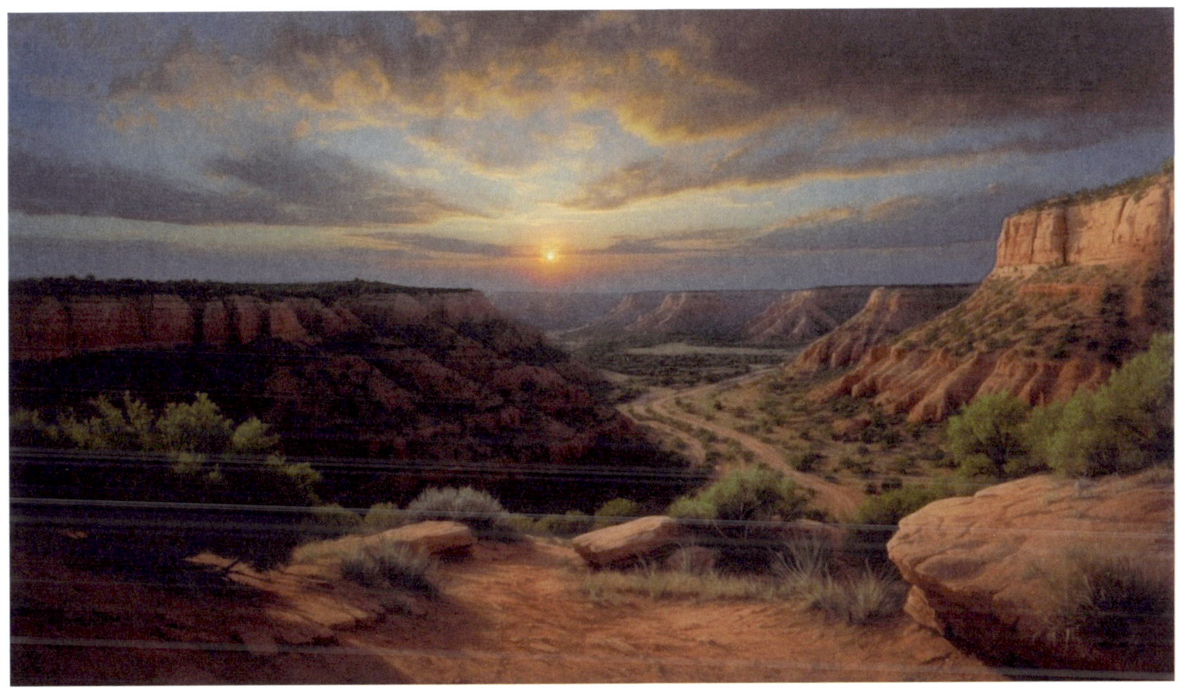

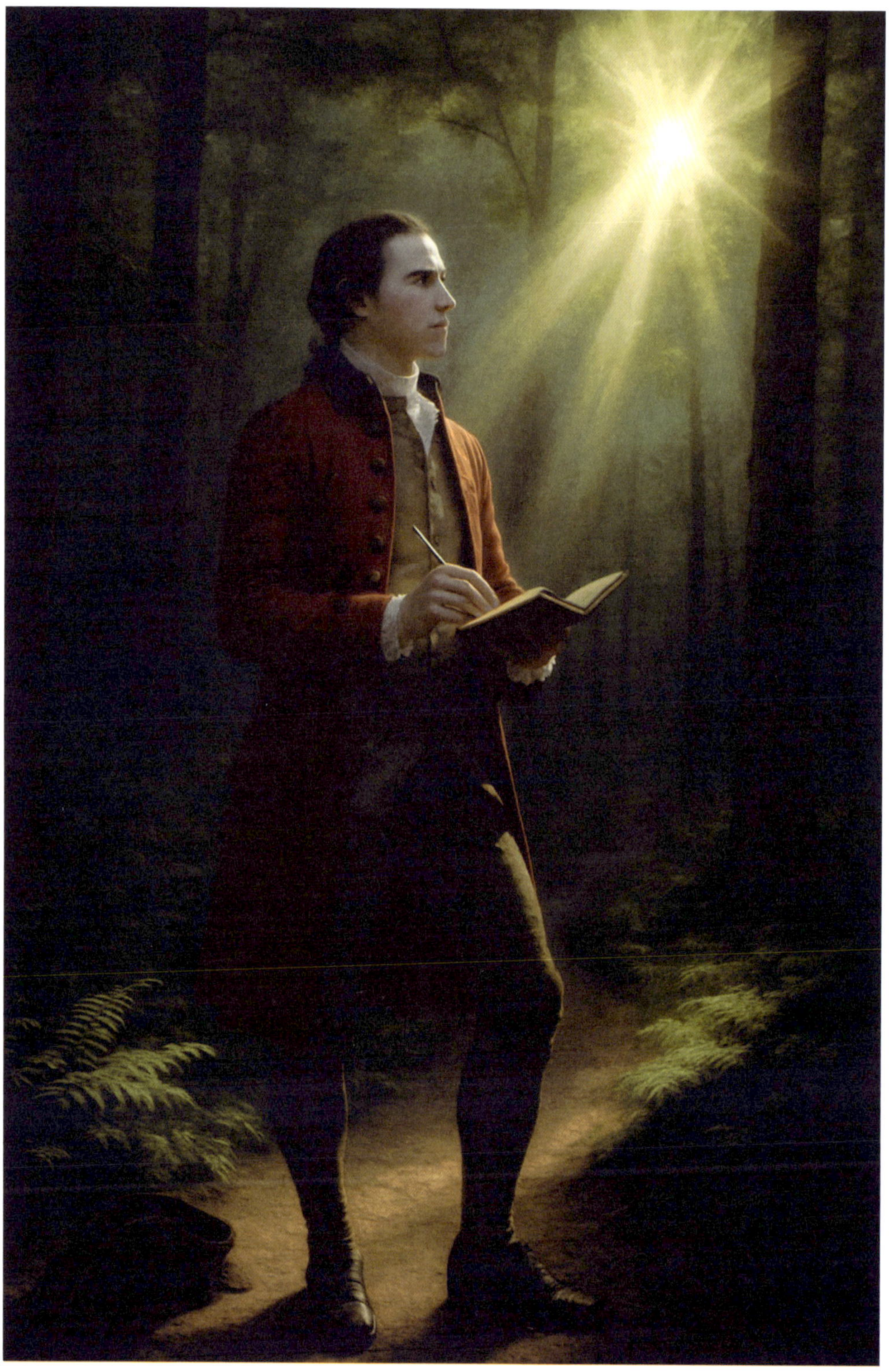

A modern interpretation of George Washington surveying the wilderness in the 1750s

PROVIDENTIAL BEGINNINGS

A STANDING MIRACLE

"The singular interpositions of Providence in our feeble condition were such, as could scarcely escape the attention of the most unobserving, while the unparalleled perseverance of the armies of the United States, through almost every possible suffering and discouragement, for the space of eight long years, was little short of a standing miracle."[18] ~ George Washington, Farewell Address to the Army, November 2, 1783

When he said goodbye to his soldiers at the end of the Revolutionary War in 1783, General George Washington was thankful. He described their victory over the greatest army at the time, the British military, as "little short of a standing miracle." Washington gratefully credited Providence, which ministers defined as God's Presence, for their victory.

Washington was no stranger to miracles. He had used similar words three decades earlier in 1755 when he experienced a miraculous survival on the battlefield at the age of 23 as a colonel in what historians call the French and Indian War, which pitted the English and their native allies against the French and their native allies.

"As I have heard since my arrival at this place, a circumstantial account of my death and dying speech, I take this early opportunity of assuring you that I have not, as yet, composed the latter. But by the all-powerful dispensation of Providence, I have been protected beyond all human probability and expectation for I had four bullets through my coat and two horses shot under me, yet although death was levelling my companions on every side of me, escaped unhurt," Washington wrote his brother Jack on July 18, 1755.[19]

Colonel Washington was part of a joint force of Virginia militia and regular British soldiers, who were ambushed by the French and their native allies on July 9, 1755, in the Ohio River Valley near what is now Pittsburg. A few weeks later, Presbyterian minister Samuel Davies preached to soldiers in Hanover, Virginia. Davies, who had been part of the Great Awakening spiritual movement, gave a prophetic word about Washington's survival. "As a remarkable instance of this, I may point out to the public that heroic youth Colonel Washington, whom I cannot but hope Providence has hitherto preserved in so signal a manner, for some important service to his country."[20]

Davies was not the only one to predict that Washington's life had been spared for future service to a great nation. Years later in 1770, when Washington returned to the Ohio River Valley, a chief visited Washington and gave him a prophetic oracle.

The chief remembered Washington from the July 1755 battle because Washington's towering height caused him to stand out among the officers. Back then, he had told his young warriors to aim for Washington, but they'd repeatedly missed. Their attempt to kill him "was all in vain, a power mightier far than we, shielded him from harm."[21] This miraculous protection led him to predict that Washington would not die in battle but would lead a nation. “Listen! The Great Spirit protects that man, and guides his destinies — he will become the chief of nations, and a people yet unborn will hail him as the founder of a mighty empire.”

The chief’s oracle made a strong impression on Dr. James Craik, a physician who was with Washington at the time. Craik later accompanied Washington during the Revolutionary War. “Yes, I do believe, a Great Spirit protects that man — and that one day or other, honored and beloved, he will be the chief of our nation, as he is now our general, our father, and our friend. Never mind the enemy, they cannot kill him, and while he lives, our cause will never die,” Craik declared in 1777. Believing in the justice of America’s cause, Washington’s perseverance and commitment to preserve the army led to America’s miraculous founding.

“You gave me life and showed me kindness, and in your Providence, watched over my spirit,” Job 10:12

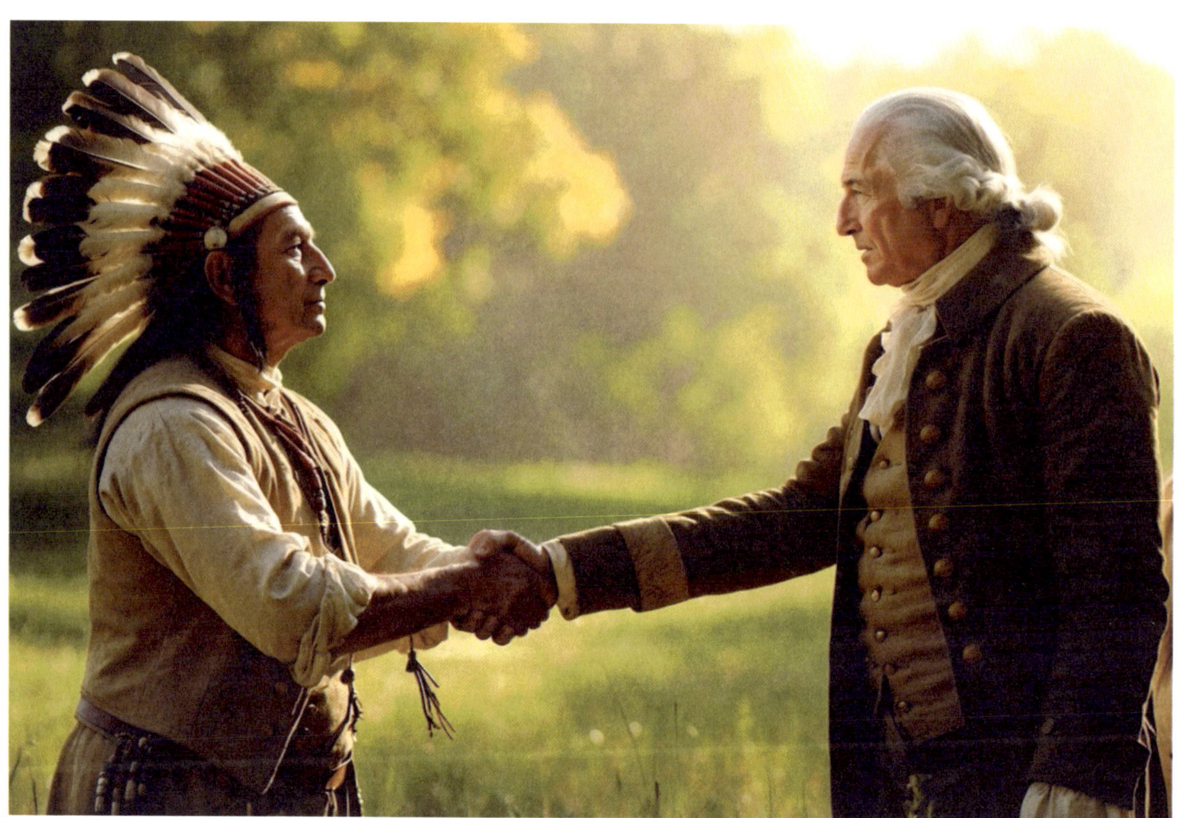

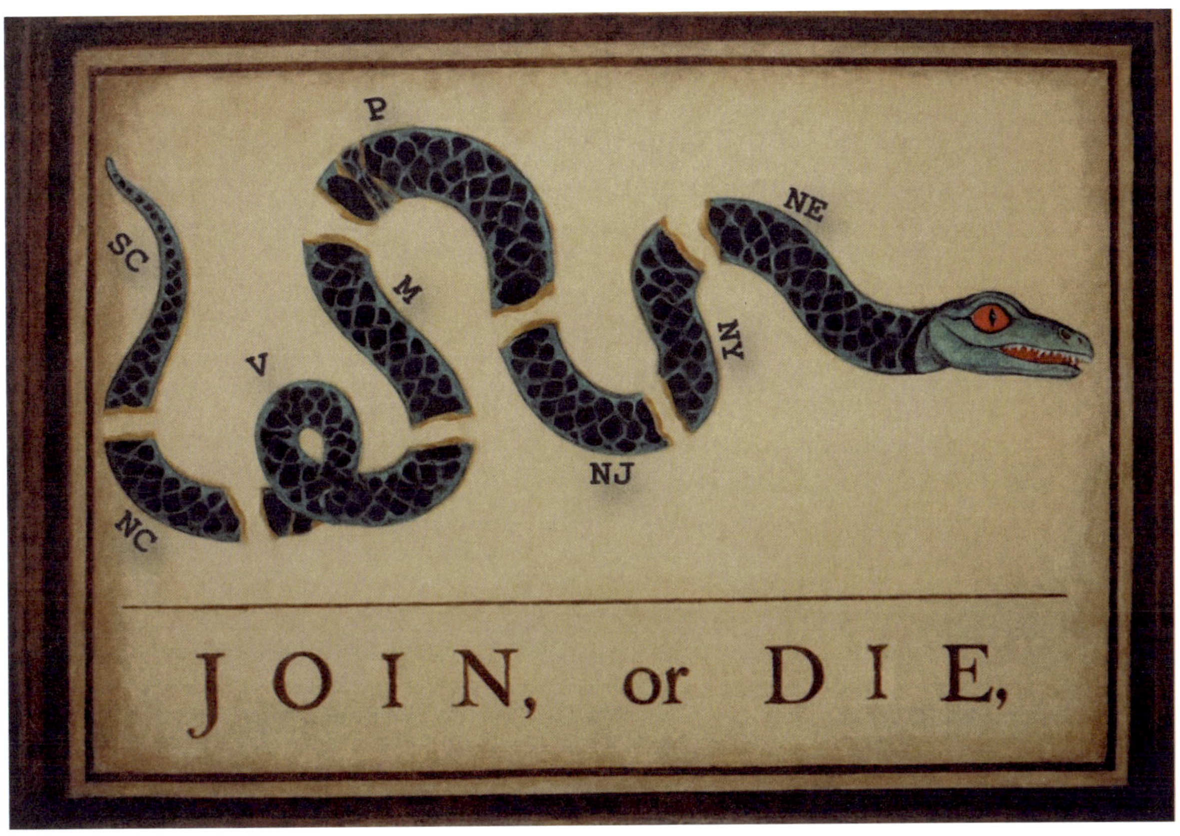

A modern rendering of Benjamin Franklin's Join or Die graphic depicting the 13 original states through segments of a snake.

JOIN OR DIE

Ben Franklin created and published the *Join or Die* graphic, the first political newspaper cartoon in America, in the *Pennsylvania Gazette* on May 9, 1754. Franklin used the word *join* three times to make his point that Britain's American colonies needed to join together and unite to fight the French.

"In the present disunited state of the British colonies and the extreme difficulties of bringing so many different governments and assemblies to agree in any speedy and effectual measures for our common defense and security," he wrote, noting that in contrast "our enemy have the very great distinction of being under one direction with one council and one purse."[22] The article accompanying this graphic was about a report from the newsmaker of the era, George Washington.

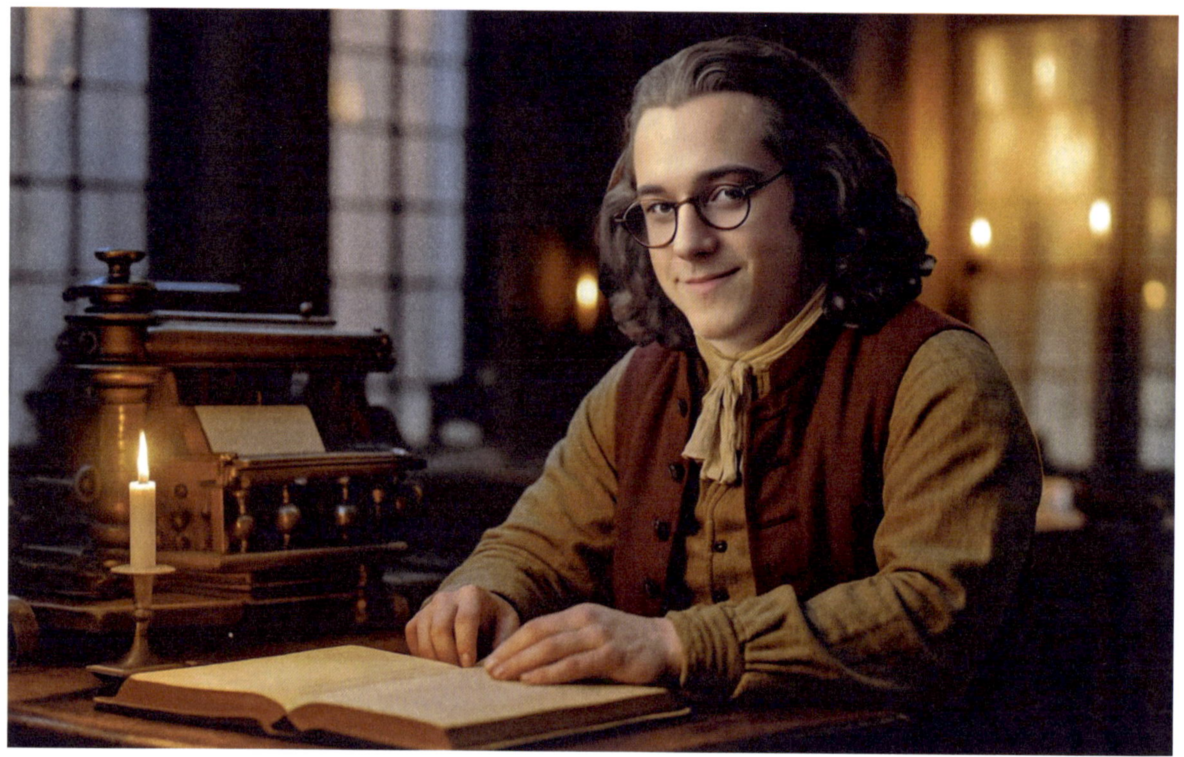

A modern rendition of Benjamin Franklin at work

COLONIAL CANCEL CULTURE & FREE SPEECH

Decades before the first shots of the French and Indian War in the 1750s and the American Revolution in the 1770s were fired, newspaper publisher Ben Franklin experienced colonial-style cancel culture. Newspapers were new in America in the 1720s and 1730s. The rise of this new social media presented challenges in the culture and to the government. Franklin's response and practices set the standards for enacting freedom of the press and freedom of speech in newspapers that endured for centuries in America.

"Being frequently censur'd and condemn'd by different persons for printing things which they say ought not to be printed, I have sometimes thought it might be necessary to make a standing apology for myself, and publish it once a year,"[23] Franklin printed in a newspaper article on June 10, 1731, in his *Pennsylvania Gazette*.

Franklin was being culturally canceled because he had published an advertisement from a ship captain that insulted the clergy by comparing them to loud birds. "Men are very angry with me on this occasion, that it could proceed from nothing but my abundant malice against religion and the clergy. They therefore declare they will not take any more of my papers, nor have any further dealings with me; but will hinder me of all the custom they can. All this is very hard!"

Denying him custom meant that they were socially ostracizing him. "I request all who are angry with me on the account of printing things they don't like, calmly to consider these following particulars," he wrote, appealing to their logic. "That the business of printing has chiefly to do with men's opinions; most things that are printed tending to promote some, or oppose others," he explained, believing that "the opinions of men are almost as various as their faces." He noted that most professions, such as carpenters and shoemakers, sold their products to everyone of all persuasions, religions, and ethnicities, without risk of "suffering the least censure or ill-will" or offending them.

"That it is as unreasonable ... to expect (everyone) to be pleas'd with everything that is printed, as to think that nobody ought to be pleas'd but themselves." His job was not to tell people what to think but to give people a chance to make up their own minds through conflicting opinions.

"Printers are educated in the belief that when men differ in opinion, both sides ought equally to have the advantage of being heard by the public," Franklin wrote. "Being thus continually employ'd in serving all parties, printers naturally acquire a vast unconcernedness as to the right or wrong opinions contain'd in what they print," he explained of tolerance. "They print things full of spleen and animosity, with the utmost calmness and indifference, and without the least ill-will to the persons reflected on." Franklin's role was to allow others to communicate without controlling them.

"That it is unreasonable to imagine printers approve of everything they print, and to censure them on any particular thing accordingly; since in the way of their business they print such great variety of things opposite and contradictory." What would happen if publishers and editors only printed opinions they agreed with? "An end would thereby be put to free writing, and the world would afterwards have nothing to read but what happen'd to be the opinions of printers."

In his view, freedom of speech would end and the world would only know one point of view, that of the publishers. Franklin avoided items that would "do real injury to any person, how much soever I have been solicited, and tempted with offers of great pay."

What did he believe would happen when different hypotheses were presented, whether in science, literature, or religion? The truth would win in the end. "That when truth and error have fair play, the former is always an overmatch for the latter." Thus, Franklin set standards for free speech and freedom of the press. He believed that truth and evidence would win instead of error and falsehoods. His printing presses were the neutral referee. Franklin declared that he would not be canceled. "I shall continue my business. I shall not burn my press and melt my letters."

INJUSTICES BEHIND THE FIRST AMENDMENT

Years earlier Franklin had witnessed government tyranny as the British authorities tried to cancel the business of his older brother, James. When officials in Boston didn't like James's newspaper, they threw him in jail for not having a government license to publish. Though he was only 16, Benjamin took over printing his brother's paper, the *New England Courant*. Using the nickname Silence Dogood to conceal his identity, Ben published a series of essays promoting freedom of speech and freedom of the press.

"Without freedom of thought there can be no such thing as wisdom and no such thing as public liberty without freedom of speech. ... Whoever would overthrow the liberty of a nation, must begin by subduing freeness of speech . . ."[24] he published in his jailed brother's newspaper on July 9, 1722.

Although government officials freed James, they published a resolution against him and attempted to control what he and others published. "Resolved, that no such weekly paper be hereafter printed or published without the same be first perused and allowed by the secretary, as has been usual (for other papers)."[25]

Ben never forgot this censorship lesson. Moving to Philadelphia, he bought a newspaper business and published the *Pennsylvania Gazette*. Because the Southern colonies had few printing presses, he also published *Poor Richard's Almanac* for all the colonies. Through these publications, Franklin vaulted the newspaper industry into a golden age. Newspapers opened the colonists' minds to knowledge about each other and played a key role along the road to revolution. For these reasons, Franklin deserves to be called the father of freedom of speech and the press in America.

A CULTURE OF GRATITUDE

Following the habits of the pilgrims and first settlers, giving thanks to God was an important part of Franklin's culture. First, thanksgiving was a regular part of weekly worship, whether the worshippers were Maryland's Catholics, Rhode Island's and Philadelphia's Jews, or Protestants from New England to Georgia.

Second, celebrating an annual harvest and listening to Thanksgiving sermons were important times of giving thanks. Though not a widespread national observance in Franklin's day, showing gratitude through feasting and worship remained common.

Third, giving thanks was a private practice. Franklin wrote a personal liturgy that he used in place of attending public worship. His liturgy included adoration, petition, and thanks to God. "I had some years before compos'd a little liturgy or form of prayer for my own private use, viz, in 1728 entitled Articles of Belief and Acts of Religion."[26]

Franklin thanked God for life's essentials. "For peace and liberty, for food and raiment, for corn and wine, and milk, and every kind of healthful nourishment—Good God, I thank thee." Fittingly for this freedom of speech advocate, he also focused on God's gift of words, which he loved. "For knowledge and literature and every useful art; for my friends and their prosperity, and for the fewness of my enemies,—Good God, I thank thee. For all thy innumerable benefits; for life and reason, and the use of speech, for health and joy and every pleasant hour,—my Good God, I thank thee."

GRIEVANCES & TYRANNY ~ THE ROAD TO REVOLUTION

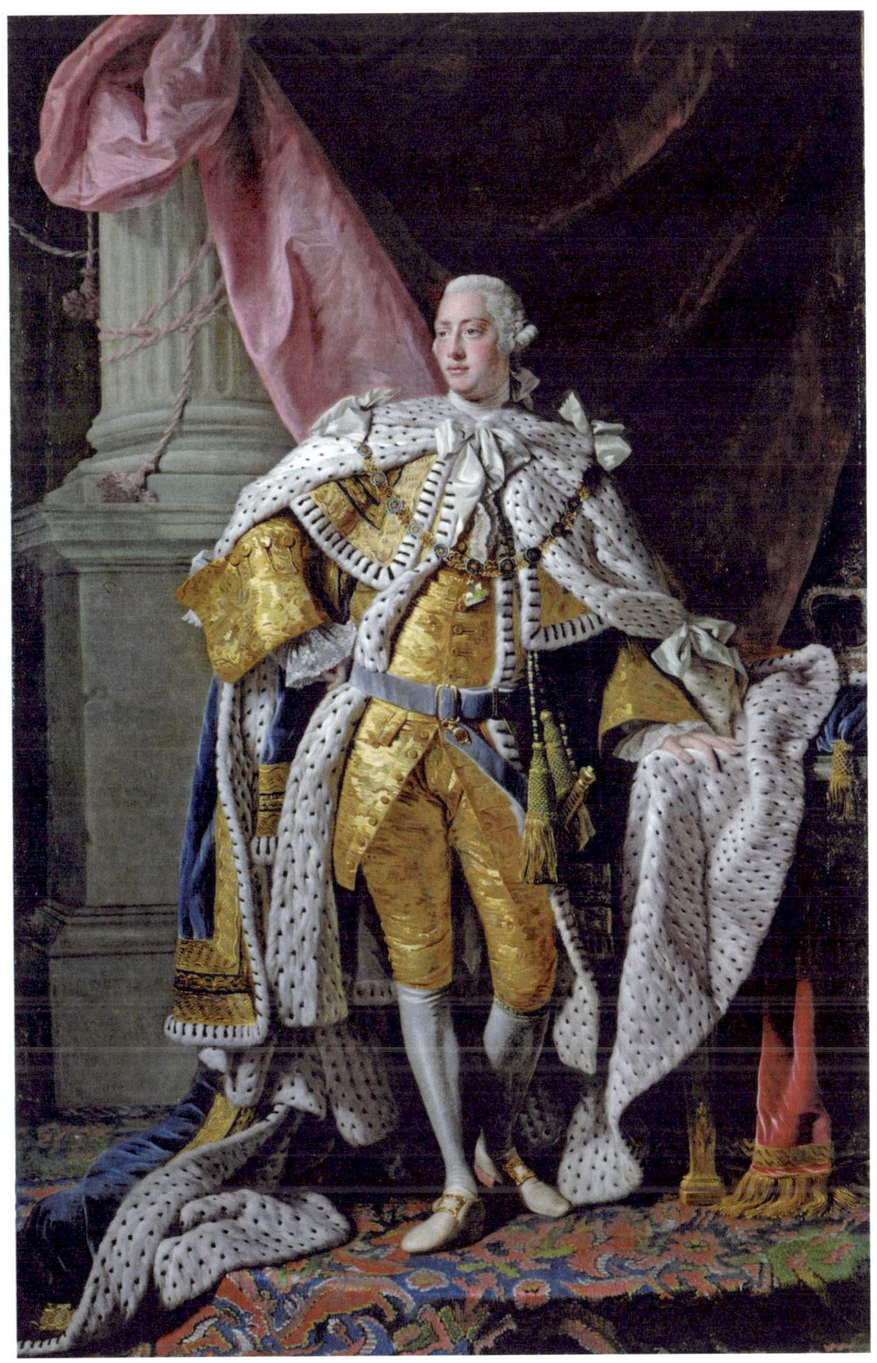

King George III by Allan Ramsey

KING GEORGE III ASCENDS TO THE THRONE–1760

"Born and educated in this country, I glory in the name of Britain,"[27] King George III said upon becoming king in 1760 after the death of his grandfather, King George II, who spoke English with a German accent. At the start of his reign, the new king wanted to prove that he was not a German but a true son of England.

"Do not stand up for a bad cause, for the king will do whatever he pleases," Ecclesiastes 8:3

TYRANNICAL TAXES–1764

Though the colonists were used to paying transportation costs for imported items from England, they were not accustomed to pay the king taxes on top of these conveyance costs. Because the colonists governed themselves through town councils and legislatures this was a radical shift. Unlike British subjects in England, British subjects in America were not represented by members of Parliament.

THE STAMP ACT–1765

Conflict with King George III intensified in 1765 because of the Stamp Act, which imposed a tax on all papers and official documents in the American colonies. From petitioning Parliament to threatening Stamp Tax collectors, many colonists refused to buy the stamps and place them on their paper documents.

"The Stamp Act, imposed on the colonies by the Parliament of Great Britain, engrosses the conversation of the speculative part of the colonists, who look upon this unconstitutional method of taxation, as a direful attack upon their liberties, and loudly exclaim against the violation ... the advantage accruing to the mother country will fall greatly short of the expectations, for certain it is, our whole substance does already in a manner flow to Great Britain,"[28] George Washington wrote to his wife's uncle in England.

"And the eyes of our people, already beginning to open, will perceive, that many luxuries, which we lavish our substance in Great Britain for, can well be dispensed with, whilst the necessaries of life are (mostly) to be had within ourselves," Washington wrote.

INJUSTICES BEHIND THE FOURTH AMENDMENT

To enforce his taxes, the king allowed British authorities to search Boston homes for smuggling evidence without a judicial warrant. Decades later in 1791, these warrant abuses led Americans to approve the Constitution's Fourth Amendment to prevent warrantless searches in the future.

THE SONS OF LIBERTY

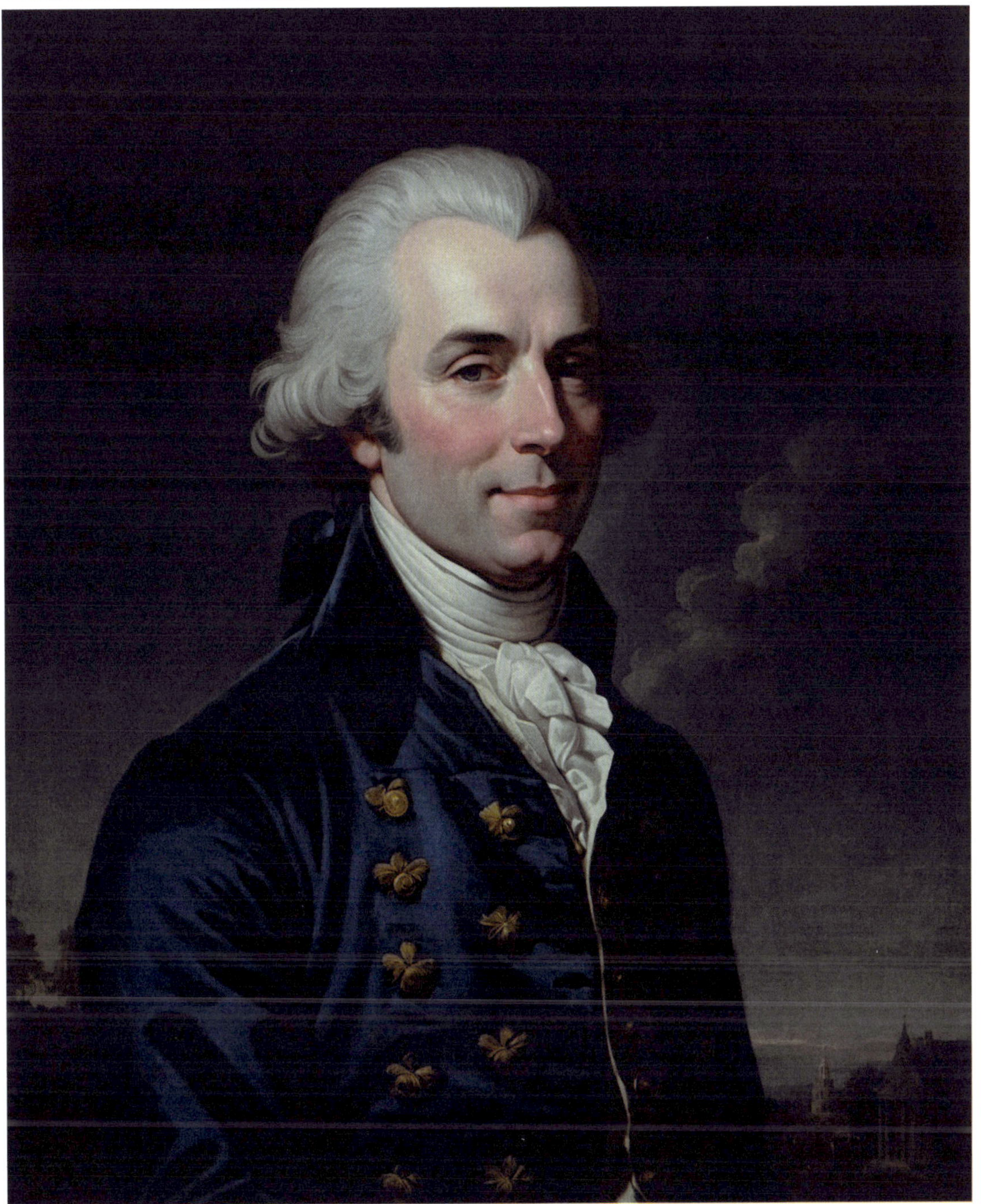

Remixed from a public domain image, John Hancock led the Sons of Liberty.

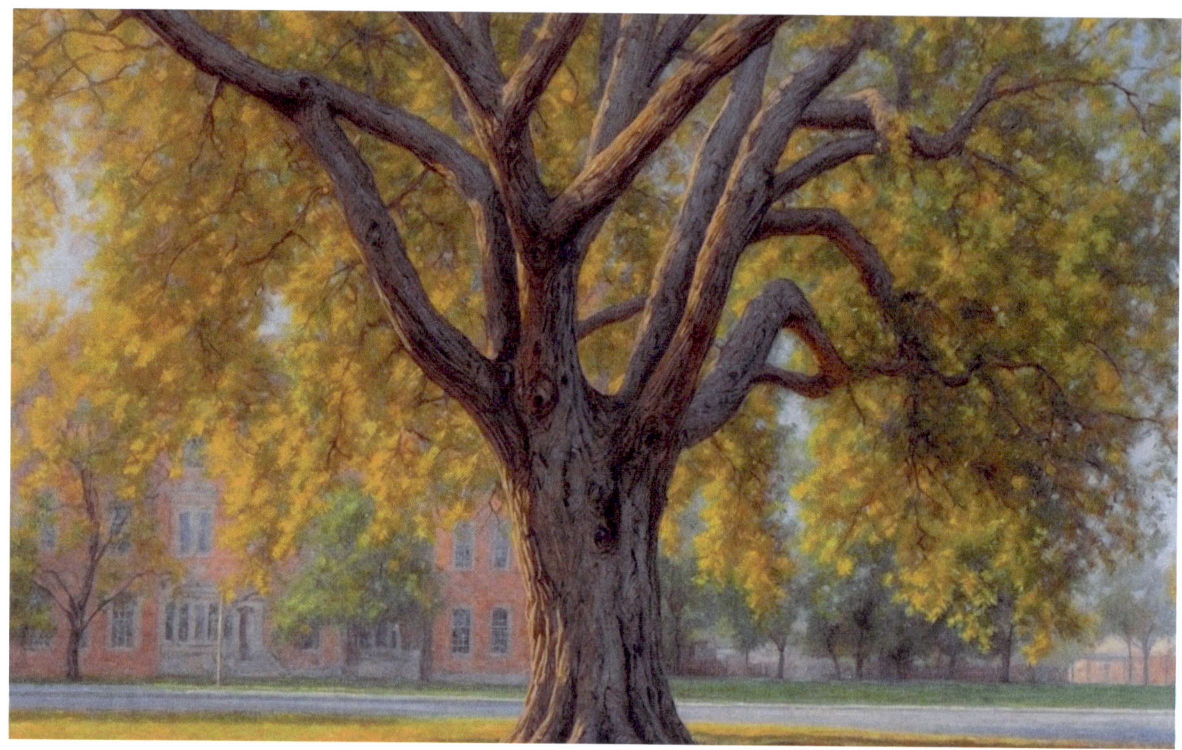

A large elm tree in Boston, the Liberty Tree was where the Sons of Liberty met and protested starting in 1765. British soldiers cut the tree down in 1775 during their siege of Boston.

John Hancock and Samuel Adams led the Sons of Liberty, an underground network who resisted King George's policies through newspapers, demonstrations, protests, and riots. Hancock was a successful Boston merchant who cared deeply about trade issues. Rather than a duty on traded goods, the Stamp Act became the first direct tax on commerce within the colonies. This paradigm-shift greatly concerned Hancock.

"I would advise you to be careful who you trust, times are very bad and precarious here and take my word, my good friends, the times will be worse here, in short such is the situation of things here that we do not know who is and who (is) not safe. I hardly know who to trust,"[29] John Hancock wrote in 1765. "It is very cruel, we were before much burdened oh, we shall not be able much longer to support trade, and in the end Great Britain must feel the ill effects of it."

As clerk for the lower house of the Massachusetts Assembly, Samuel Adams wrote official letters to protest these new taxes. He also wrote newspaper articles under nicknames to conceal his identity. "It seems to be generally agreed, that every man who is

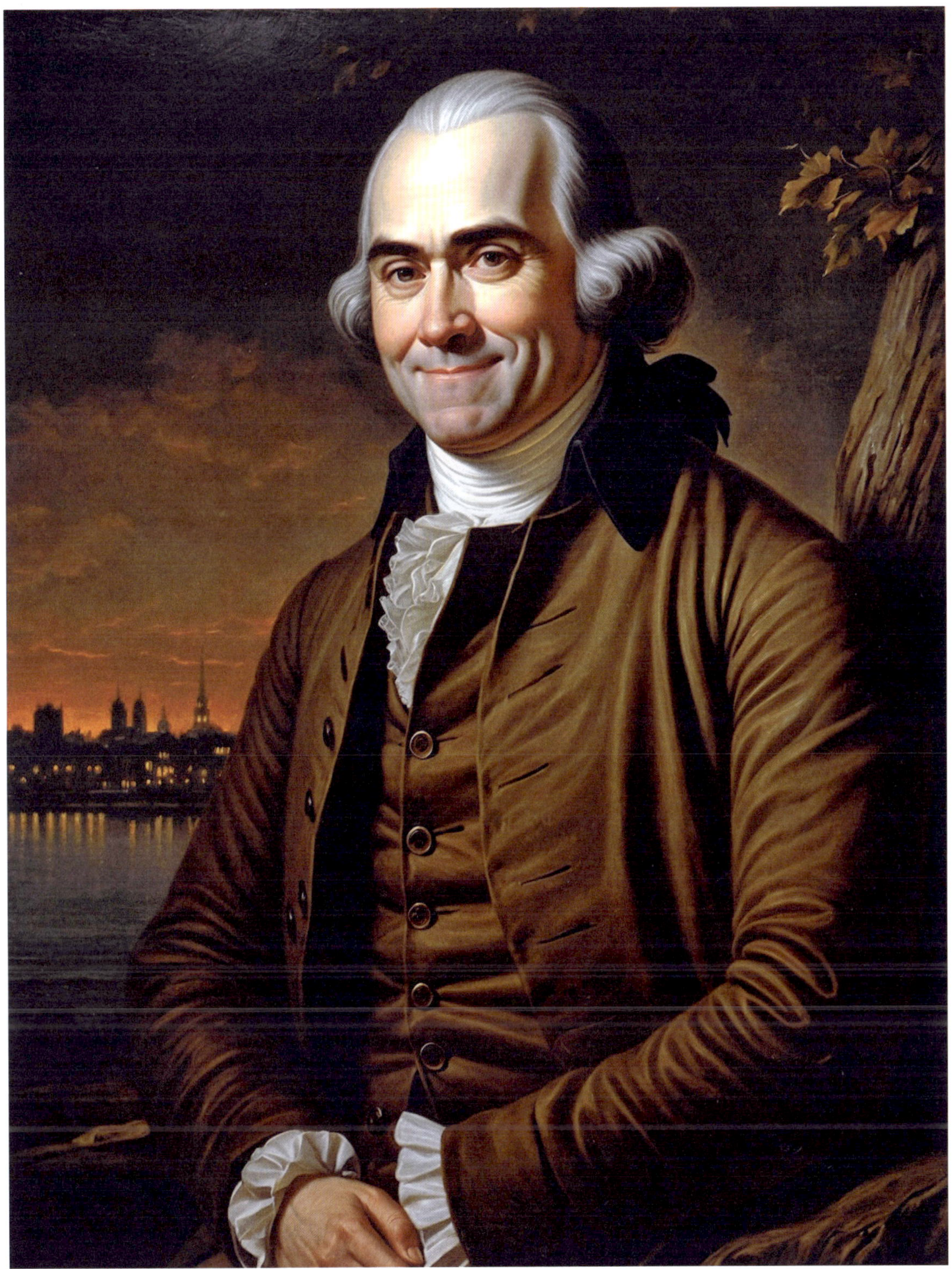

This new rendering of Samuel Adams is adapted from public domain portraits.

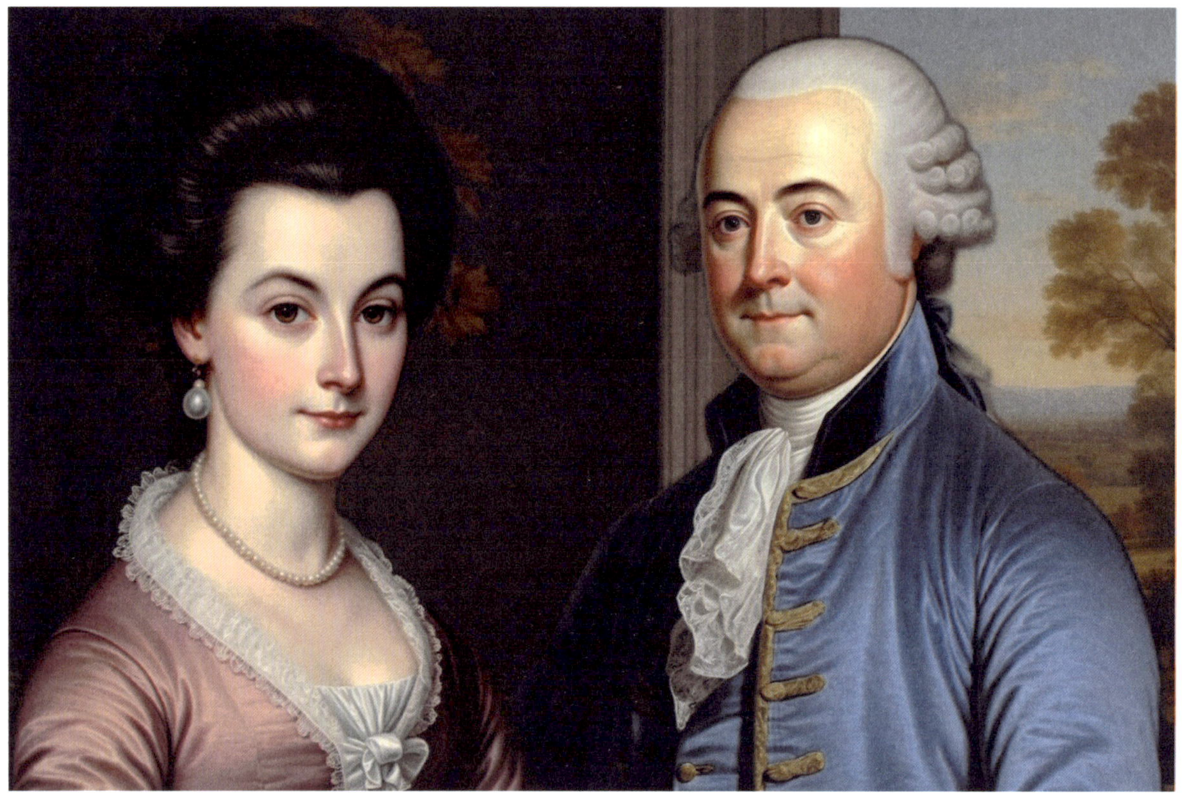

Modern rendering of Abigail and John Adams based on their portraits as young adults

taxed has a right to be present in person or by his own representative, in the body that taxes him; or as Lord Camden has expressed it, that 'taxation and representation are inseparable,'"[30] Samuel Adams wrote of the concept known today as no taxation without representation.

"A man's property is the fruit of his industry; and if it may be taken from him under any pretense whatever, at the will of another, he cannot be said to be free, for he labors like a bond slave, not for himself, but for another," Adams wrote about basic human freedoms. "Or supposing his property comes by inheritance or free gift, it is absolutely his own, and it cannot rightly be taken from him without his consent. This I take to be the commonly received opinion, concerning liberty, as it regards taxation: And it is moreover generally understood, that upon this opinion the very being of a free government depends." In December 1765, the Sons of Liberty summoned Andrew Oliver, who'd recently received his official papers to become the Stamp Master or collector of the Stamp Tax, to Boston's Liberty Tree. Oliver resigned his commission.

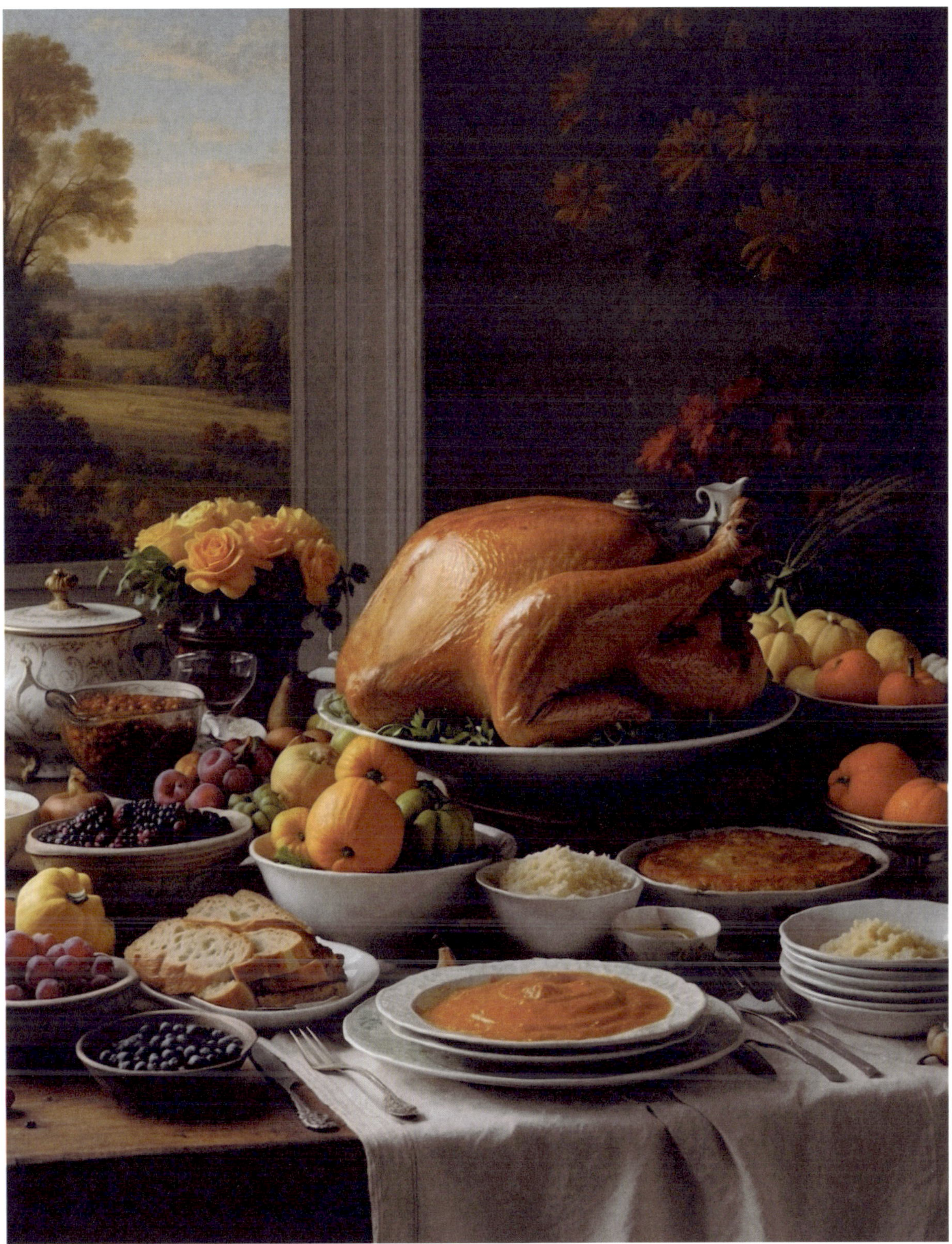

INJUSTICES BEHIND THE FIFTH-EIGHTH AMENDMENTS

Taxation without representation was not the only new injustice and grievance affecting the colonists. To face accusations of noncompliance with the king's taxes, many were forced to travel burdensome distances to attend trials by a judge instead of a jury of their peers. These judges' salaries came from the crown and not the colonists. Through these grievances, the king corrupted the colonists' court system. This led to the 5th to 8th Amendments in the Bill of Rights decades later.

THANKSGIVING DINNER CONFLICT

The Stamp Act caused conflict at Thanksgiving dinner tables in Massachusetts in 1765. Newlyweds John and Abigail Adams dined for Thanksgiving at the house of her father, William Smith, who was a minister. Reverend Smith often alternated the pulpit with Reverend Ebenezer Gay. John and Samuel Adams were cousins.

"Went to Weymouth with my wife. Dined at Father Smith's. Heard much of the uneasiness among the people of Hingham, at a sermon preached by Mr. Gay, on the day of Thanksgiving, from a text in James,"[31] John Adams recorded in his diary in December 1765.

Strongly advocating submission to the Stamp Act, Reverend Gay believed the weapons of the church were prayers not protests. "We have tried prayers and tears, and humble begging and timid tame submission as long as trying is good—and instead of redress we have only increased our burdens and aggravated our condemnation," Adams wrote.

The Smith and Adams families believed that "Mr. Gay would do very well for a (stamp) distributor, and they believed he had the stamps in his house." In contrast, John's father-in-law, Reverend Smith, had recently preached a different sermon, which the people had "admired very much, and talk of printing as the best sermon, they ever heard him preach." While Smith called for his people to "render therefore to Caesar, the things that are Caesars and unto God the things that are God's," he supported civil objection. "The tenor of it was to recommend honor, reward, and obedience to good rulers; and a spirited opposition to bad ones, interspersed with a good deal of animated declamation upon liberty and the times."

A RHODE ISLAND THANKSGIVING 1765: POLITICS OR PIETY?

Governor Samuel Ward, like John Adams, was also dealing with politics during Thanksgiving. Ward was the only governor of one of the thirteen colonies who refused to take an oath supporting the Stamp Act. When Rhode Island's general assembly designated Thursday, November 28, 1765, as a day of Thanksgiving, Governor Ward then issued a Thanksgiving proclamation, becoming the only governor to do so that season.

Was Ward's Thanksgiving proclamation a political move or a spiritual act? It was both. "I do also exhort all persons to offer up their most sincere and fervent prayers to Almighty

God, that He will be graciously pleased to continue his kind and favorable regard to the kingdoms of Great Britain and Ireland, and their dependencies,"[32] Ward wrote.

His proclamation accomplished the goal of calling on people to turn to God and give thanks during the Stamp Act crisis. After he defied the crown on the Stamp Act, the proclamation also provided an opportunity to publicly support King George III by congratulating him on the birth of a new prince. It also gave Ward an opportunity to emphasize that both civil and religious rights and liberties were precious to God.

FIRST PUBLISHED JEWISH THANKSGIVING PRAYER

Rhode Island's *Newport Mercury* published a Thanksgiving prayer by Isaac Touro, who led Newport's Jewish synagogue. Touro wrote the prayer in Hebrew for the general Thanksgiving set aside on the last Thursday in November 1765. This was the first Jewish Thanksgiving prayer published in America. Describing God as the Lord of Lords, Touro prayed for mercy and compassion and thanked God for their great bounty.

He also recognized the tumult caused by the Stamp Act and sought peace. "Grant, we beseech thee, that we may enjoy internal peace in this land; and that peace may subsist between all states and potentates; that thy holy word, spoken by the prophet, may be fulfilled; 'and I will give peace in the land.' Be graciously pleased to grant, that we may hear glad tidings of our neighbors who inhabit round about us." He closed by recognizing their "most gracious Sovereign, King George the Third" and the royal family.[33]

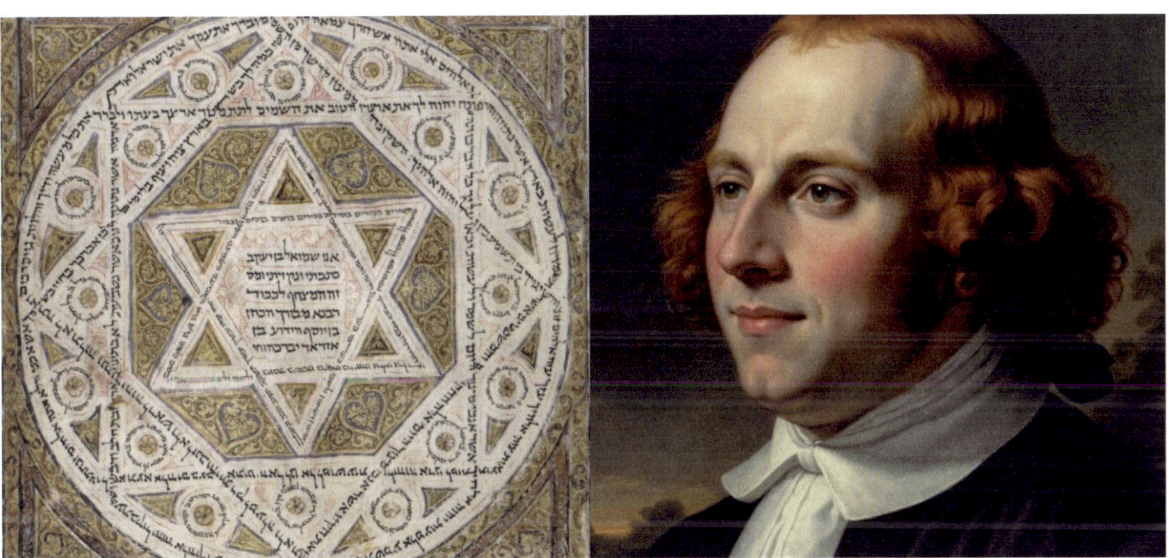

On the left is the Leningrad Codex, the oldest complete manuscript of the Hebrew Bible. On the right is a modern rendition from a sketch of Isaac Touro.

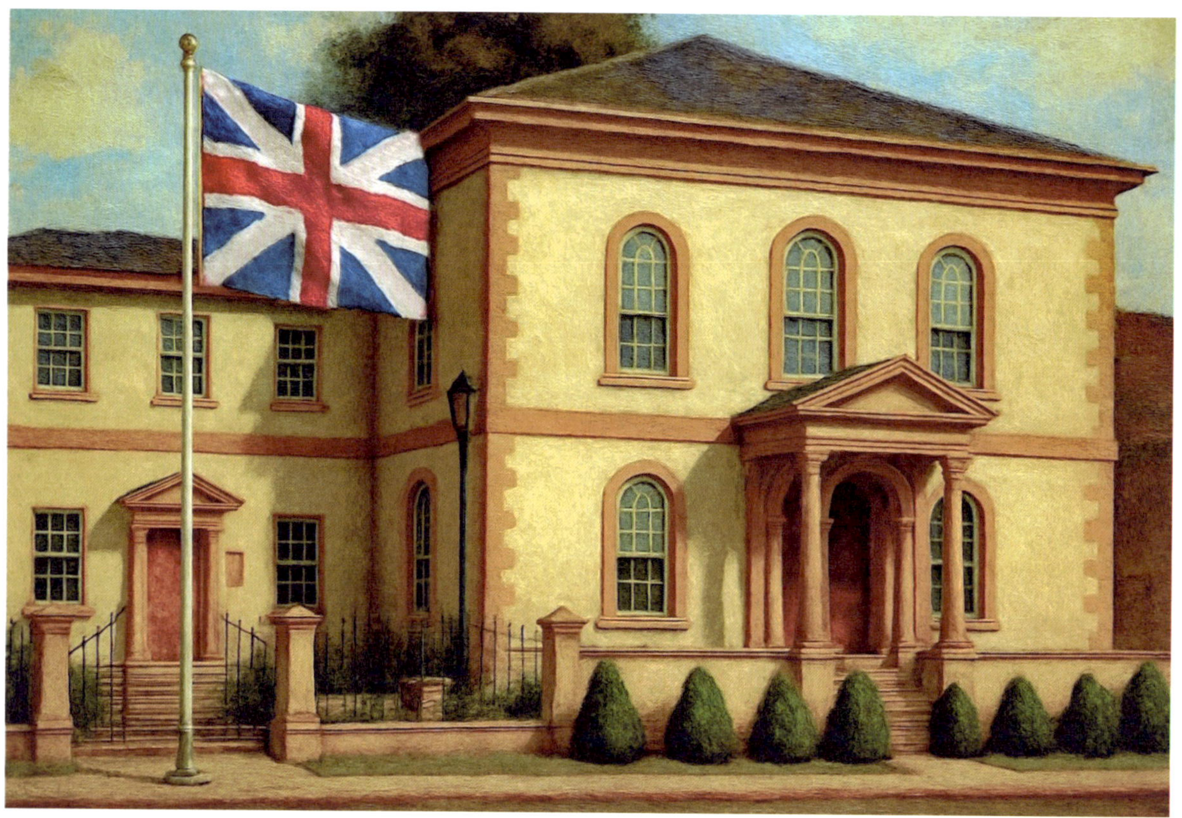

Touro Synagogue as it might have looked in 1765

THANKSGIVING IN JULY

Why were John and Abigail Adams celebrating Thanksgiving in July 1766? "We talked of keeping Thanksgiving with you,"[34] Abigail wrote on July 15, 1766, to her sister Mary Cranch in Salem, Massachusetts. After word arrived that Parliament had repealed the Stamp Act, the colonists set aside a day in July to give thanks.

"Thanksgiving for the repeal of the Stamp-Act. Mr. Smith's text was 'The Lord reigneth, let the Earth rejoice, and the multitude of the isles be glad thereof,'"[35] John wrote in his diary on July 24, 1766, about his father-in-law's message from the pulpit for the special day of thanks set aside for the Stamp Act's repeal.

Adams also heard another minister's Stamp Act Thanksgiving message. This sermon compared the American people to Joseph in the Bible and likened the king and Parliament to Joseph's brothers because they sold him into slavery. "But as for you, ye thought evil against me; but God meant it unto good, to bring to pass, as it is this day, to save much people alive," Adams wrote, paraphrasing Genesis 50:20 (KJV) and pointing out Joseph's perspective and reflection on how God had turned his personal hardship into the public salvation of his people, the Israelites.

Years later, Adams explained this New England tradition to a Dutch immigrant this way:

"Yesterday the anniversary festival, which we in New England call by the technical term Thanksgiving, I heard from my Reverend Pastor, Mr. Peter Whitney, an excellent sermon upon patriotism from Psalm 137:5-6."[36]

For John Adams, Thanksgiving was not merely a New England tradition. Thanksgiving was also a part of his family history. Adams had a direct connection to New England's first Thanksgiving because he was a direct descendent of two *Mayflower* pilgrims, John and Priscilla Alden, who celebrated the historic 1621 Thanksgiving in Plymouth, Massachusetts.

"Let us come before him with thanksgiving and extol him with music and song." Psalm 95:2

OBLIGATIONS OF GRATITUDE & THE TOWNSHEND ACTS

Giving thanks should be free, not obligatory. *Obligations of gratitude* was how John Adams described what would happen if he took a job in King George III's government. In 1768, Adams refused a lucrative appointment as advocate general in Boston's Court of Admiralty. Not wanting to be dependent financially on the king for a salary, he rejected the offer because of the "unsettled state of the country, and my scruples about laying myself under any restraints, or *obligations of gratitud*e to the government for any of their favors."[37] Likewise, Adams opposed Parliament's new "duties on glass, paint &c." He could see no end to grievances.

Adams referred to Parliament's new Townshend Acts, which taxed chinaware, glass, lead, paper, wine, fruits, and tea in the colonies. These laws also prevented New Yorkers from denying housing to British soldiers, called quartering, and established a customs board in Boston, which became corrupt.

John Hancock also vehemently opposed the Townshend Acts. "The articles of glass etc., I find has a new duty fixed upon it. I will sooner shut up my windows or undergo many inconveniences before I will import a single box,"[38] he complained to his London agent.

Around the same time, Benjamin Franklin wrote a letter asking why grievance petitions from Massachusetts had not reached the king. "It had been revealed there that the late provincial applications for redress of grievances had been somehow strangely obstructed." Likewise, Maryland's assembly complained that their grievances had failed to reach "the royal ear."[39] In other words, men who served the king slow-walked if not stopped supplications and grievance documents from arriving on the king's desk from America.

MILITARY OCCUPATION–1768

"The ships of war came up and arranged themselves on the northeast side of the metropolis, as if intended for a formal siege,"[40] the *Boston Evening Post* reported of the British troops' arrival in Boston on October 3, 1768. The king sent the troops to squelch opposition to his policies.

INJUSTICES BEHIND THE THIRD AMENDMENT

Mr. Brown, a businessman, was one of the first to refuse to house or quarter British troops in Boston. "It was Colonel Dalrymple's positive orders to have the factory cleared in two hours for the reception of the soldiers." An upset Brown "complained to him (Dalrymple) of the hardship of being turned out of doors from a house he had been placed in by the province ... without legal warning." The troops instead camped at Boston Common, Faneuil Hall, and the barracks at Castle William. Decades later, this led to the Constitution's third amendment that prohibits the government from requiring Americans to house soldiers in their homes.

THE BOSTON MASSACRE–1770

Tension over the weekend between British soldiers housed in the town of Boston and teenage boys throwing snowballs culminated in a tragedy on Monday, March 5, 1770. British soldiers fired upon the crowd, killing Sam L. Gray, Sam L. Maverick, James Caldwell, Crispus Attucks, and Pat K. Carr. Attacks was a runaway slave who worked on a ship under the alias "Michael Johnson" and defended the teenage boys against the soldiers.

"We have had a tragical scene of military execution in our town, which is unprecedented by anything hitherto have happened in English America, but though perhaps it is but a prelude of what we may expect in the future,"[41] a Bostonian wrote to a friend about the Boston Massacre.

CORRUPTION

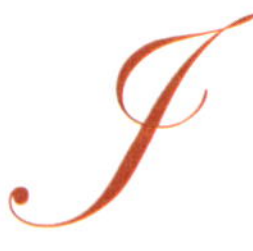

John Adams had served as the British officers' defense attorney during their trial over the Boston Massacre. Why? Because he believed they had a right to a fair trial. Yet, he concluded that corruption was taking over his local government through the king's hand.

"But when a government becomes totally corrupted, the system of God Almighty in the government of the world and the rules of all good government upon Earth will be reversed, and virtue, integrity and ability will become the objects of the malice, hatred and revenge of the men in power, and folly, vice, and villainy will be cherished and supported,"[42] Adams wrote. He knew that the king now paid the salaries of judges instead of the people paying their salaries through their legislatures. As a result, the officials were not accountable to the people but owed their "gratitude" to the crown. He predicted that the "consequence of this will be that the iron rod of power will be stretched out vs. the poor people..."

THE BOSTON TEA PARTY–1773

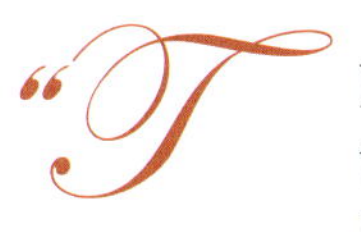

hat they would, to the utmost of their power, prevent the landing of the tea," the *New York Gazette* published on December 13, 1773 of the results of a Boston town meeting. The people's anger was greater than during the Stamp Act conflict eight years earlier.[43]

By this time, Parliament had repealed the Townshend Acts except for the tax on tea, which remained firmly in place. On December 16, 1773, dozens of the Sons of Liberty dressed as Mohawks and boarded the newly-arrived East India ships. Instead of burning the ships and denying the owner an ability to make a living, they dumped 342 chests of tea into Boston Harbor to protest Parliament's tea tax. They left all other goods on the ships.

Hundreds of miles away in Virginia, George Washington explained to a friend that their grievances were not about tea but about the principle of taxation without representation.

"For Sir what is it we are contending against? Is it against paying the duty of 3d. per lb on tea because (it is) burthensome? No." Washington wrote, noting that they objected to being taxed by a government that did not represent them. "We have already petitioned His Majesty in as humble, and dutiful a manner as subjects could do ... we applied to the House of Lords, and House of Commons in their different legislative capacities,"[44] Washington wrote. Though he disliked the tactics of the Boston Tea Party, he supported the sentiment of civil opposition.

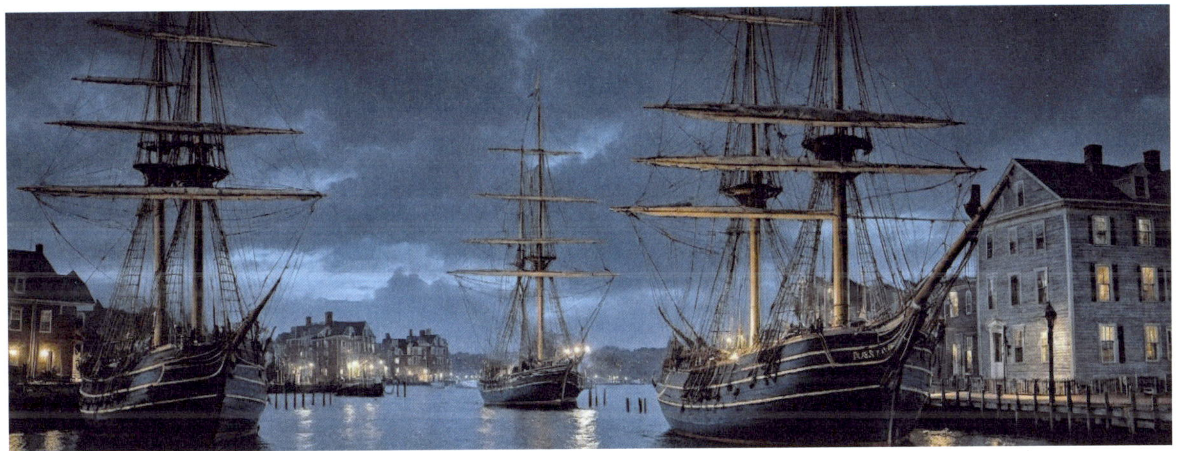

FALLOUT FROM THE TEA PARTY

On Christmas Day in 1773, Ben Franklin, who resided in London and served as postmaster for the colonies, published a confession in a newspaper in London, where he'd been living after retiring from newspaper publishing in Philadelphia. Franklin publicly admitted that he'd transmitted Massachusetts Governor Thomas Hutchinson's letters to patriots in Boston. Why did he confess? Integrity. He'd learned that two Englishmen had fought a duel after accusing each other of publicizing Hutchinson's embarrassing letters. Franklin confessed giving the letters to patriots in Boston before someone died over the matter.

"There must be an abridgement of English liberties, you wish to see further restraint of liberty in the colony,"[45] Hutchinson had written. Franklin believed Boston's patriot leaders needed to know Hutchinson's true position. Hutchison publicly declared he supported American liberties but privately argued for ways to increase their dependency. Hence, Franklin forwarded Hutchinson's letters to Boston's patriotic leaders so they could know the governor's true intentions.

Franklin's problems increased when news of the Boston Tea Party reached London on January 20, 1774. Because King George III and Parliament were furious that chests of tea were dumped into Boston Harbor, they wanted to hear from Franklin as America's representative in England. Hence, Franklin was ordered to an unofficial hearing by members of the King's Privy Council, which was the British Crown's private committee made up of cabinet and Parliament members.

Accompanied by two attorneys and clad in a formal velvet suit, Franklin arrived at London's Cockpit Tavern on January 29, 1774. With thirty-five Privy Council members watching, the solicitor general gave Franklin an epic English tongue lashing. He accused Franklin of stealing Hutchinson's letters and blamed him for the Boston Tea Party.

"My Lords, Dr. Franklin's mind may have been so possessed with the idea of a Great American Republic, that he may easily slide into the language ... of a foreign independent state." He compared Franklin to a bribed villain who stole state secrets. Then he accused him of being a spy.

How did Franklin respond? He was silent. This longtime gentleman known for his wit and way with words sat stock still. All he could do was absorb their multiple oral lightning bolts. Franklin left Cockpit Tavern a different man. Gone was the noted scientist and postmaster devoted to his king. Replacing him was an independent American with a renewed commitment to liberty. No longer welcome in London, Franklin returned to Philadelphia. Parliament imposed the harshest punishment possible on Massachusetts after the Boston Tea Party.

King George III revoked the charter of Massachusetts, dissolved the Massachusetts legislative assembly, replaced the civilian governor with a military general, locked down the Boston economy by forbidding merchants from buying and selling goods on ships in Boston Harbor, and implementing martial law.

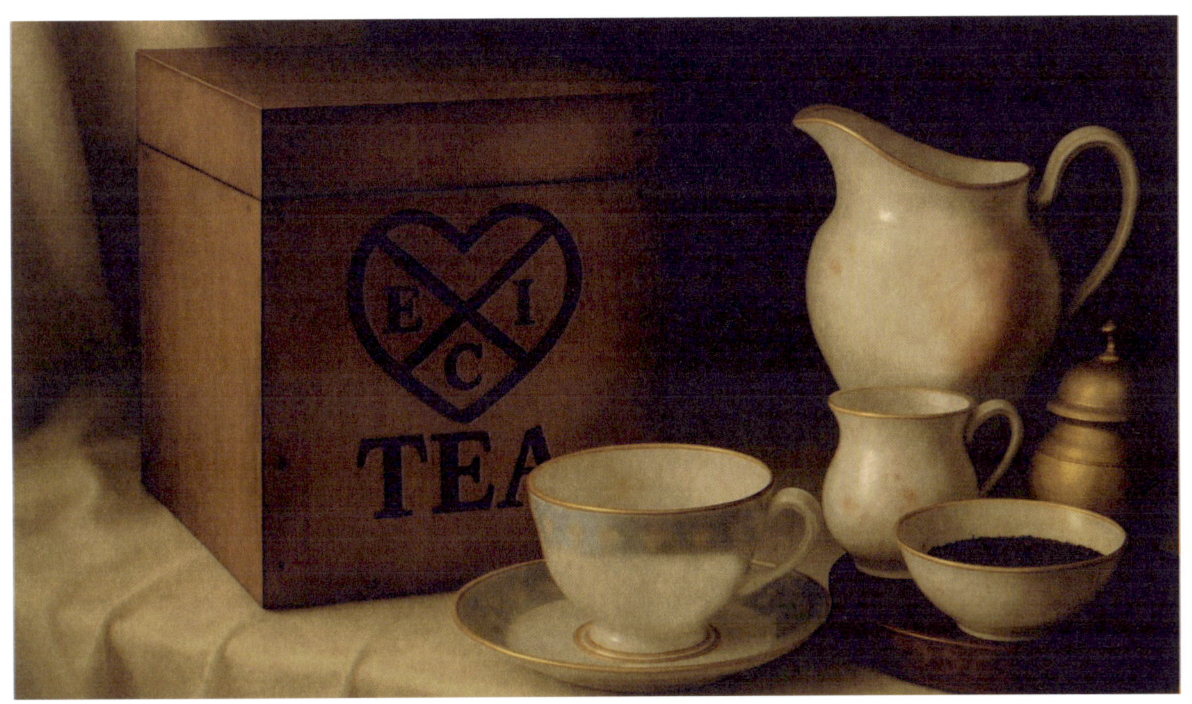
E I C
TEA

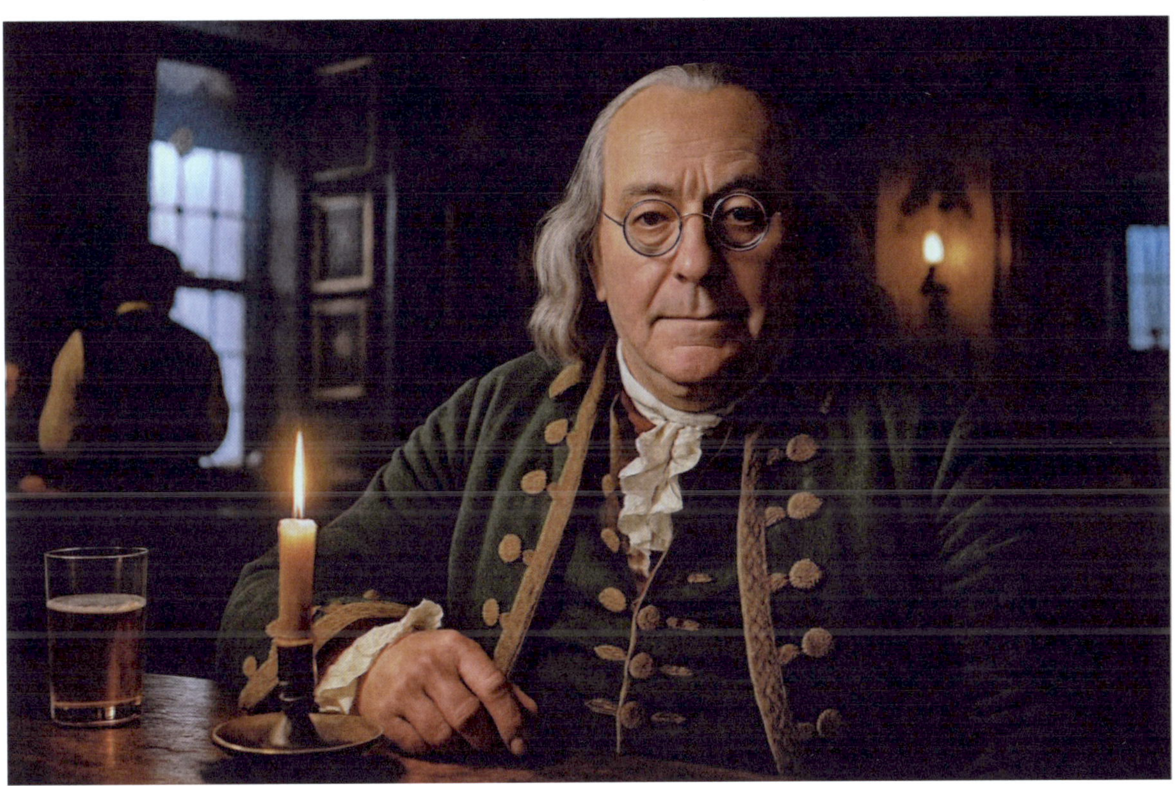

AMERICA'S WAR FOR INPENDENCE STARTS–1775

George Washington believed the consequences of the Boston Tea Party, especially depriving Massachusetts of its charter, were not equal to the crime. "The conduct of the Boston people could not justify the rigor of their (Parliament's) measures."[46] He decried this "despotic system of tyranny." Soon Washington, Franklin, Hancock, and cousins Samuel and John Adams, took their seats at the Continental Congress in 1774. Representatives from twelve of the thirteen colonies met to address the worsening problems with the king and Parliament. Under the spirit of Patrick Henry's declaration that he was not a Virginian but an American, they united and passed a boycott of English goods.

"Woe to those who make unjust laws, to those who issue oppressive decrees." Isaiah 10:1

LEXINGTON & CONCORD–APRIL 19, 1775 & INJUSTICES BEHIND THE SECOND ADMENDMENT

Warned by Paul Revere and other horse-backed messengers, minutemen came out to defend Lexington and Concord, Massachusetts, from the British military, who tried to seize the patriots' gunpowder and ammunition stores on April 19, 1775.

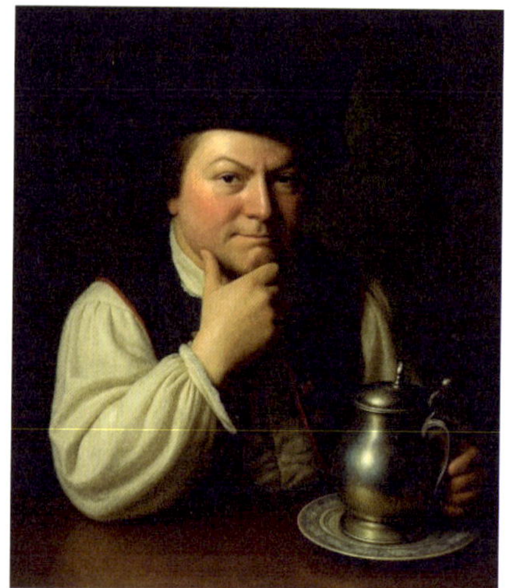

A modern rendering of Paul Revere, the messenger and silversmith

A Boston silversmith, Paul Revere served as a courier for the Boston Committee of Public Safety. On the night of April 18, 1775, Revere and others rode to Lexington to warn John Hancock and Samuel Adams that British soldiers were coming to arrest them in Lexington and to seize gunpowder stores in Concord.

The sexton of Boston's North Church signaled that British forces had left Boston by way of the Charles River instead of a land-only route. Revere was captured and then released by the British before the battles began.

A month after the Battles of Lexington and Concord, Abigail Adams wrote a thank you letter to a London bookseller from her home outside of Boston at Braintree. Her husband, John Adams, who was away at the Continental Congress in Philadelphia, had asked her to write this letter. In addition to thanking this Londoner for a shipment of books, she sought to persuade him to support the plight of Bostonians, who were in lockdown by an army of 30,000 British soldiers.

"The state of the inhabitants of the town of Boston and their distresses no language can paint—imprisoned with their enemies, suffering hunger and famine, obliged to endure insults and abuses from breach of faith plighted to them in the most solemn manner by the General," Abigail declared, dipping her quill pen in ink as she wrote on the parchment paper. On May 22, 1775, Abigail explained that the British general had ordered them to surrender their guns. She revealed that British soldiers were so brutal that they took away biscuits and chocolate from "the pockets of distressed women."[47]

She also revealed her belief that liberty was for men and women, all classes and ethnicities. "The spirit that prevails among men of all degrees, all ages and sexes is the spirit of liberty. For this they are determined to risk all their property and their lives 'nor shrink unnerved before a tyrants face' but meet this luring insolence with scorn . . .Tis thought we must now bid a final adieu to Britain," she wrote of her desire for independence over a year before her husband and the Congress declared independence from England.

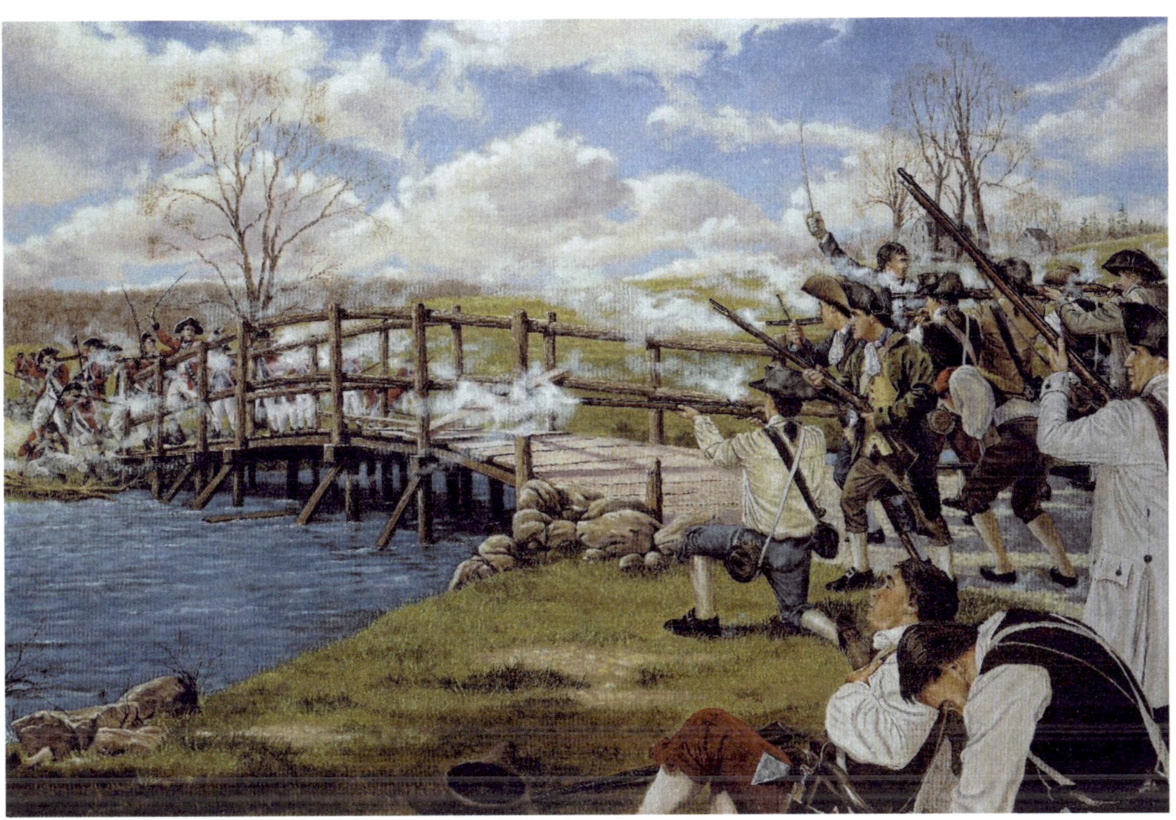

***The Shot Heard around the World*, public domain by Domenick D'Andrea**

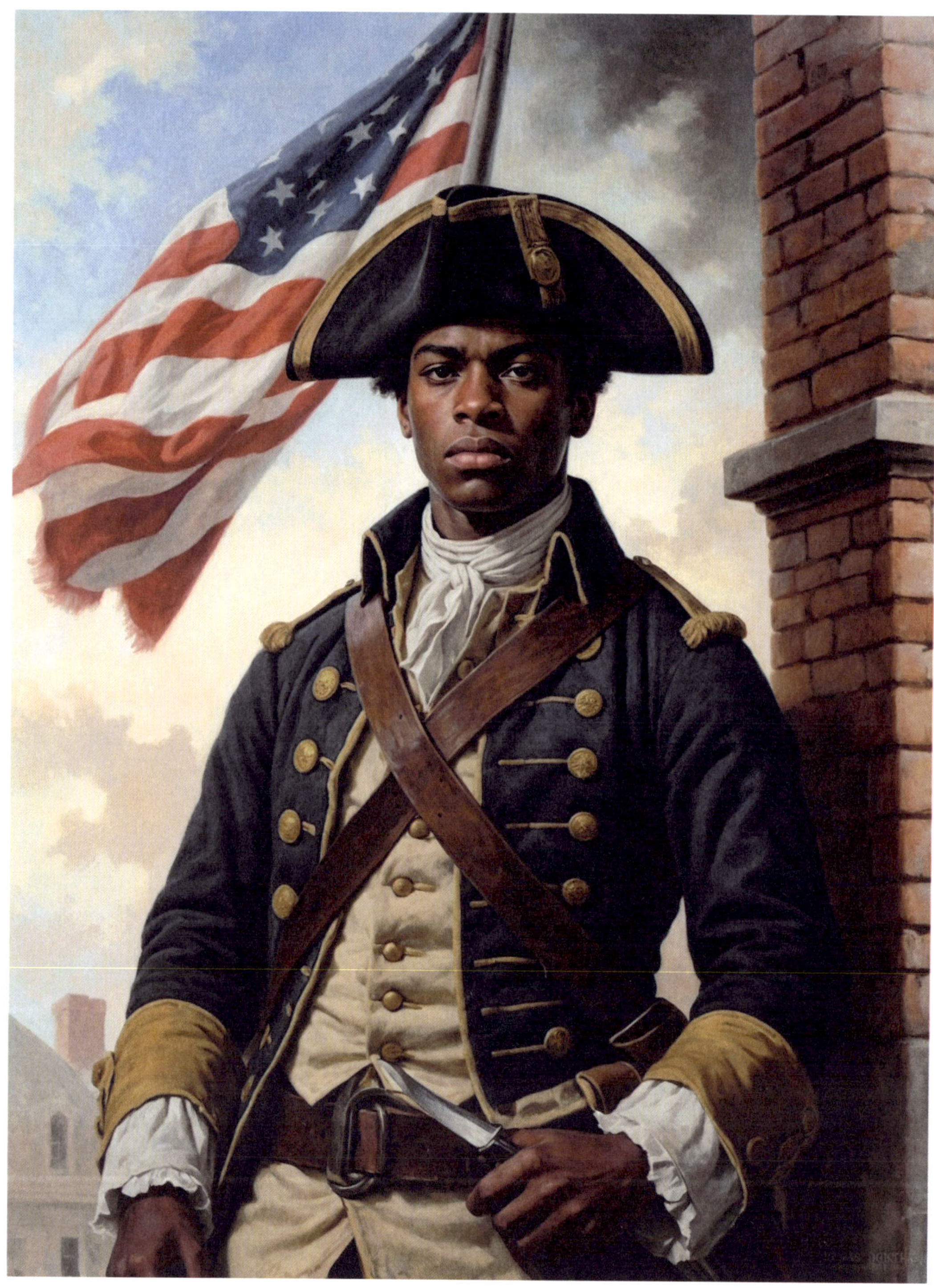

Peter Salem was a free black minuteman who fought at the Battle of Concord, the Battle of Bunker Hill, and many others throughout the war.

BATTLE OF BUNKER HILL–JUNE 17, 1775

"The day; perhaps the decisive day is come on which the fate of America depends. My bursting heart must find vent at my pen. I have just heard that our dear friend Dr. Warren is no more but fell gloriously fighting for his country—saying better to die honorably in the field than ignominiously hang upon the gallows. Great is our loss ... The race is not to the swift, nor the battle to the strong, but the God of Israel is he that giveth strength and power unto his people. Trust in him at all times, ye people pour out your hearts before him. God is a refuge for us.—Charlestown is laid in ashes. The battle began upon our intrenchments upon Bunker's Hill, a Saturday morning about 3 o'clock and has not ceased yet and tis now 3 o'clock Sabbath afternoon,"[48] *Abigail Adams wrote to John on June 18, 1775.*

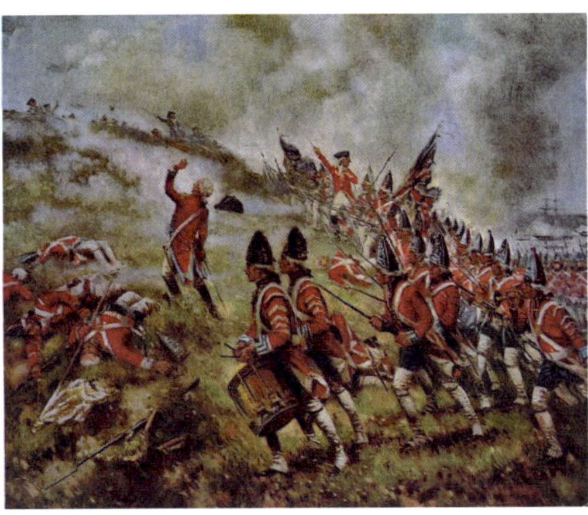

Battle of Bunker Hill by E. Percy Moran

The Battle of Bunker Hill, which took place on Boston's Charlestown peninsula, was fought on June 17, 1775. Though the patriots lost the battle, they inflicted numerous casualties on the British military and proved they could fight. The standoff between the city of Boston and the surrounding countryside continued for many more months.

Freed slave Peter Salem was one of the minutemen who defended Concord's Old North Bridge. Fighting at Bunker Hill, he is credited for taking out Major John Pitcairn, the British officer whom the continentals believed was responsible for ordering his men to fire the first shots of the American Revolution at Lexington two months earlier.

WASHINGTON'S FIRST THANKSGIVING

The Continental Congress commissioned George Washington as commander-in-chief in June 1775. He took charge of the army in Cambridge, Massachusetts. When Massachusetts celebrated Thanksgiving that fall, General Washington, asked his soldiers to join in this tradition, which made November 23, 1775 the army's first Thanksgiving. It was also the first time that Washington wrote the word *thanksgiving*. He explained that "The Honorable Legislature of this Colony" had "set apart Thursday the 23rd of November instant, as a day of public thanksgiving 'to offer up our praises, and prayers, to Almighty God, the source and benevolent bestower of all good." He looked to God to "smile upon our endeavors, to restore peace, preserve our rights ... and avert the calamities of a civil war."[49]

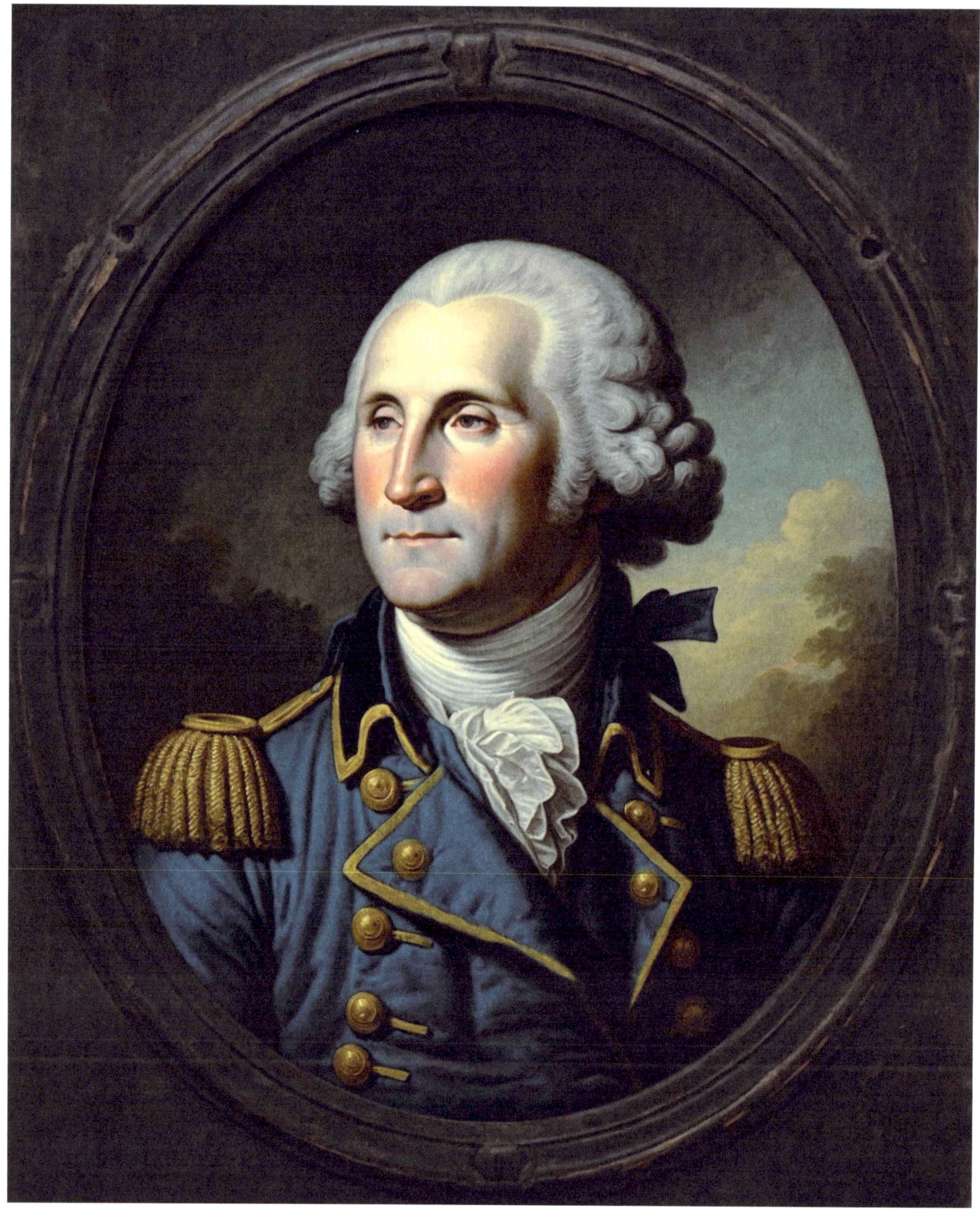

Adapted from several portraits, a modern rendering of a slightly smiling George Washington

THE MIRACULOUS YEAR OF 1776

AMERICA'S BOLDEST NEW YEAR'S RESOLUTION

Benjamin Towne, editor of the *Pennsylvania Evening Post,* was discouraged as the New Year began in 1776. After all, his world had gone mad in April 1775, when the first shots of the American Revolution were fired at the Battles of Lexington and Concord. For months since then, the British military had locked down the city of Boston while Washington's rag-tag militia controlled the surrounding countryside.

In response to the chaos of his world, Towne published a poem in the *Pennsylvania Evening Post* on January 1, 1776, called "Poor Tom's A-Cold."[50]

Poor Tom's a-cold referred to Shakespeare's *King Lear* in which a character disguised himself as Tom O'Bedlam to symbolize madness or a storm of chaos in the social world. Despite this theme of insanity, Towne's New Year's Day poem concluded with hope for good news in 1776. "But now, alas! Poor Tom's a-cold. But you, who live with hearts at ease, will surely never let him freeze. Sweet Madam, gentle Sir, good morrow; God keep you free from pain and sorrow. And let me hope, are long to boast: Good news! -- good news! -- in *The Evening Post.*"

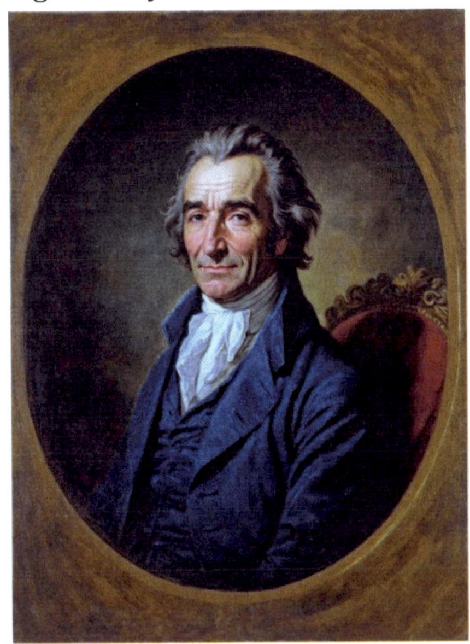

A modern rendering of Thomas Paine adapted from public domain portraits

Towne didn't let poor Tom freeze. Within days, his paper became the first newspaper to announce the publication of a fiery, brand-new pamphlet. "*Common Sense* addressed to the inhabitants of America, on the following interesting subjects"[51] was first printed on January 9, 1776, anonymously by an unknown poor Tom —Thomas Paine.

Common Sense discussed the Bible's view of a Republic under Moses, the English Constitution, monarchy, hereditary succession, and the present state of America. At the heart of *Common Sense* was Paine's New Year's resolution for America for 1776.

"The blood of the slain, the weeping voice of nature cries, 'TIS TIME TO PART,"[52] Paine wrote of the boldest possible New Year's resolution.

Paine's *Common Sense* lit a fire. Soon printers in Virginia and New York were printing thousands of copies. *Common Sense* became so popular so quickly, that the *Virginia Gazette* published an extract of it in early February 1776. Why were the colonists drawn to it? Paine gave them the solution they wanted but had been scared to openly support. He gave them logical reasons for America to become independent of England, and thus to begin the world again. "I challenge the warmest advocate for reconciliation to show a single advantage that this continent can reap by being connected with Great Britain," he wrote.

"Everything that is right, or reasonable, pleads for separation. The blood of the slain, the weeping voice of nature, cries, 'It is time to part.' Even the distance at which the Almighty hath placed England and America is a strong and natural proof that the authority of one over the other was never the design of Heaven." Reminding readers that Bostonians were living in lockdown by the British military, Paine viewed America's situation as precarious.

"But let our imaginations transport us for a few minutes to Boston; that seat of wretchedness will teach us wisdom, and instruct us forever to renounce a power in whom we can have no trust,' he wrote. "The inhabitants of that unfortunate city, who but a few months ago were in ease and affluence, have now no other alternative than to stay and starve or turn to beg."

How did Bostonians receive Paine's solution and New Year's resolution? With glee. "I am charmed with the sentiments of *Common Sense*; and wonder how an honest heart, one who wishes the welfare of their country, and the happiness of posterity can hesitate one moment at adopting them," Abigail Adams wrote to her husband.

George Washington also agreed with *Common Sense's* logic and doctrine. He believed that more people would agree with it, especially after the British military burned Falmouth, Massachusetts, and Norfolk, Virginia. These atrocities would drive hundreds to "decide upon the propriety of a separation,"[53] Washington wrote about *Common Sense* from Cambridge. "[B]y private letters which I have lately received from Virginia, I find *Common Sense* is working a powerful change there in the minds of many men."[54]

Soon the conclusion was clear. Americans wanted to begin the world over again as an independent nation. "The public in general having read, and (excepting a few timid Whigs or disguised Tories) loudly applauded,"[55] the *New England Chronicle* published on March 21, 1776. Within months, Thomas Paine's New Year's resolution came true through the words of another Tom—Thomas Jefferson. Poor Tom was no longer cold but on fire with patriotism.

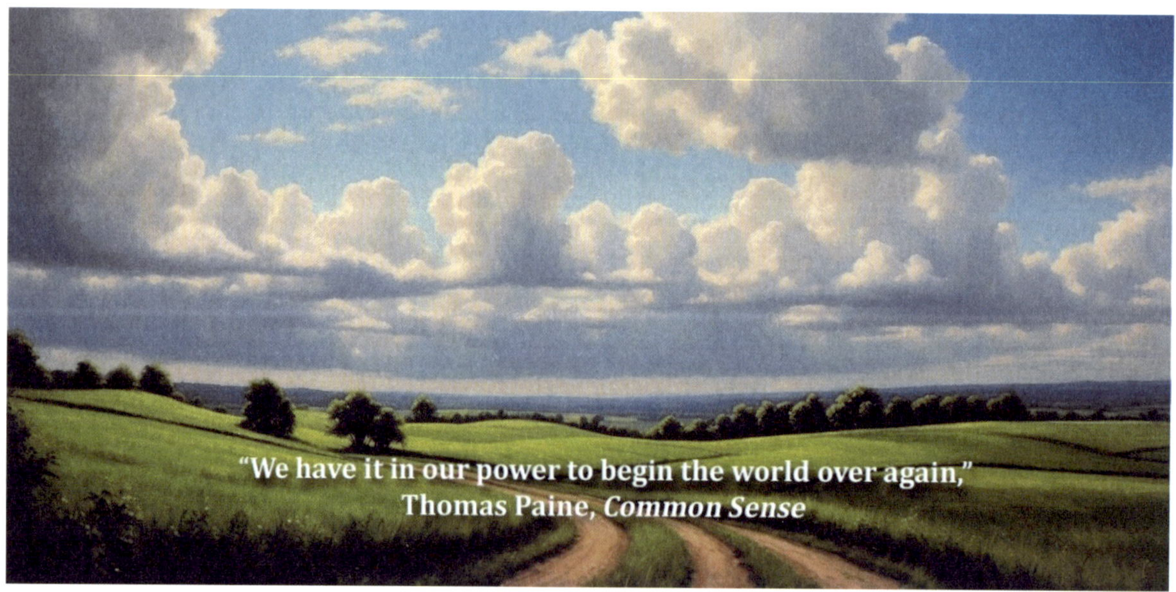

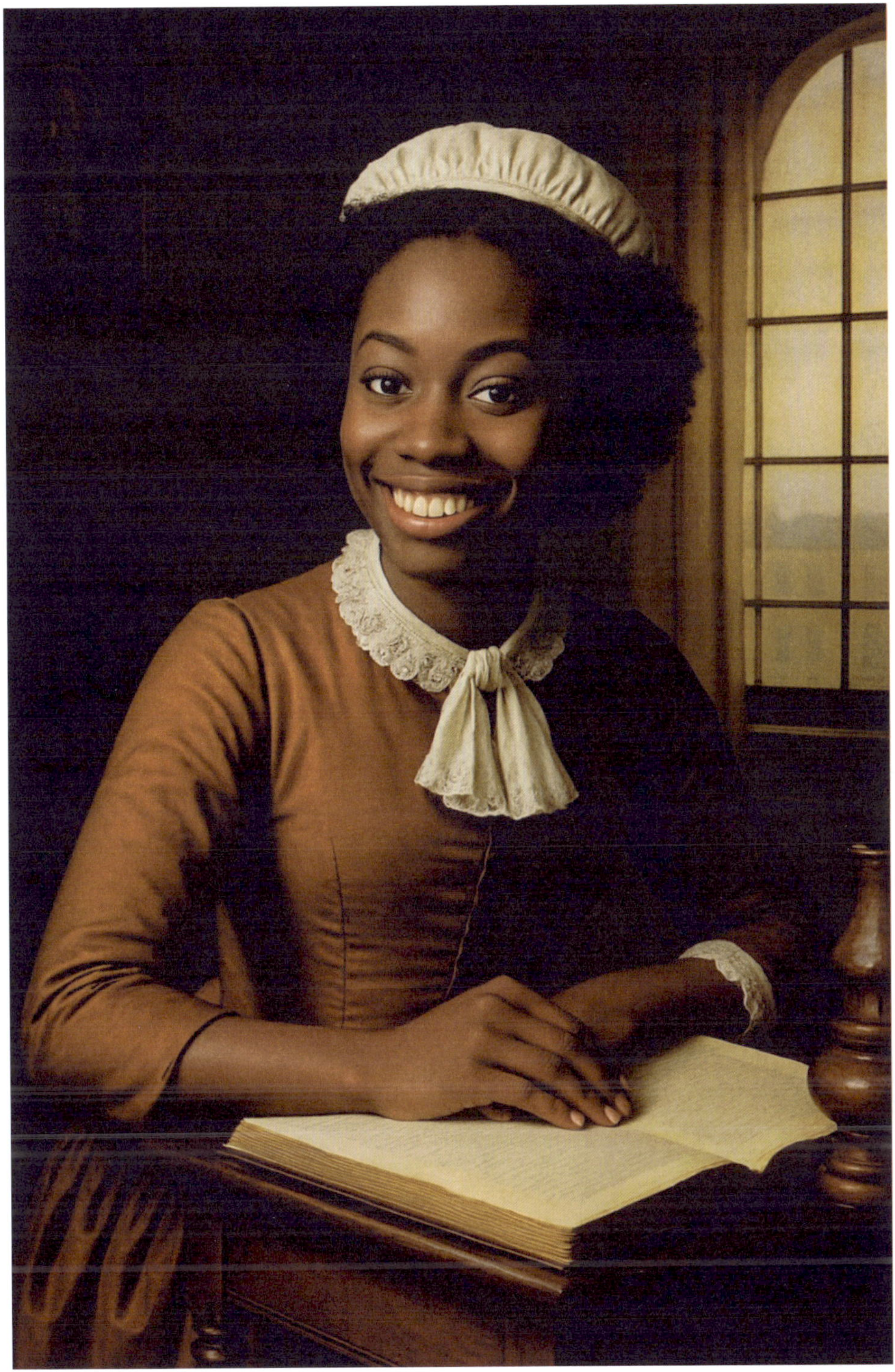

A modern rendering of what Phillis Wheatley might have looked like in 1776.

WINTER CAMP & PHILLIS WHEATLEY

From the Continental Army's winter camp at Cambridge, Massachusetts in January 1776, General Washington played a waiting game. Armed with a surprise plan, he believed that his army would soon drive the British military from Boston.

While he waited for the winter snow to give way to spring rain, Washington re-read a 1775 "letter and poem addressed to me by Mrs. or Miss Phillis Wheatley."[56] By this time Wheatley had become the first published black author in America. A wealthy British patron in England had published her poetry in a 1773 book called *Poems on Various Subjects, Religious and Moral*. She was likely the first educated black American that Washington had ever interacted with. What he may not have realized as he read her new poem, which was dedicated to him, is that Wheatley's life and poetry reflected the paths of many Americans. In just a few short years, she had transformed from a loyal subject of King George III into a full-blown patriot. Her poetry was the best witness of her transformation.

As a six- or seven-year-old child, Wheatley had left Africa on the slave ship *Phillis* in 1760, the same year that King George III ascended to the British throne. A Boston tailor, John Wheatley, and his wife Susannah bought her when she arrived in Boston the following year. Though they had intended to train her as a domestic servant to care for them in their old age, Phillis also reminded them of their daughter who'd died as a child around the same age. When Phillis took an interest in reading and writing, they made a counter-cultural decision. They did what others would not do: They gave Phillis an education. She learned to read the Bible and classic literature, including many of the same books that the young men of Harvard read.

As a result, Wheatley began writing poems at an early age. She honed her craft by writing obituary poems for family, friends, and community leaders. Though she wasn't freed from slavery until adulthood, she became a free thinker who transformed politically like those around her. Wheatley wrote a poem praising the king for ending the Stamp Act.

"Your subjects hope, dread Sire—The crown upon your brows may flourish long, and that your arm may in your God be strong! O may your septre num'rous nations sway, and all with love and readiness obey!" she wrote of King George III. She hoped that his subjects would remember both his "favors past" and "remember the last," referring to the Stamp Act's repeal. She showed that God would "guard him from on high, and from his head let ev'ry evil fly!"

Yet, instead of smiling on his free subjects, King George III sent British soldiers to Boston. Conflict between the troops and colonists led to the killing of eleven-year-old Christopher Snider by a loyalist on February 22, 1770.

Deeply moved and revealing her emerging loyalty to the American cause, Phillis wrote a poem memorializing Snider. "In heavens eternal court it was decreed, how the first martyr for the cause should bleed."[57] Thirteen days later the Boston Massacre took place on King Street, the street where the Wheatleys lived.

By 1775, Wheatley had switched to the patriot side. Overflowing with hope for liberty, she wrote a poem depicting America as a female goddess named Columbia and Washington as the army's chief. She expressed hope for personal freedom — which she had received — and for America's freedom through lines such as, "The land of freedom's heaven-defended race!"[58] In this poem, she defined race as a spiritual and aspirational belief in freedom. Her switch from loyalty to the king to support of the patriots was evident in the last lines of her poem to Washington:

"Proceed, great chief, with virtue on thy side,
Thy ev'ry action let the goddess guide.
A crown, a mansion, and a throne that shine,
With gold unfading, Washington! be thine."

Wheatley courageously mailed this poem to Washington at his camp in nearby Cambridge. How did Washington, a slave owner, respond? "I thank you most sincerely for your polite notice of me, in the elegant lines you enclosed; and however undeserving I may be ... the style and manner exhibit a striking proof of your great poetical talents,"[59] he wrote Wheatley on February 28, 1776.

While hesitant to directly ask a newspaper to publish a self-promoting poem, he saw the value of giving "the world this new instance of your genius." Washington asked Colonel Joseph Reed to send the poem to the newspapers. From Philadelphia to Virginia, newspapers published her poem and noted its presentation to Washington.

"If you should ever come to Cambridge, or near headquarters, I shall be happy to see a person so favored by the muses, and to whom nature has been so liberal and beneficent in her dispensations," Washington wrote, ending his letter to Wheatley the same way he did anyone else. "I am, with great respect, your obedient humble servant." Whether they met or not is lost to history.

Washington soon drove the British from Boston and moved to New York to fight the British there. Wheatley's poem showed Americans that Washington appreciated the talents and education of a black woman. The long-term results aided the cause of abolishing slavery when Wheatley's poems were sold to raise money for abolition decades later.

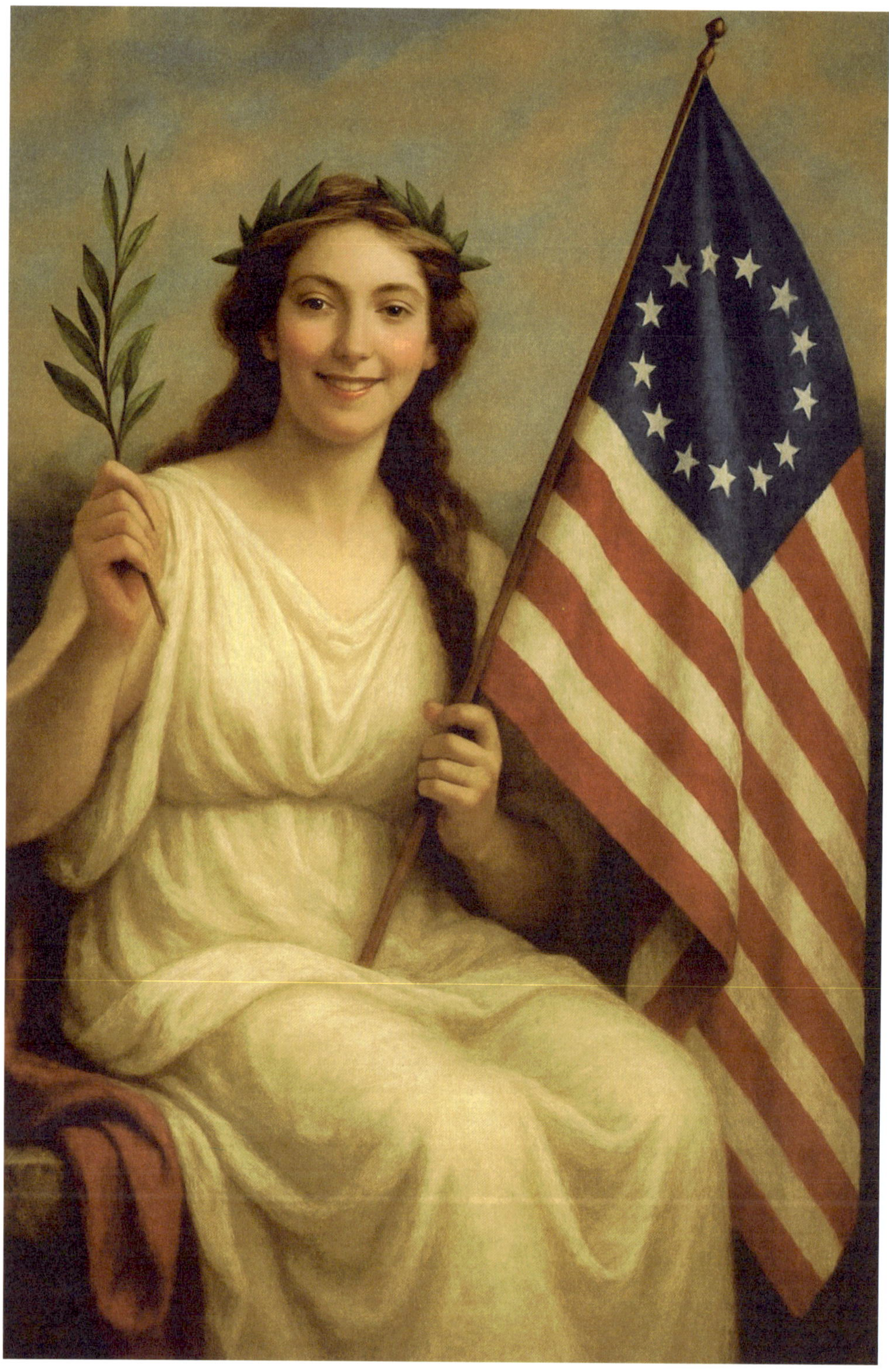

A modern rendition of a political cartoon from the 1770s of Columbia resembling a Greek Goddess with an olive branch in one hand

WONDER WOMAN 1776-STYLE

A*merica* is the female Latin word of the name *Amerigo Vespucci,* an Italian explorer who determined that the new world wasn't East Asia as Christopher Columbus had concluded. Instead Vespucci decided that the new world was another continent. Following the tradition of using female names for land, mapmakers named this continent *America* after Vespucci. Artists in the 1500s personified this paradise as a woman, often as a naked Mother Earth.

By the 1770s, this image of had transformed into a female fighter. A Boston almanac published a map-like drawing featuring two women: Britannia and America. Under a devil's influence, Britannia was weeping next to her discarded shield while trade ships from other countries sailed toward the independent America. In contrast to Britannia, America was a confident and resilient Grecian female sitting under the U.S. flag. She held a staff topped by a liberty cap in one hand and an olive branch in the other. This woman warrior was known by two names: America and Columbia.

WASHINGTON'S FIRST MIRACULOUS VICTORY– DORCHESTER HEIGHTS

Born into poverty, General Henry Knox became a Boston bookseller who loved volumes of military history. Against the wishes of his loyalist father-in-law, Knox joined the Continental Army and became chief of artillery.

Colonel Henry Knox orchestrated the transportation of the cannon and artillery from New York's Fort Ticonderoga to Massachusetts in December 1775. Facing treacherous conditions, he fulfilled Washington's request and arrived in mid-January 1776.

"It is not easy to conceive the difficulties we have had in getting them (cannons) over the lake owing to the advanced season of the year and contrary winds—three days ago it was very uncertain whether we could have gotten them over until next spring, but now please God they shall go—I have made forty-two exceeding strong sleds and have provided eighty yoke of oxen to drag them as far as Springfield where I shall get fresh cattle to carry them to camp,"[60] Knox wrote to Washington on December 17, 1775.

When spring broke on March 4, 1776, Washington ordered his men to place the largest artillery pieces on top of Boston's Dorchester Heights. From this position, the Continental Army could target British ships bringing supplies into Boston. Caught off guard by the large cannons and left puzzled as to where the Continentals acquired them, the British military launched an attack. When a storm stopped their ships, the British military and loyalists gave up. They evacuated Boston on March 17, 1776.

"General Howe is driven from Boston pretty equally for the neglect of the government in not sending him any supplies for several months, and by the rebel army which received the end of last month great reinforcement, and among other articles a train of twenty-four pounders (they had, only 12 and 14 before and 13-inch mortars),"[61] a British officer wrote while on a ship after leaving Boston. "Where they got the latter, our generals have no conception. They bombarded the town from Dorchester-neck from whence the general tried in vain to dislodge them, but suffered severely in the attempt."

Overflowing with thankfulness, Abigail Adams was thrilled to learn the siege of Boston was over. From their farmhouse outside of the city, she discovered from a friend that though their Boston townhouse was dirty, it was not damaged by the British physician who had occupied it. "The town in general is left in a better state than we expected, more owing to a precipitate flight than any regard to the inhabitants,"[62] she wrote to John on March 31.

Her outlook was once again hopeful. "I feel very differently at the approach of spring to what I did a month ago. We knew not then whether we could plant or sow with safety, whether when we had toiled, we could reap the fruits of our own industry, whether we could rest in our own cottages, or whether we should not be driven from the sea coasts to seek shelter in the wilderness, but now we feel as if we might sit under our own vine and eat the good of the land ... I think the sun looks brighter, the birds sing more melodiously, and nature puts on a more cheerful countenance. We feel a temporary peace, and the poor fugitives are returning to their deserted habitations."

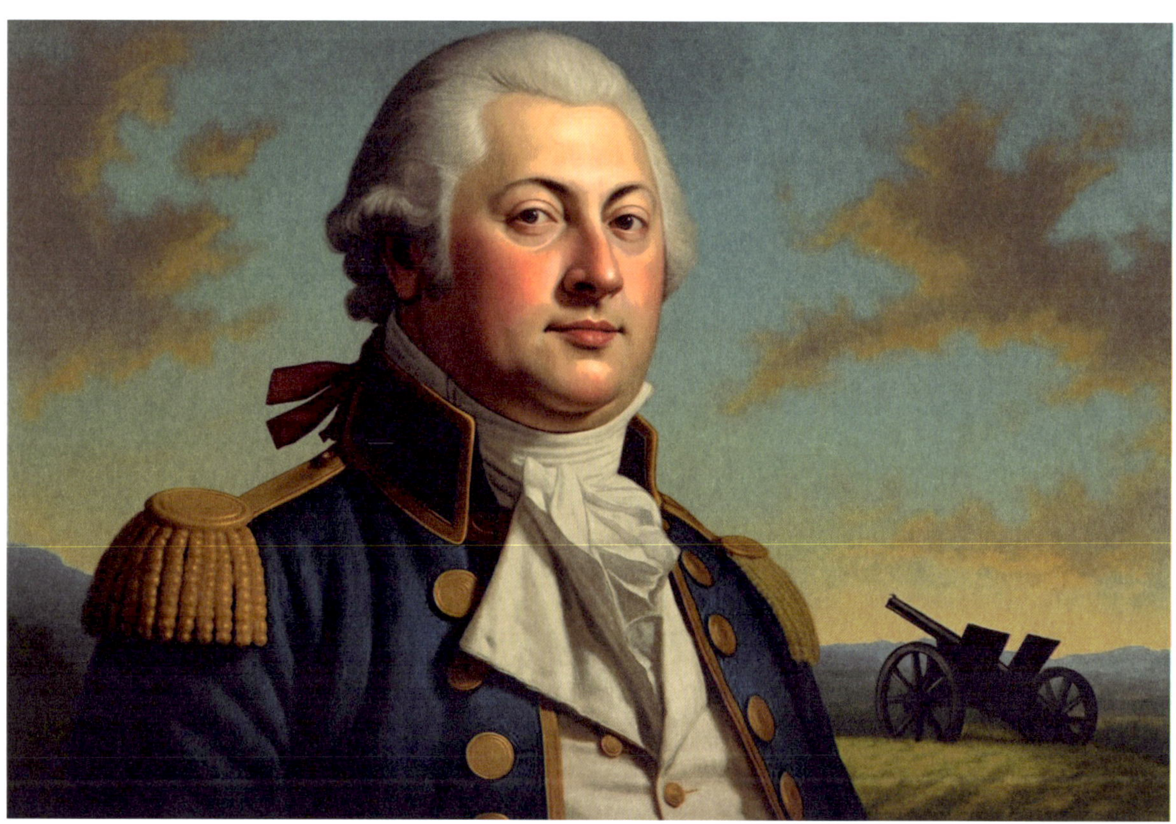

A modern rendering based on portraits of General Henry Knox, who commanded the artillery

'TIS TIME TO PART–INDEPENDENCE

FAITH IN INDEPENDENCE

By the spring of 1776, independence had become both a matter of faith as well as a challenge to faith. "I long to hear that you have declared an independency,"[63] Abigail Adams had written, expressing her faith in independence in a letter to her husband John on March 31, 1776, just days after the British had evacuated Boston. A month later, John had heard that the people of North Carolina and Virginia were also devoted to independence.

"Mr. John Penn, one of the delegates [to the Continental Congress] from North Carolina, lately returned home to attend the convention of that colony, in which he informs, that he heard nothing praised in the course of his journey, but *Common Sense* and Independence. That this was the cry, throughout Virginia,"[64] he had written a friend in April 1776.

Thomas Paine's New Year's Resolution for 1776, *Common Sense,* had given many people the courage to begin the world again through independence. But an important question remained. Were the clergy ready? Was declaring independence consistent with the colonists' Christian faith, whose dimensions and denominations were vast in their eyes?

After all, English monarchs believed in the divine right of kings. At minimum, this meant that God had ordained the king or queen to rule over the English people as part of their Christian faith. King Charles I, who'd reigned in the previous century, went further and believed in the divinity of kingship. Not only was Charles destined by God to rule in his opinion, but he was also divine like God, which made him an extension of God in his sovereign mind.

Abigail's and John's ancestors were Puritans who left England during Charles I's reign and settled in the Massachusetts Bay Colony. The Puritans disagreed with the king's claims to divinity and objected to many of the Church of England's practices.

Charles Chauncy of Boston's First Church had a healthy perspective on their ancestors. "They would hazard everything dear to them, their estates, their very lives, rather than suffer their necks to be put under that yoke of bondage, which was so sadly galling to their fathers, and occasioned their retreat into this distant land, that they might enjoy the freedom of men and Christians," he had written in the 1760s.[65]

Many, from the descendants of the Puritans to those from the Church of England who were born in America to the Jews in Rhode Island, were wrestling with their traditions and beliefs. "When I consider these things and the prejudices of people in favor of ancient customs and regulations, I feel anxious for the fate of our monarchy or democracy or whatever is to take place. I soon get lost in a labyrinth of perplexities, but whatever occurs, may justice and righteousness be the stability of our times, and order arise out of confusion,"[66] Abigail had written in November 1775.

Loyalist clergy frequently pointed to Romans 13:1-2. "Let every soul be subject unto the higher powers," was Paul's direction to the Romans,[67] wrote Charles Inglis, the associate rector of New York's Trinity Church in a pamphlet countering Paine's *Common Sense*. "For there is no power 'but of God; the powers that be, are ordained of God.' I seem inclined to think that Paul did not believe with our author [of *Common Sense*], that 'Government by kings, was the invention of the Devil!'"

John Adams soon discovered that some members of the clergy also had faith in independence and had found a Biblical example to follow, one that would also appeal to Jewish patriots in Philadelphia.

"I have this morning heard Mr. Duffield upon the signs of the times. He ran a parallel between the case of Israel and that of America, and between the conduct of Pharaoh and that of [King] George,"[68] Adams wrote to his wife, Abigail, on May 17, 1776.

While living in Philadelphia, Adams had enjoyed listening to George Duffield, the Presbyterian minister of Pine Street Church, because he was a man "whose principles, prayers and sermons more nearly resemble, those of our New England clergy than any that I have heard." Duffield had spoken to the Continental Congress.

When ministers preached on political topics, they did so when the issue was of great importance. Duffield's comparison between Pharaoh and King George III also showed Adams that a minister had concluded that the king was a tyrant. Pharaoh's despotic measures were the result of his fear. Pharaoh's "jealousy that the Israelites would throw off the government of Egypt made him issue his edict that the midwives should cast the children into the river, and the other edict that the men should make a large revenue of brick without straw."

King George III had mimicked Pharaoh by responding to the colonists' objections and petitions with increasing tyrannical measures, from sending troops to Boston in 1768 to seeking to seize their guns and ammunition at Lexington and Concord in 1775.

For her part, Abigail believed that power was corrupting. "I am more and more convinced that man is a dangerous creature, and that power whether vested in many or a few is ever grasping, and like the grave cries give, give. The great fish swallow up the small ... ,"[69] she had written.

What was Duffield's solution to the king's tyranny? "He concluded that the course of events, indicated strongly the design of Providence that we should be separated from Great Britain,"[70] Adams reported. "[Great Britain] has at last driven America, to the last step, a complete separation from her, a total absolute independence, not only of her Parliament but of her crown," he concluded, noting that there was something very "unnatural and odious" in a government that was "1,000 leagues" away. "Confederation will be necessary for our internal concord, and alliances may be so for our external defense."

Simeon Howard of Boston's West Church agreed and cited Galatians 5:1 as the authority for responding to tyrants: "Stand fast therefore in the liberty wherewith Christ hath made us free, and be not entangled again with the yoke of bondage."[71]

"It is the duty of all men to stand fast in such valuable liberty, as Providence has conferred upon them,"[72] Howard proclaimed. "But in what way can a man be more justly chargeable with this neglect, than by suffering himself to be deprived of his life, liberty, or property, when he might lawfully have preserved them?" This is how the descendants of Puritans and other Christians justified taking up arms against their God-ordained king. If ministers were ready for Americans to declare independence, then they would encourage their congregations to call for it. A large question still loomed over Adams as he considered his position as a member of the Continental Congress after listening to Duffield. What role would he play in this great question of independence?

"Is it not a saying of Moses, who am I, that I should go in and out before this great people? When I consider the great events which are passed, and those greater which are rapidly advancing, and that I may have been instrumental of touching some springs, and turning some small wheels ... I feel an awe upon my mind, which is not easily described,"[73] Adams confided in Abigail as he grasped the gravity of the situation in one hand and hope for liberty in the other.

Was he to play the role of Moses, or Aaron, who paved the way for his brother Moses, to lead the Israelites? Before he learned the answer to that question and fulfilled his purpose, he would make a prediction that seemed inspired by some Virginians who held a parade the same day that he wrote Abigail about Duffield's faith in independence.

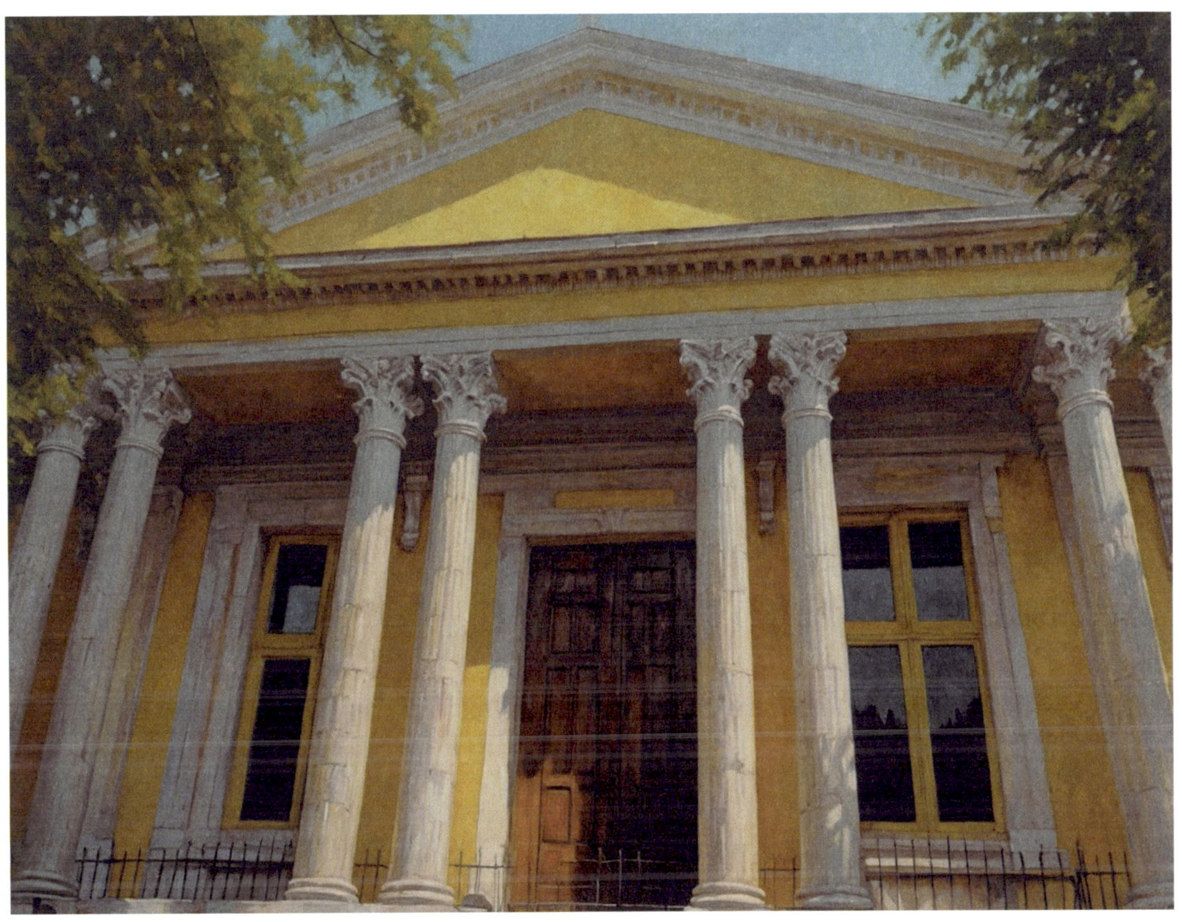

A modern rendering of Pine Street Church

VIRGINIA'S FIRST FIREWORKS FOR INDEPENDENCE

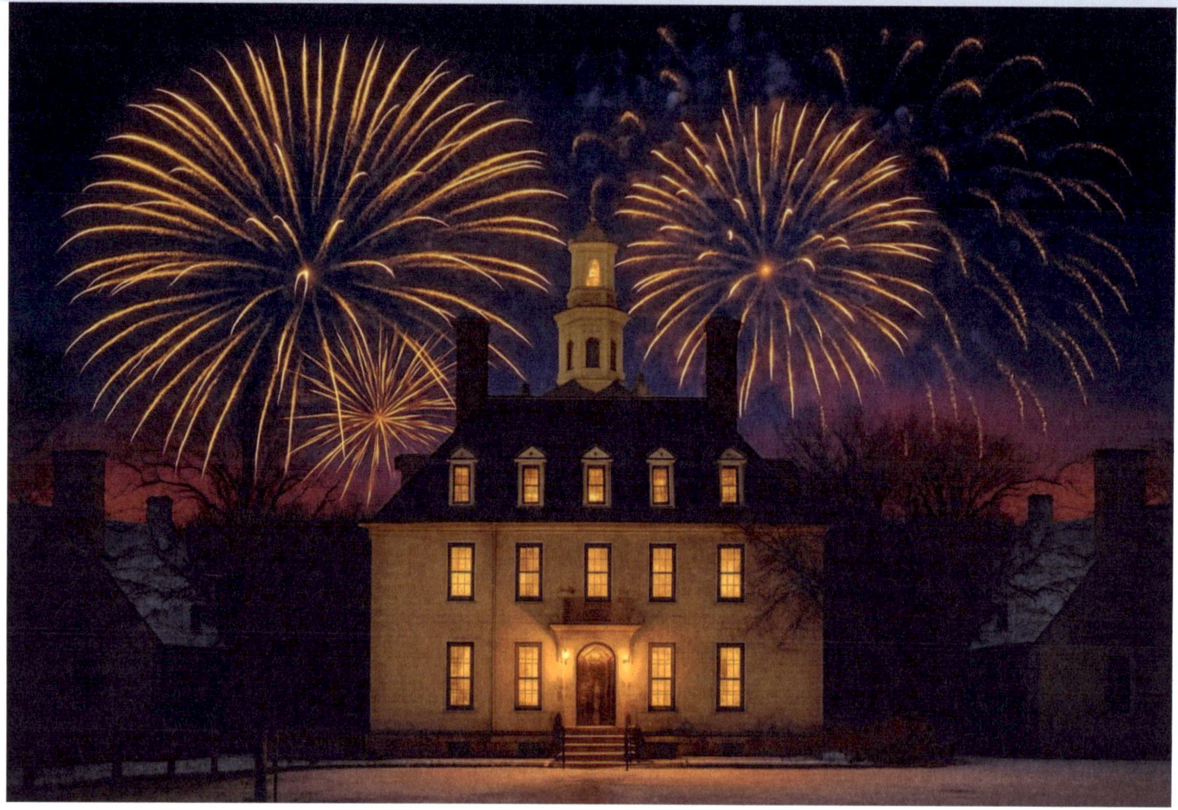

A reenactment of golden fireworks in Williamsburg, fireworks were usally gold in this eara.

Around the same time that John Adams wondered to Abigail if he was being called to be a type of Moses, Virginians held the first parade and fireworks display weeks before the Continental Congress made the final decision on the matter. On May 15, 1776, 112 men attended a convention in Williamsburg, Virginia. Their goal was to give instructions to the Virginia delegates for the Continental Congress in Philadelphia. They cited their attempts to reconcile with King George III.

"For as much as all the endeavors of the United Colonies, by the most decent representations and petitions to the King and Parliament of Great Britain, to restore peace and security to America under the British government, and a reunion with that people under just and liberal terms, instead of a redress of grievances, have produced, from an imperious and vindictive administration, increased insult, oppression, and a vigorous attempt to affect our total destruction,"[74] the *Pennsylvania Ledger* published on June 1, 1776. A year earlier the Continental Congress had sent King George III an Olive Branch Petition. Without even reading it, the king had declared war on the colonies.

Virginians had had enough. "By a late act, all these colonies are declared to be in rebellion, and out of the protection of the British Crown, our properties subjected to confiscation, our people ... compelled to join in the murder and plunder of their relations and countrymen, and all former rapine and oppression of Americans declared legal and just," the Virginia resolution declared on May 15, 1776. "Fleets and armies are raised, and the aid of foreign troops engaged to assist these destructive purposes."

At the time of the convention, Virginia's royal governor was aboard an armed ship. He was seizing property on Virginia's rivers and coast. The delegates' choices were dire. "In this state of extreme danger, we have no alternative left but an abject submission to the will of those overbearing tyrants, or a total separation from the Crown and government of Great Britain, uniting and exerting the strength of all America for defense, and forming alliances with foreign powers for commerce and aid in war."

These Virginians unanimously voted on declaring independence for Virginia. "That the delegates appointed to represent this colony in General Congress be instructed to propose to that respectable body TO DECLARE THE UNITED COLONIES FREE AND INDEPENDENT STATES." They proposed that the Continental Congress issue a declaration of rights to "secure substantial and equal liberty to the people."

These Virginians were so happy that they collected money for a celebration. The first independence parade, fireworks and a feast took place on May 16, 1776, the day after their decision for Virginia to leave England and less than two months before July 4. The soldiers in Williamsburg "... paraded in Waller's Grove, before Brigadier General Lewis, attended by the gentlemen of the Committee of Safety, the members of the General Convention, the inhabitants of this city..." After reading the resolution aloud to the Virginia militia, they toasted America's independent states, the Continental Congress, General Washington and victory to America. They discharged artillery and small arms, and shouted acclamations.

Instead of flying the Union Jack of Great Britain, they raised a new flag with thirteen red and white stripes with a small version of the British flag in the upper left-hand corner. How did their celebration end? With fireworks, of course!

"...[T]he evening concluded with illuminations (fireworks), and other demonstrations of joy, everyone seeming pleased that the domination of Great Britain was now at an end, so wickedly and tyrannically exercised for these twelve or thirteen years past, notwithstanding our repeated prayers and remonstrances of redress."

Four Pennsylvania newspapers soon reported on these festivities, which may have inspired John Adams to make a prediction to Abigail a few weeks later:

"The second day of July 1776, will be the most memorable epocha, in the history of America.—I am apt to believe that it will be celebrated, by succeeding generations, as the great anniversary festival. It ought to be commemorated, as the day of deliverance by solemn acts of devotion to God Almighty. It ought to be solemnized with pomp and parade, with shows, games, sports, guns, bells, bonfires and illuminations from one end of this continent to the other from this time forward forever more."[75]

Why did Adams say that July 2 would be the nation's birthday? How did he get this date wrong? And is July 4, 1776, the true birthday of the United States of America?

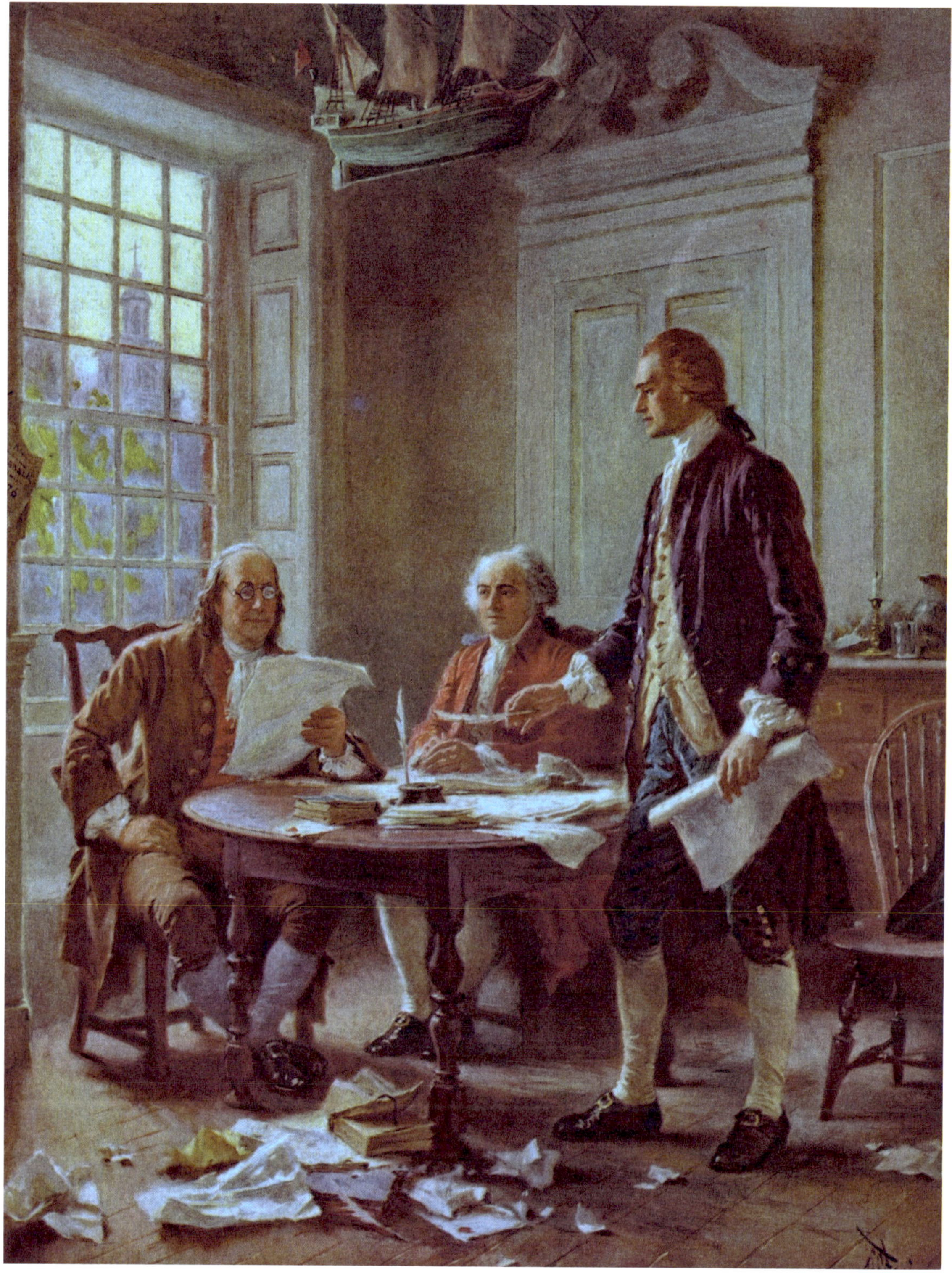

Writing the Declaration of Independence **by Jean Gerome Leon Ferris, Library of Congress.**

WHY IS JULY 4 THE BIRTHDAY OF THE UNITED STATES OF AMERICA?

The Continental Congress issued the Declaration of Independence on July 4, 1776 and signed the document weeks later. But why wasn't another date from the Revolutionary War designated as the nation's start? After all, the first shots of the American Revolution were fired on April 19, 1775, when the British military attempted to seize gunpowder stores at Lexington and Concord in Massachusetts. Wouldn't April 19 have been a better birthdate?

The problem with this date is that not enough Americans were ready for independence in 1775. The new phrase *united colonies* was used in newspapers only three dozen times before the Battles of Lexington and Concord, according to GenealogyBank.com. In the following year, *united colonies* appeared more than 1,800 times in newspapers. The colonists were clearly united against King George's tyranny, but weren't united in what to do about it. Many were terrified at separating from England.

"They raise prejudices in the minds of people and serve to create in their minds a terror at a separation from a people (in England) wholly unworthy of us,"[76] Abigail wrote to John Adams in December 1775, after the Continental Congress urged New Hampshire to create an independent legislature. Not enough colonists were ready for independence.

What had changed? In August 1775, King George had declared the colonies were in rebellion and ordered farms seized. On the same day that Philadelphia had learned about the king's war declaration, Thomas Paine had published *Common Sense*.

When the Continental Congress reconvened in the summer of 1776, Adams became one of the strongest advocates for independence. He also met a red-headed Virginian who had a strong command of the pen and wrote with great felicity. Thomas Jefferson brought "a reputation for literature, science, and a happy talent for composition,"[77] as Adams later reflected. "Writings of his [Jefferson's] were handed about, remarkable for the peculiar felicity of expression. Though a silent member in Congress, he was so prompt, frank, explicit, and decisive upon committees and in conversation ... that he soon seized upon my heart."

"The delegates from Virginia moved in obedience to instructions from their constituents that the Congress should declare that these united colonies ... be free and independent states," Jefferson reflected of the actions of Virginia's elder statesman, Richard Henry Lee.

In June 1776, Lee put forward three resolutions, which led Congress to appoint committees to consider each resolution: one committee drafted the declaration of independence, one wrote a treaty with France, and the third committee took on the arduous task of drafting a new constitution. Adams recognized his talent and recommended that Thomas Jefferson draft the Declaration of Independence, with Benjamin Franklin and himself providing editorial support. "The committee for drawing the

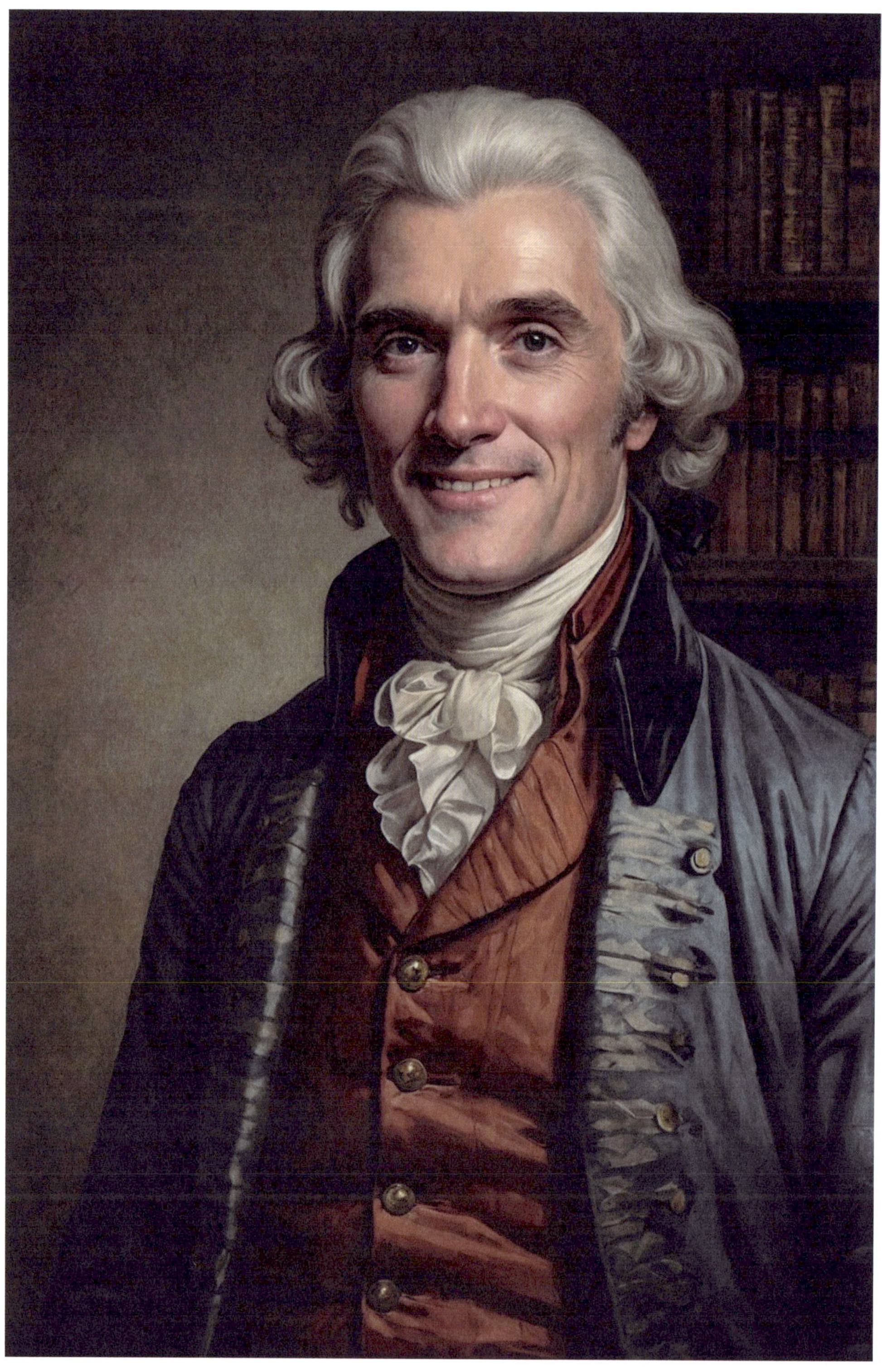

A modern rendition of Thomas Jefferson smiling, generated from public domain paintings.

Declaration of Independence desired me to do it," Jefferson reflected.

Adams also revealed how the committee's youngest member was tasked with writing the declaration: "You inquire why so young a man as Mr. Jefferson was placed at the head of the committee for preparing a Declaration of Independence? I answer: It was ... to place Virginia at the head of everything."

Just as Adams had nominated George Washington, another Virginian, for the post of commander-in-chief, so he also named a Virginian to write the declaration. He believed that independence had a greater chance of succeeding if the South and New England were united with each taking leadership roles. In this way, Jefferson became the metaphorical Moses while Adams played the part of Aaron. As the brother of Moses Aaron paved the way for Moses to take the lead of freeing the Israelites from Pharaoh.

"Before I reported it to the committee, I communicated it separately to Dr. Franklin and Mr. Adams, requesting their corrections, because they were the two members of whose judgments and amendments, I wished most to have the benefit,"[78] Jefferson reflected.

How did Adams respond to Jefferson's draft? "I was delighted with its high tone and the flights of oratory with which it abounded ..."[79] Adams recalled.

Jefferson's original draft addressed the issue of slavery and blamed the king's desire for profit as the motive behind it. "He has waged cruel war against human nature itself, violating its most sacred rights of life and liberty in the persons of a distant people who never offended him, captivating and carrying them into slavery in another hemisphere, or to incur miserable death in their transportation thither. This piratical warfare, the opprobrium of infidel powers, is the warfare of the Christian king of Great Britain determined to keep open a market where MEN should be bought and sold, he has prostituted his negative for suppressing every legislative attempt to prohibit or to restrain this execrable commerce,"[80] Jefferson wrote about slavery in his original draft of the Declaration.

Adams was pleased with this passage "... especially that concerning [abolishing] ... slavery, which, though I knew his southern brethren would never suffer to pass in Congress, I certainly never would oppose."[81] Adams was correct.

Congress received Jefferson's draft on June 28, 1776. The older Benjamin Franklin peppered Jefferson with wit as he sat next to him during the tense three-day debate. Jefferson noted that Franklin had "observed that I was writhing a little under the acrimonious criticisms on some of its parts."[82]

Jefferson was "a passive auditor of the opinions of others, more impartial judges than I could be, of its merits or demerits." The debate focused on two major issues: criticism of the common people in England and slavery. Several members wanted to distinguish the British government from the English people. "For this reason those passages which conveyed censures on the people of England were struck out, lest they should give them offence," Jefferson explained. "The clause too, reprobating the enslaving the inhabitants of Africa, was struck out in complaisance to South Carolina and Georgia."

Though the passage was struck from the final draft because of opposition from Southern states, it shows both the efforts of Jefferson and Adams to address the issue of slavery and their understanding that slavery violated the sacred rights of life and liberty.

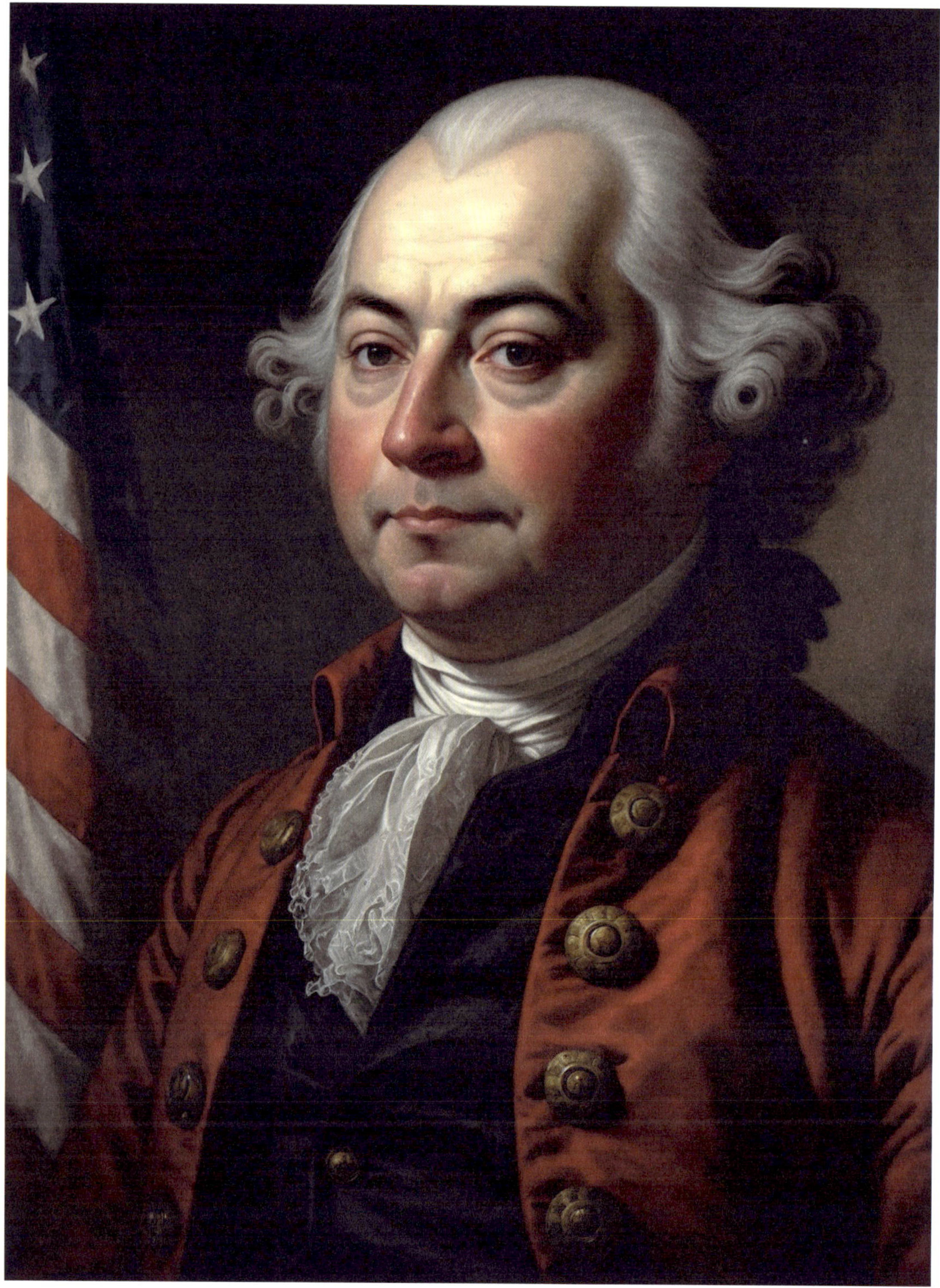

A modern rendition of John Adams adapted from public domain art.

The Continental Congress approved Richard Henry Lee's resolution for independence on July 2, 1776, which led Adams to initially predict that July 2 would be the nation's anniversary date.

The Continental Congress approved the Declaration of Independence on July 4, 1776. This marked the moment that Americans were united in declaring independence from England and the birth of the United States of America.

"People, I am told, recognize the resolution (of independence) as though it were a decree promulgated from Heaven,"[83] Samuel Adams wrote on July 27, 1776.

Samuel also tapped another reason that July 4 is America's birthdate. In addition to unity, the Declaration gave Americans a new identity. Gone were the colonies. Replacing them were states. In this letter, Samuel habitually chose the word *colonies* before correcting himself. "Or as I must now call them *states*."

Evidence of this new identity is also found in historical newspapers. The phrase *United States* appeared a handful of times in newspapers between 1773 and July 4, 1776, to describe an alliance between two nations, such as Spain and Morocco. Hence, by using the phrase *states* instead of *colonies*, the founders carved a new identity of a nation of equal powers. The phrase *United States* appeared over 600 times from July to December 1776.

"Time has been given for the whole people, maturely to consider the great question of independence and to ripen their judgments, dissipate their fears, and allure their hopes, by discussing it in newspapers and pamphlets, by debating it in assemblies ... (and) in private conversations, so that the whole people in every colony of the 13, have now adopted it, as their own act,"[84] John Adams wrote, reflecting on the advantage of the timing. "This will cement the Union, and avoid those heats and perhaps convulsions which might have been occasioned, by such a declaration six months ago."

Yet, another birthdate option remains. Why didn't the founders designate September 3, 1783, marking the peace treaty between America and Britain, as America's birthdate?

A sermon celebrating this peace treaty by Continental Congress chaplain George Duffield concluded that America was born in a day — not after an eight-year war.

"Who since time began, hath seen such events take place so soon?"[85] Duffield proclaimed, paraphrasing Isaiah 66:8. "The earth has indeed brought forth, as in a day. A nation has indeed been born, as at once."

In the days and decades to come, Americans would reflect with pride on the Declaration of Independence and July 4 as the nation's rightful birthday. They embraced the idea that their liberty had been born in a day—on July 4, 1776. The September 3, 1783 peace treaty was the day the king finally acknowledged it.

NEW YORK CAMPAIGN–1776

"This morning we have been alarmed with a party of the enemy landing on Staten Island and proceeding to the point within two miles of this town, where they took off the plank of a drawbridge and retreated to a house about a mile from the bridge. From the best intelligence we can get, there are several parties on the island,"[86] Isaac Woodruff, a barracks master at Elizabethtown, New Jersey, reported to George Washington in early July 1776.

British General William Howe, and his brother, Admiral Richard Howe, had arrived on New York's Staten Island with an intimidating sea of red in their wake—thousands of British redcoats on ships. Knowing the British fleet was arriving, Washington exhorted his men to bravery. "The time is now near at hand which must probably determine, whether Americans are to be, freemen, or slaves; whether they are to have any property they can call their own; whether their houses, and farms, are to be pillaged and destroyed, and they consigned to a state of wretchedness from which no human efforts will probably deliver them,"[87] George Washington wrote in general orders for his army in New York on July 2, 1776. This commander-in-chief knew his men would soon face the British military on the battlefield.

"The fate of unborn millions will now depend, under God, on the courage and conduct of this army—Our cruel and unrelenting enemy leaves us no choice but a brave resistance, or the most abject submission; this is all we can expect—We have therefore to resolve to conquer or die: Our own country's honor, all call upon us for a vigorous and manly exertion, and if we now shamefully fail, we shall become infamous to the whole world," Washington concluded.

"Let us therefore rely upon the goodness of the cause, and the aid of the Supreme Being, in whose hands victory is, to animate and encourage us to great and noble actions," Washington wrote, reflecting on God's Providence. He focused on the enemy's tyranny.

"The eyes of all our countrymen are now upon us, and we shall have their blessings and praises, if happily we are the instruments of saving them from the tyranny meditated against them. Let us therefore animate and encourage each other, and show the whole world, that a freeman contending for liberty on his own ground is superior to any slavish mercenary on earth."

After listening to their first public reading of the Declaration of Independence in New York, Washington's soldiers pulled down King George III's statue on July 9, 1776, on Manhattan's Bowling Green. "Though the General doubts not the persons, who pulled down and mutilated the statue, in the Broadway, last night, were actuated by zeal in the public cause; yet it has so much the appearance of riot and want of order, in the army, that he disapproves the manner, and directs that in future these things shall be avoided by the soldiery, and left to be executed by proper authority."

THE BATTLE OF LONG ISLAND

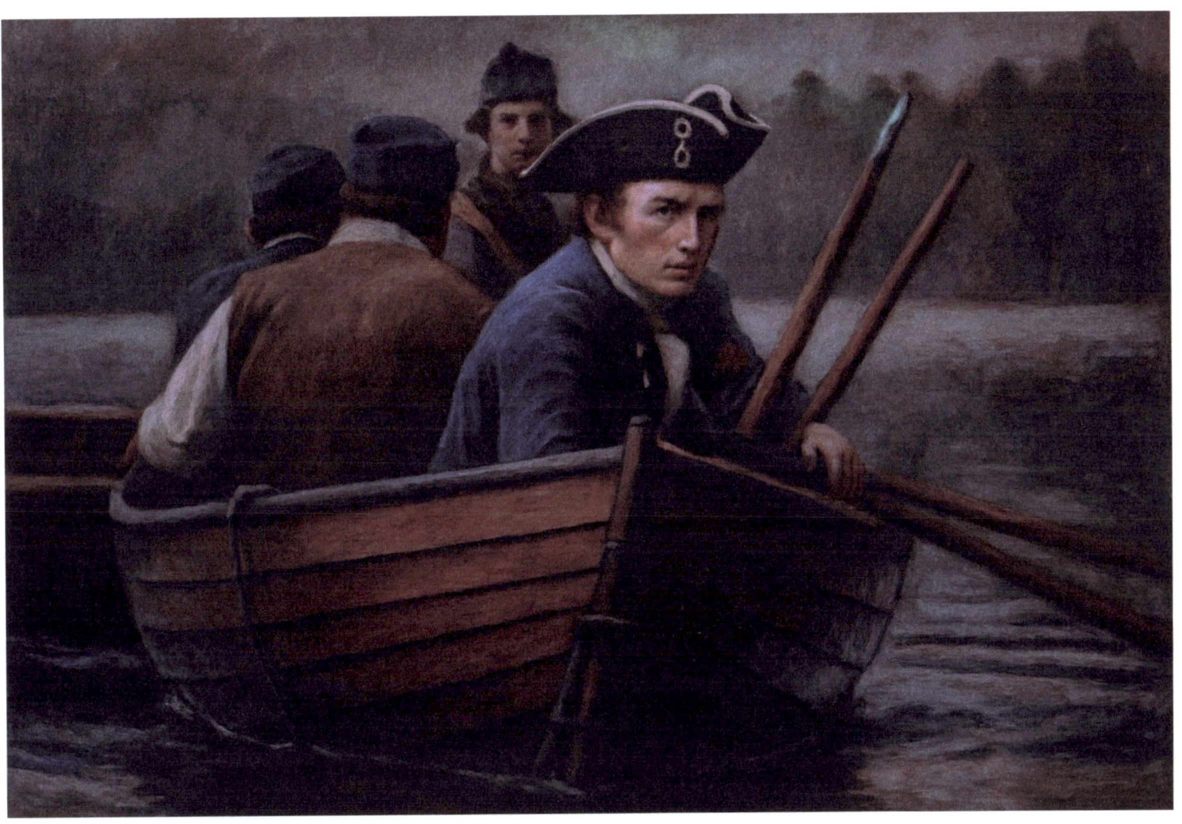

George Washington's men evacuated in boats overnight after losing the Battle of Long Island.

Over several weeks in the summer of 1776, British ships carrying 32,000 soldiers arrived at Staten Island, while General Washington's army constructed fortifications on both lower Manhattan Island and Long Island. Then British General Howe landed 22,000 soldiers at Long Island's Gravesend Bay on August 22 and attacked Washington's army of 10,000 on August 27.

"We have had a glorious day against the rebels,"[88] a British field officer wrote to his wife about the Battle of Long Island, which is also known as the Battle of Brooklyn Heights. While some of his forces attacked the Continental Army on August 27 at the island's Gowanus Heights, General Howe brought his main column around the patriot's rear on the rarely used Jamaica Pass and attacked the patriot's flank. American General William Alexander, known as Lord Stirling, and 400 Marylanders held off the British so the rest of the Continental troops could retreat to safety at Brooklyn Heights. The British captured Stirling but later exchanged him.

"As the action became warm, General Washington passed over to the camp at Brooklyn, where he saw, with inexpressible anguish, the destruction in which his best troops were involved, and from which it was impossible to extricate them,"[89] historian and soldier John

Marshall described of the 300 soldiers killed, 1,100 captured and 700 wounded. "Should he [Washington] attempt anything in their favor with the men remaining within the lines, it was probable the camp itself would be lost, and that whole division of his army destroyed," he said.

"Should he bring over the remaining battalions from New York, he would still be inferior in point of numbers; and his whole army, perhaps the fate of his country, might be staked on the issue of a single battle thus inauspiciously commenced." Washington tapped common sense. Victory on Long Island was no longer achievable. The preservation of his army became paramount.

MIRACULOUS ESCAPE

"The brigades were ordered to be in readiness with bag and baggage to march at such a time, but they knew not for where or what; the second did not know where the first was gone, nor the third the second,"[90] an American wrote to a woman in England in a letter that he purposely published in Boston's *Independent Chronicle* on September 19, 1776, so the British military would read about their miraculous escape from Long Island.

As the British camped within 600 yards of the Americans' outermost redoubt at their Brooklyn Heights position on the night of August 28, 1776, Washington evaluated the situation. At the next fair wind, British warships could enter the East River and cut off his ability to communicate with his troops on Manhattan, enact a siege of his troops on Long Island, wipe out or capture his entire army and win the war.

"His Excellency General Washington ... most wisely concluded upon evacuating the island: he concealed his intention, while he got the boats ready." Experienced fisherman from Marblehead, Massachusetts rowed all the troops safely to Manhattan.

"Last night our forces were ordered to evacuate Long Island and retreat to New York, when our regiment, two others from Pennsylvania, and the remainder of the Maryland regiment, were ordered to secure the retreat. We remained at the extent of our lines, within musket shot of the enemy, by whom we were surrounded until sunrise, and had not an excessive fog arose, which concealed the retreat of our main body, we must have fallen into their hands,"[91] an officer with the regiment closest to the enemy reported.

Many viewed the fog as a miracle from God because it concealed their evacuation from the British at sunrise. Newspapers published letters they received from soldiers who witnessed the fog. "Providence favored us. The night was remarkably still; the water was as smooth as glass, so that all our boats went over safe, tho' many of them were but about three inches out of the water. At sunrise a great fog came up. The enemy did not discover that we had evacuated our lines, till we were all over ... This evacuation is a masterpiece,"[92] a soldier explained in a letter published in the *Independent Chronicle*.

"May we not say in the language of the sacred writer, our soul is escaped as a bird out of the snare of the fowler; the snare is broken and we are escaped. We are bound to, and I trust shall always honor the instrument; but as it is the inspiration of the most High that giveth understanding, let God have the chief glory," the soldier continued.

"Providentially for us, a great fog arose, which prevented the enemy from seeing our retreat from their works, which was not more than a musket shot from us, had we been discovered we must have been unavoidably cut off, as we were on a neck of land which could have been taken possession of buy them before we could have got out,"[93] another soldier wrote. Staying with his troops at the Long Island ferry until the end of the evacuation, Washington saved the army from capture. "The manner in which our retreat was performed reflects the highest credit upon our commander-in-chief, and the officers in general,"[94] the *Philadelphia Evening Post* reported on August 31, 1776.

There was a second miracle, as noted by historian William Jackman. A British loyalist lived near the ferry that Washington's army used to escape from Long Island to Manhattan. Seeking to tell the British soldiers about their evacuation, she sent her African servant to the nearest British post, which was guarded by Hessians, who were German-speaking soldiers hired by the British.

"He reached the Hessian outposts in safety, but they did not understand his language, and detained him a close prisoner till morning. Then an English officer learned the truth from him, but it was too late. The British did not reach the ferry till the last boat was beyond musket shot."[95]

The Continentals were gone. Both a miraculous fog and a language barrier were the miracles of the moment. "The safe retreat of the patriot army was by many attributed to a peculiar Providence. It was a trust in this Providence, a calm assurance of ultimate success under its guiding care that strengthened the hearts of the patriots in their darkest hour of trial," Jackman reflected.

The war continued on Manhattan. On September 16, the Continental Army secured a victory at the Battle of Harlem Heights. Weeks later Washington sought to establish an orderly evacuation from Manhattan by taking a stand on high ground. General Howe defeated the patriots at the Battle of White Plains on October 28, 1776.

Weeks later, attacked from three sides, the Continental Army surrendered Fort Washington to the British on November 16, 1776, and abandoned Fort Lee four days later. "The misfortune of losing Fort Washington, with between two and three thousand men, will reach you before this, if it has not already,"[96] General Nathanael Greene wrote to Henry Knox, who'd retreated with the rest of the army. "I feel made vexed, sick and sorry. Never did I need the consoling voice of a friend more than now. Happy should I be to see you. This is a most terrible event: its consequences are justly to be dreaded." Washington divided his army and retreated across New Jersey, where he would reach the lowest point of 1776.

MIRACULOUS CROSSING

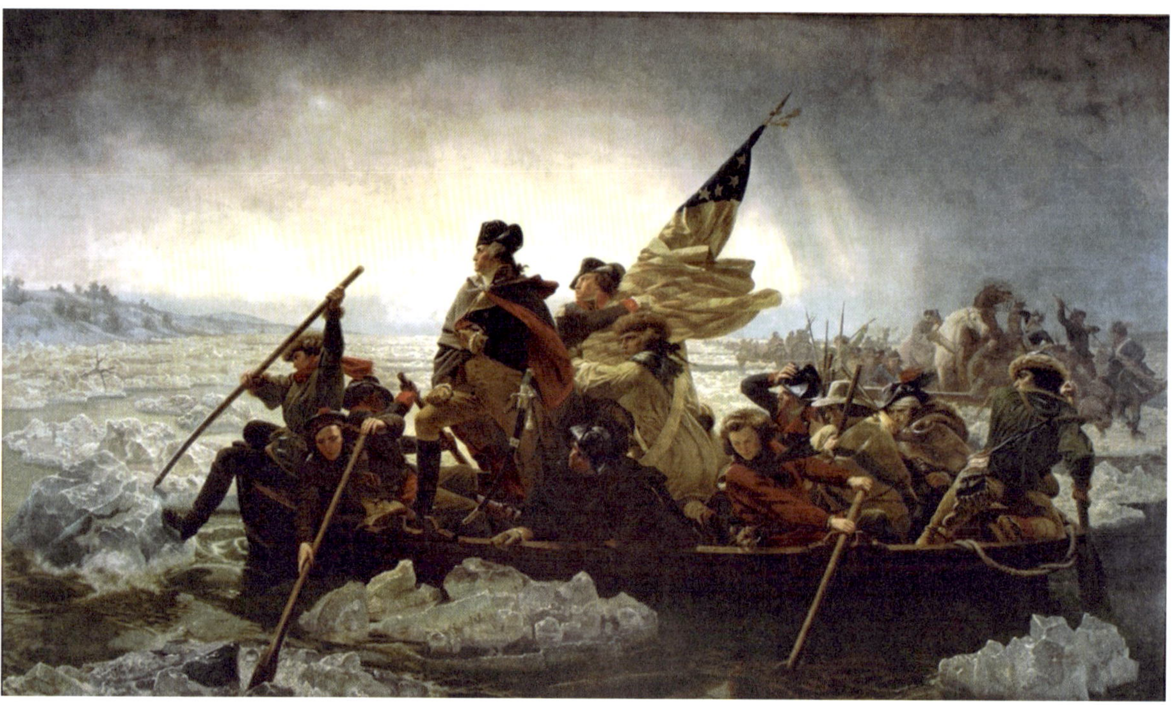

***Washington Crossing the Delaware* by Emanuel Leutze, public domain**

"We are in a very disaffected part of the province; and, between you and me, I think our affairs are in a very bad situation,"[97] General Washington wrote to his brother Samuel on December 18, 1776. The enemy had pushed his army across New Jersey, where many unfriendly loyalists lived, until they crossed the Delaware River and camped in Pennsylvania. He had "less than 3,000 men fit for duty, owing to the dissolution of our force by short enlistments; the enemy's numbers, from the best accounts exceeding ten and by some 12,000 men."

"In a word, my dear Sir, if every nerve is not strained to recruit the new army with all possible expedition, I think the game is pretty near up," Washington explained to Samuel. Many of his men's enlistment terms would expire in a few days on December 31, 1776. The British had also recently captured his second in command, General Charles Lee.

"You can form no idea of the perplexity of my situation. No man, I believe, ever had a greater choice of difficulties, and less means to extricate himself from them." The commander-in-chief may have been discouraged but he believed in independence. "However, under a full persuasion of the justice of our cause, I cannot entertain an idea, that it will finally sink, tho' it may remain for some time under a cloud."

Washington needed to convince his men to stay in the army and regain the confidence of the members of Congress who questioned his leadership after losing New York.

"The evening of the [December] twenty-fifth, I ordered the troops intended for this service to parade back to McKonkey's Ferry, that they might begin to pass [over the Delaware River] as soon as it grew dark, imagining we should be able to throw them all over, with the necessary artillery, by twelve o'clock, and that we might easily arrive at Trenton by five in the morning, the distance being about nine miles,"[98] Washington wrote to John Hancock, the president of the Continental Congress, on December 27, 1776.

Once again, Washington launched a surprise. This time he'd planned to attack the British post at Trenton, which was guarded by the Hessians, hired mercenaries. "But the quantity of ice, made that night, impeded the passage of the boats so much, that it was three o'clock before the artillery could all be got over; and near four before the troops took up their line of march," Washington recorded.

The delay put the army in danger of someone seeing them at sunrise and alerting the Hessians, who were thought to be about 2,000 in number. "This made me despair of surprising the town, as I well knew we could not reach it before the day was fairly broke. But as I was certain there was no making a retreat without being discovered and harassed on repassing the river, I determined to push on at all events."

Dividing his men into two columns, Washington ordered them to approach the Hessian post from different directions. A captain asked a man along the road for directions to the Hessians' advance guard house. At first the man was reluctant to answer but did so willingly upon learning that General Washington's army had arrived.

Within minutes, Washington's advance party overtook the Hessians' picket-guards. Within an hour, his army had captured the surprised Hessians, who were still recovering from Christmas frivolity.

"I have the pleasure of congratulating you upon the success of an enterprise, which I had formed against a detachment of the enemy lying at Trenton, and which was executed yesterday morning," Washington wrote. "Finding from our disposition, that they were surrounded, and that they must inevitably be cut to pieces if they made any further resistance, they agreed to lay down their arms. The number that submitted in this manner was 23 officers and 886 men."

"Colonel Rahl, the commanding officer, and seven others were found wounded in the town. I do not exactly know how many were killed; but I fancy twenty or thirty, as they never made any regular stand. Our loss is very trifling indeed, only two officers and one or two privates wounded." This commander could not have been prouder of his men's behavior. They had not panicked as many had at Long Island. Instead, they answered the call of duty. "In justice to the officers and men, I must add, that their behavior upon this occasion reflects the highest honor upon them," he explained.

"The difficulty of passing the river in a very severe night, and their march through a violent storm of snow and hail, did not in the least abate their ardor; but, when they came to the charge, each seemed to vie with the other in pressing forward; and were I to give a preference to any particular corps, I should do great injustice to the others." His men re-enlisted and stayed with him. Not only had crossing the Delaware River led to a victorious surprise attack but it had also enabled him to preserve the army so they could fight in the future. The cause of independence lived on. How did the people respond?

One newspaper publisher, Thomas Greene of New Haven, Connecticut, had already started printing his January 1, 1777 edition of the *Connecticut Journal* when he received an express letter from New Jersey about the Battle of Trenton. Filled with relief at finally receiving good news after months of losses by the Continental Army in New York, Greene ripped out a block of text, leaving an article incomplete and replaced it with the good news.

"That early on the 26th of December General Washington with about 3,000 men crossed the Delaware [River], and at 8 o'clock in the morning engaged the enemy at Trenton, who were about 1,600 in number, and in 35 minutes routed the whole, taking 919 prisoners, exclusive of killed and wounded."[99]

A few days later, he received an officer's letter that conveyed the emotion of the hour. "A colder or icier season I never felt. Rain and hail, with high winds – but no difficulties were too much for our worthy commander to surmount at this important crisis," he wrote, noting that he appreciated Washington's willingness to lead by example. "His Excellency commanded in person ... Too much praise cannot be given to our brave troops. His Excellency was pleased at their undoubted courage; not a soul was found cowardly skulking, but was fierce for the battle."

BATTLE OF PRINCETON

The Battle of Princeton took place on January 3, 1777, when both sides stumbled upon each other and engaged in battle, including on the grounds of the College of New Jersey, which is now Princeton. Washington lost his friend, Hugh Mercer, who was mortally wounded when his brigade ran headlong into the British forces at William Clarke's farm. Personally leading the counterattack that broke the British line, Washington ended the day with his army achieving victory.

Despite this success, the patriots were often reminded of the brutality of the British. Dunlap's *Pennsylvania Packet* published an account on April 29, 1777, of the burial of a member of a military chaplain, whose death had violated the rules of warfare. Reverend George Duffield, a chaplain for the Continental Congress, reported on the death of Mr. Rosborough, a military chaplain assigned to a Pennsylvania battalion. He died on January 2, 1777, following the Battle of Trenton and right before the Battle of Princeton.

"That as a party of the Hessian jagers (hunters) marched down the back of the town, after our troops had retreated, they fell in with Mr. Rosborough, who surrendered as a prisoner,"[100] Duffield wrote in a published affidavit. The jagers were hunting for food when they came across Rosborough. When he surrendered as a prisoner, they knew he was a minister and a chaplain, but they showed him no mercy.

"Notwithstanding, which one of them struck him on the head with a sword or cutlass and then stabbed him several times with a bayonet, while imploring mercy and begging for his life at their hands. That this account was given by a Hessian who said he had killed him. (Save only he did not know Mr. Rosborough's name but called him a d___ rebel minister.)" Their brutality increased after they killed him. "That after he was massacred, he was stripped naked, and, in that confusion, left lying in an open field." Local residents buried the military chaplain in a nearby cemetery.

SEEDS OF CIVIL RIGHTS SOWN IN THE AMERICAN REVOLUTION

How soon did the Declaration of Independence's signature phrase inspire men of all degrees, as Abigail had described?

VOTING

Who could vote in Old England? Initially, the only vote that mattered was the King of England's vote. Then the Magna Carta opened the door for barons to influence the king, which led to the formation of Parliament. However, the king chose the members of Parliament until 1265, when elites from various counties began to hold elections. The 1432 Knights of the Shire Act defined the qualification for a voter as someone who[101] owned land and paid the crown at least 40 shillings a year. During the time of the American Revolution, only about three percent of the population in the United Kingdom could vote. This land-owning requirement was similar in Britain's colonies.

Prior to the American Revolution, voters were the only ones in society who were economically independent. If you did not own land, you were dependent on someone who did own land. Therefore, your vote would reflect the interests of your landlord or husband or father. This influence would theoretically corrupt the votes of non-landowners.

This was the belief system that had existed for centuries among Englishmen and Englishwomen. But as the ideals of the American Revolution took hold, some began to see the dissonance between economic independence and the belief that all were created in the image of God and should be a part of the consent of the governed, regardless of their economic status.

"Laws and government are founded on the consent of the people, and that consent should by each member of society be given in proportion to his right. Every member of society has a right to give his consent to the laws of the community or he owes no obedience to them,"[102] Massachusetts attorney James Sullivan wrote in May 1776, to his friend Elbridge Gerry.

"And yet a very great number of the people of this colony have at all times been bound by laws to which they never were in a capacity to consent not having (an) estate worth 40 shillings per annum (year)," Sullivan explained, knowing that the colonial voting system was based on the medieval voting system in Old England.

While anticipating a meeting to form a new government in Massachusetts, Sullivan concluded that it was time to think about a new way of voting to be true to the emerging republican system. "In order to do it must we not lay aside our old patched and unmeaning form of government?"

Prior to the War for Independence, in order to vote in Massachusetts, a person had to own land worth forty shillings a year. The result was that only about 15 percent of the population was eligible to vote. Of those eligible, only 3.5 percent of the population had voted in the decade before 1774, when the king abolished the Massachusetts legislature and implemented martial law under a British general. Sullivan saw the contradiction. If only landowners could vote in America, then more than 80 percent of the people (both men and women, free and slave) had no voice in choosing their representatives. The resulting system favored upper class men and excluded men who didn't own land, as well as women, free blacks, and slaves.

When John Adams read Sullivan's letter to Gerry, he wrote Sullivan a letter offering his opinion on expanding voting rights to non-landowners. "The same reasoning, which will induce you to admit all men, who have no property, to vote, with those who have, for those laws, which affect the person will prove that you ought to admit women and children: for generally speaking, women and children, have as good judgment, and as independent minds as those men who are wholly destitute of property," Adams wrote on May 26, 1776. Why was he discussing women's voting rights?

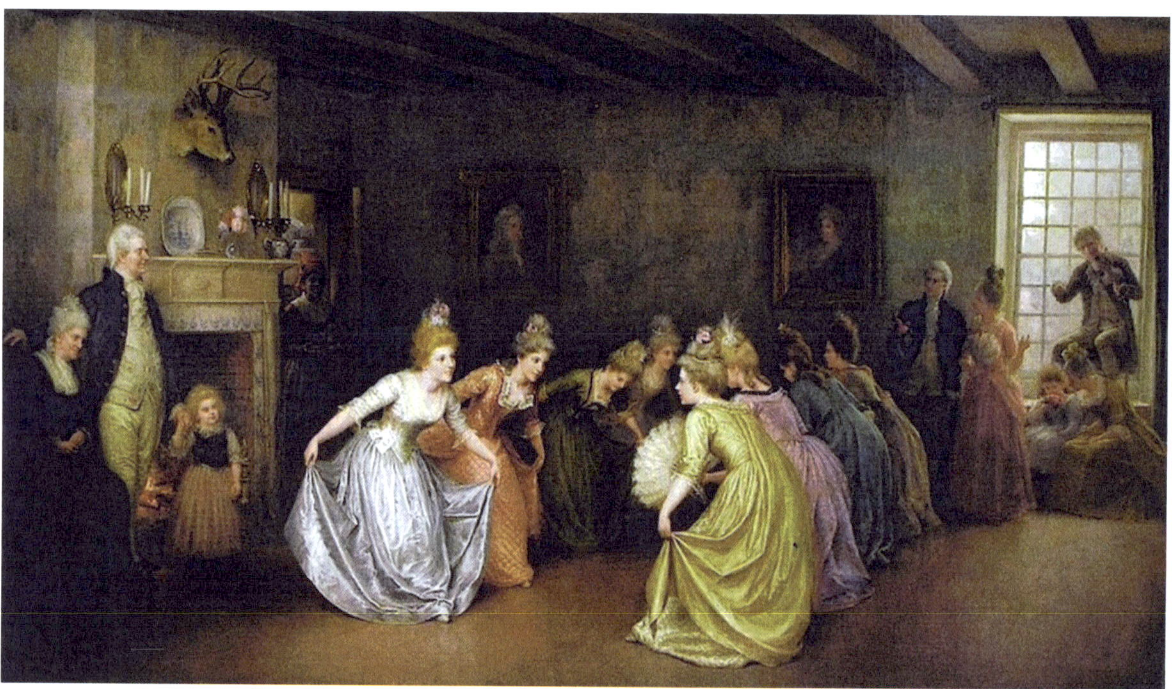

Ladies bowing by Jennie Augusta Brownscombe

REMEMBER THE LADIES

What Sullivan didn't know, is that two months earlier, Abigail Adams had written her husband with a request. She knew that if the Continental Congress declared independence, they would have to make a new code of laws. "... I desire you would remember the ladies, and be more generous and favorable to them than your ancestors,"[103] she had written to John on March 31, 1776.

"Do not put such unlimited power into the hands of the husbands. Remember all men would be tyrants if they could. If particular care and attention is not paid to the ladies, we are determined to foment a rebellion, and will not hold ourselves bound by any laws in which we have no voice or representation," she'd warned, before expressing concerns.

"That your sex are naturally tyrannical is a truth so thoroughly established as to admit of no dispute, but such of you as wish to be happy willingly give up the harsh title of master for the more tender and endearing one of friend. Why then, not put it out of the power of the vicious and the lawless to use us with cruelty and indignity with impunity. Men of sense in all ages abhor those customs which treat us only as the vassals of your sex," she wrote referring to John Locke's philosophy that viewed both men and women as created in the image of God.

"Regard us then as beings placed by Providence under your protection and in imitation of the Supreme Being make use of that power only for our happiness."

John had responded by teasing her. But his correspondence with Sullivan two months later showed that he'd been thinking about Abigail's concerns. Adams had concluded that if men without land could vote, so should women. After all, he'd placed the management of their farmland in Abigail's hands, which led to praise from his neighbors.

However, John Adams was not ready to grant men or women who did not own land the right to vote. He agreed with the English philosopher James Harrington, who wrote *The Commonwealth of Oceana* in 1656. "Harrington has shown that power always follows property. This I believe to be as infallible a maxim, in politics, as, that action and re-action are equal, is in mechanics. Nay, I believe we may advance one step farther and affirm that the balance of power in a society, accompanies the balance of property in land."[104]

Adams had a different solution to the problems proposed by Sullivan and his wife: let more people own land. Expand land-ownership to other classes of people beyond the wealthy. This could be done by selling smaller tracts of land.

"The only possible way then of preserving the balance of power on the side of equal liberty and public virtue, is to make the acquisition of land easy to every member of society: to make a division of the land into small quantities, so that the multitude may be possessed of landed estates," Adams concluded.

"If the multitude is possessed of the balance of real estate, the multitude will have the balance of power, and in that case the multitude will take care of the liberty, virtue, and interest of the multitude in all acts of government."

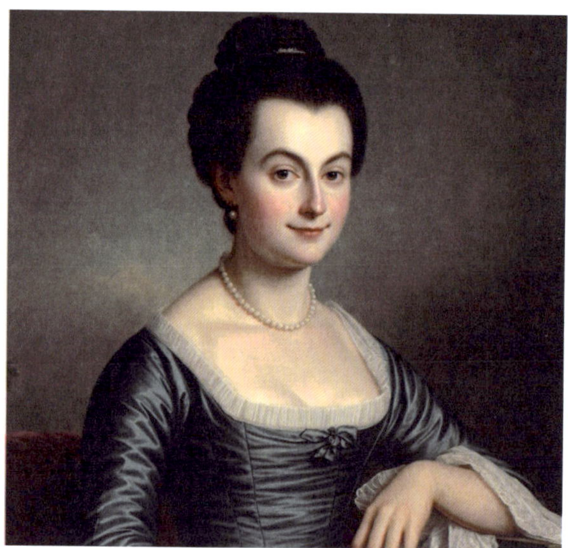

Rendering of Abigail Adams, adapted from paintings of her

Abigail's call to remember the ladies may not have succeeded with her husband, but New Jersey did. Women who owned land in New Jersey began voting in 1776. Unlike next door in New York, where women could not inherit land, women in New Jersey could own land. Usually, these women voters had inherited land when their husbands died. Women landowners could vote in New Jersey until 1808, when the vote was taken from them. Why did this happen? Politics. Too many women were voting for the Federalist party. When non-land-owning men were given the right to vote, government legislators added the word *male* to describe a voter and removed the land-owning requirement. The result was that New Jersey women who owned land lost the right to vote.

In hindsight, James Sullivan was on the right track. The American Revolution had upended the view of independence as primarily an economic concept and had put it into a political and societal concept that would release shockwaves in the centuries to come.

When George Washington left to attend the first Continental Congress in 1774, Patrick Henry and Edmund Pendleton accompanied him. "I was most pleased with Mrs. Washington and her spirit. She seemed ready to make any sacrifice and was cheerful though I knew she felt anxious. She talked like a Spartan mother to her son going to battle. 'I hope you will stand firm – I know George will,' she said,"[105] Pendleton later reflected.

"The dear little woman was busy from morning to night in domestic duties, but she gave us much time in conversation and affording us entertainment. When we set off in the morning, she stood in the door and cheered us with the good words, 'God be with you gentlemen.'"

Martha traveled to be with Washington in winter camp yearly. She stayed in a safe location, such as Mount Vernon, during the fighting season. As a result, Martha spent about fifty percent of the war with him. Later in the war, Martha and other ladies, including Thomas Jefferson's wife, raised money to clothe the Continental Army.

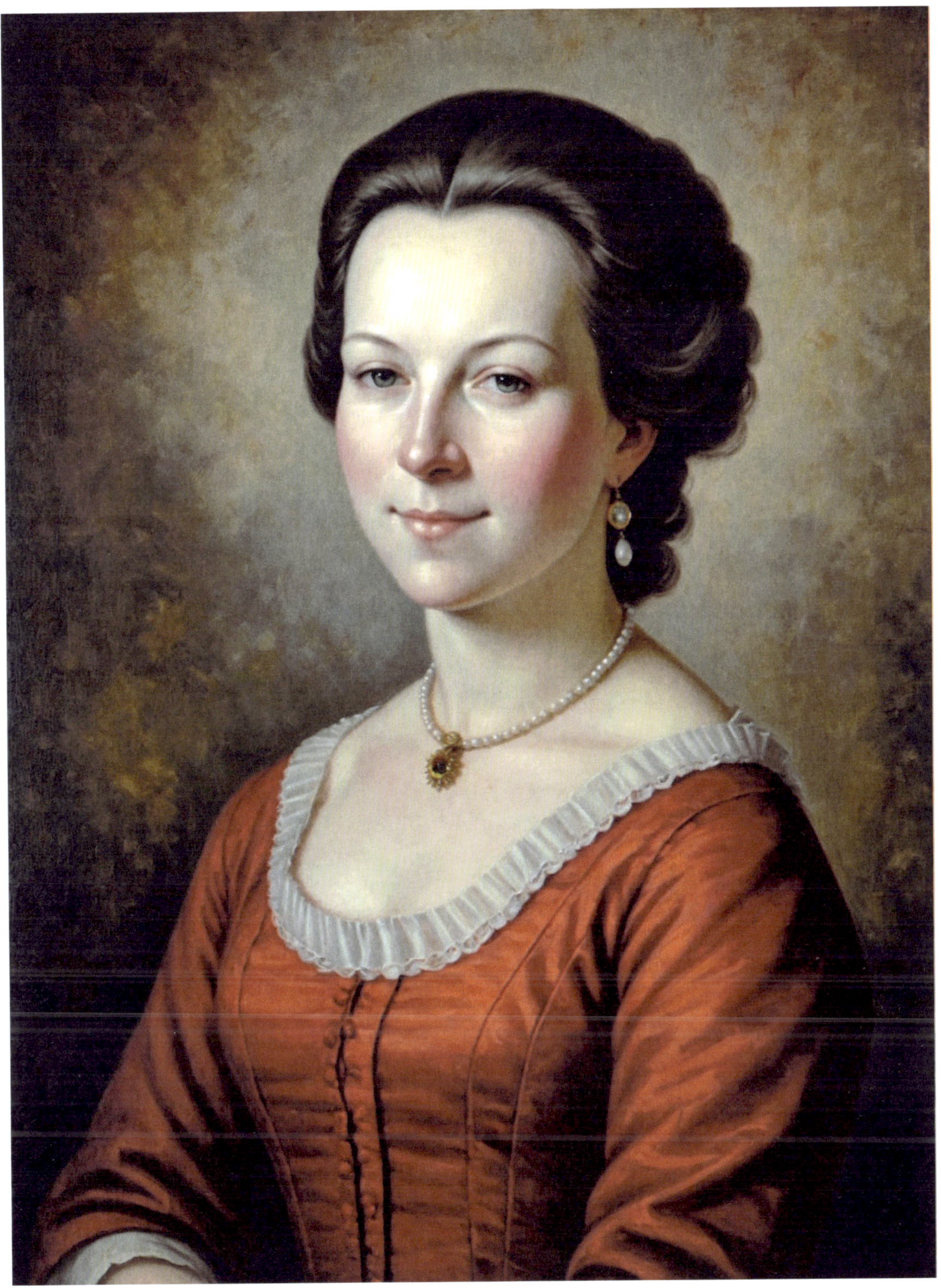

A modern rendering of Martha Washington based on her face in other portraits

THE FIRST OFFICIAL U.S. FLAG

In January 1777, Washington's army rested in camp. This gave Washington an opportunity to give the USA something it needed: a new flag. At the time, the British flag combined the English red cross of St. George with the Scottish blue cross of St. Andrew. The diagonal cross of Ireland's St. Patrick was added later. Before the War for Independence, the colonies flew the British flag but also flags with pine trees to represent New England or solid red flags with a small British flag in the left corner.

"But for those who fear you, you have raised a banner to be unfurled against the bow." Psalm 60:4

The first flag used by the Continental Army was the Grand Union Flag, which featured thirteen stripes to represent the thirteen colonies and a small version of the British flag on the top left. When General Washington flew the Grand Union flag in his effort to drive the British from Boston in March 1776, the British thought he was flying a British flag. This confusion exposed a need for a new, distinctly American flag. After Congress declared independence on July 4 and established the United States of America, Washington concluded that America, and his army, needed a new flag.

The Continental Congress passed a resolution on June 14, 1777, for the first official flag of the United States of America. "In CONGRESS, June 14, 1777. Resolved, That the FLAG of the United States be THIRTEEN STRIPES alternate red and white; that the union be THIRTEEN STARS white in a blue field, representing a new constellation."[106] The public first learned about it when the *Pennsylvania Evening Post* published the minutes from Congress's June 14 meeting on August 30, 1777.

Gone was the Grand Union flag that featured a small version of the British flag in the upper corner with red and white stripes. Though the stripes remained, gone were the thirteen British colonies. Replacing them were America's new thirteen states, which the flag's stripes and new stars represented. But these states were more than just separate entities. Whereas the colonies had almost acted as separate nations, these states were united into one nation. This was the flag's purpose: to symbolize a united nation.

The meaning of the first official United States flag had nothing to do with skin color, sex, class, race, ethnicity, religion or any other distinction. Congress intended for the flag of the United States to mean one thing: union. Through a new constellation, the white stars on the blue background depicted this unity. When the stars formed a circle, they also conveyed the equality of that union, because no state was more important than another.

Congress was busy that day. They also fired a ship captain of poor character and replaced him with a new upstart. They chose a promising new talent, Captain John Paul Jones. Unfortunately, they were too busy prosecuting the business of war to give more information about the flag. This left unanswered questions. Who had designed the flag? What did the colors mean? When did they start calling June 14 Flag Day?

Yet, today, the thirteen-star flag approved by the Continental Congress in 1777 is often called the Betsy Ross flag. How did her name become linked to this flag?

The connection of Betsy Ross to the first flag was not known to the American public for nearly 100 years – until her grandson told her story, which some historians question. This newspaper article, based on a presentation made by William J. Canby to the Pennsylvania Historical Society, reported in 1870: "The first American flag, however, according to the design and approval of Congress, was made by Mrs. Elizabeth Ross. Three of her daughters still live in our vicinity to confirm this fact, founding their belief, not upon what they saw, for it was many years before they were born, but upon what their mother had often told them. A niece of this lady, Mrs. Margaret Boggs, aged ninety-five years, now lives in Germantown, and is conversant with the fact."[107]

Canby was one of Betsy's grandsons from her third marriage to John Claypoole. She lost two husbands before having five children with Claypoole. Canby explained that Betsy Ross became involved in making the first flag through her deceased husband's uncle, Colonel George Ross.

"It is related that when Congress had decided upon the design, Colonel George Ross and General Washington visited Mrs. Ross [the colonel's widowed niece] and asked her to make it. She said, 'I don't know whether I can, but I'll try,' and directly suggested to the gentlemen that the design was wrong, in that the stars were six-cornered, and not five-cornered, as they should be."

Ross was an upholsterer who knew the ins and outs of efficient cutting and sewing techniques for patterns such as stars. Having sewn flags for ships and recognizing that the flags would need to be uniform, she straightened out George Washington as her great-granddaughter Rachel Beuhler later relayed.

"Washington wanted a flag, and he had a six-point star in mind. But Betsy said a five-pointed star would be more symmetrical. She showed them how she could fold a piece of paper and with one snip of the scissors make a perfect five-pointed star."[108] And with that, a new constellation was born, stitched into history by Betsy Ross according to family tradition. Her grandchildren were so confident in her role that they signed sworn affidavits testifying to her contribution. The first official Flag Day was not celebrated until June 14, 1916, when President Woodrow Wilson seized an opportunity to establish a patriotic observance to boost patriotism for World War I.

Why didn't Congress define the meaning of red, white, and blue when they issued the flag on June 14, 1777? They didn't know what those colors meant because they lacked perspective. They were in the middle of the chaos of the Revolution. But in the days and weeks ahead, they would come to know the meaning of the colors through the valor and perseverance of George Washington's army and others who contributed to the cause of liberty. Congress would choose another time to define the meaning of the nation's colors.

A STAR IS BORN

Washington spent the spring of 1777 rebuilding his army through new recruits. One volunteer touched Washington's heart. At age 19, the Marquis de Lafayette defied King Louis XVI by sneaking out of France and traveling to Philadelphia. He joined Washington's army as a volunteer. Lafayette, who'd served as one of the French king's

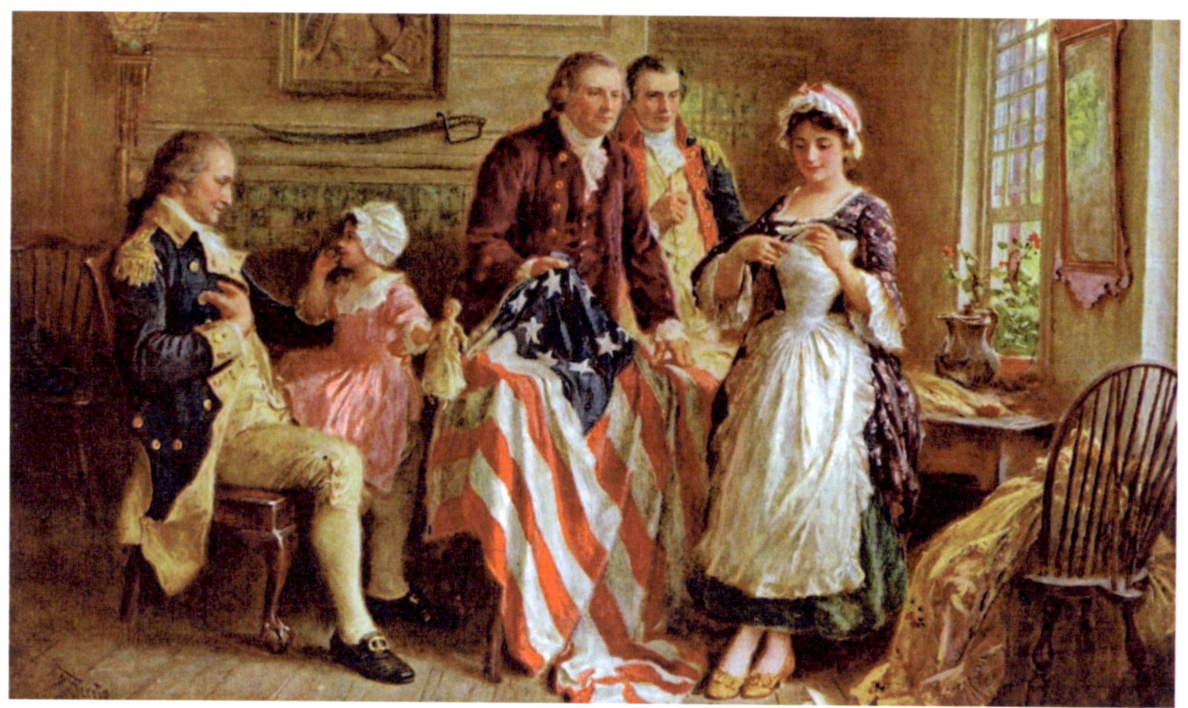

Betsy Ross and the first official flag by Jean Gerome Leon Ferris, Library of Congress

musketeers since he was 13, told Washington, "I am here to learn, not to teach."[109]

Washington sought to prevent the British from capturing Philadelphia, the nation's capital. Because Congress improved financial and other terms for enlistments, his army of 14,500 was nearly the same size as British General Howe's 15,500 force. The armies engaged in battle along Brandywine Creek on September 11, 1777. The British gained the advantage by fording the creek further north and attacking. Nathanael Greene's men served as a rear guard and made a counter attack, enabling the rest of the Continental army to withdraw. Though Lafayette was wounded at the Battle of Brandywine, he ensured an orderly retreat. Although Washington lost the battle, he preserved his army, enabling them to live to fight another day.

"I shall begin by telling you that I am well, because I must end by telling you that we fought in earnest yesterday, and we were not the victors. Our Americans, after holding firm for a considerable time, were finally routed," Lafayette wrote to his wife Adrienne.

"While I was trying to rally them, the English honored me with a musket shot, which wounded me slightly in the leg," he wrote. "But the wound is nothing, dear heart; the ball hit neither bone nor nerve, and all I have to do for it to heal is to lie on my back for a while – which puts me in very bad humor. I hope, dear heart, that you will not worry; on the contrary, you should be even less worried than before, because I shall now be out of action for some time. I intended to take good care of myself; you may be sure of that, dear heart. This battle will, I fear, have unpleasant consequences for America; we must try to repair the damage, if we can," Lafayette wrote.

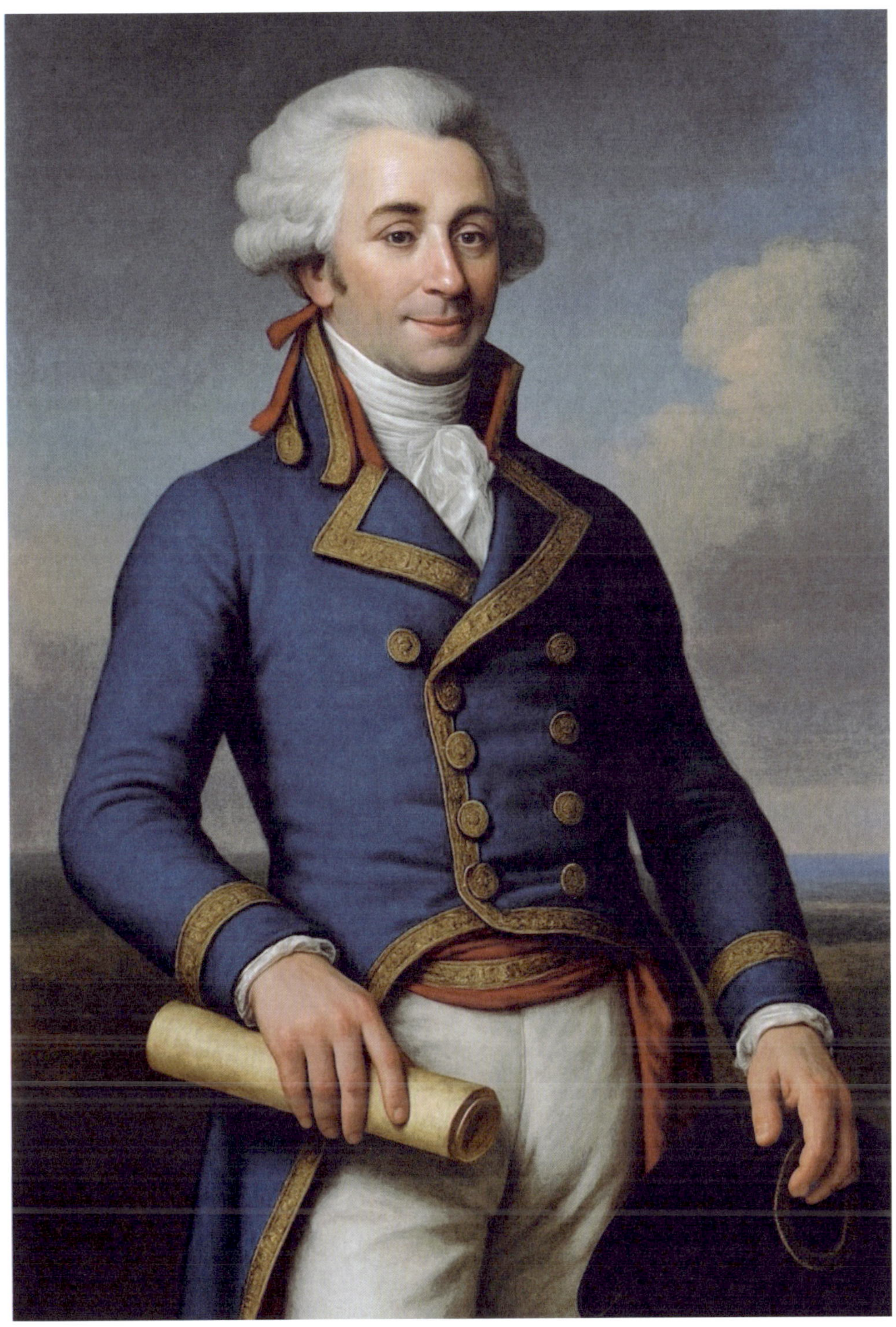

A modern rendering of the Marquis de Lafayette based on public domain portraits.

A SIZABLE VICTORY

Taking place in the Hudson River Valley in New York from September 19 until October 17, 1777, two key battles led to the surrender of British General John Burgoyne, 5,800 prisoners, 27 field pieces and 5,000 muskets at Saratoga. The most significant victory to date, Burgoyne's surrender was a turning point in the war because it gave the king of France confidence in becoming America's ally.

Led by General Horatio Gates, the Continental Army defeated British forces at Freeman's Farm and Bemis Heights. Although General Burgoyne had captured Fort Ticonderoga on his march from Canada in July, he lost a number of forces at Freeman's Farm, the first Battle of Saratoga on September 19. After unsuccessfully attacking the Continentals at Bemis Heights on October 7, Burgoyne eventually surrendered on October 17 after he failed to receive reinforcements.

General Benedict Arnold led a charge on October 7, when he was hit in the leg. Though he'd defied and argued with General Gates, he was hailed as a hero for his bravery.

THE FIRST NATIONAL THANKSGIVING PROCLAMATION

The Continental Congress released America's first national Thanksgiving proclamation on November 1, 1777, and set aside December 18, 1777, as a day for Thanksgiving after British General Burgoyne's surrender. They believed it was their "indispensable duty"[110] to adore "the superintending Providence of Almighty God." They expressed their gratitude.

"And it having pleased him in his abundant mercy, not only to continue to us the innumerable bounties of his common Providence; but also to smile upon us in the prosecution of a just and necessary war, for the defense and establishment of our unalienable rights and liberties; particularly in that he hath been pleased, in so great a measure, to prosper the means used for the support of our troops, and to crown our arms with most signal success," the proclamation declared, while listing detailed and flourishing descriptions of their gratitude. How did General Washington respond to Congress's call for giving thanks?

WASHINGTON'S ARMY GIVES THANKS–1777

"The Commander-in-Chief with the highest satisfaction expresses his thanks to the officers and soldiers for the fortitude and patience with which they have sustained the fatigues of the campaign,"[111] Washington wrote his troops in General Orders on December 17, 1777. Though they lost Germantown on October 4, they proved they could stand up to the British after the victory of Saratoga.

"Altho' in some instances we unfortunately failed, yet upon the whole Heaven hath smiled on our arms and crowned them with signal success; and we may upon the best grounds conclude, that by a spirited continuance of the measures necessary for our defense we shall finally obtain the end of our warfare—Independence—Liberty and Peace—These are blessings worth contending for at every hazard."

"Every motive therefore, irresistibly urges us—nay commands us, to a firm and manly perseverance in our opposition to our cruel oppressors—to slight difficulties—endure hardships, and contemn every danger."[112] After explaining that they would be soon setting up a new camp at Valley Forge, Washington called on them to give thanks.

"Tomorrow being the day set apart by the Honorable Congress for public Thanksgiving and praise; and duty calling us devoutly to express our grateful acknowledgements to God for the manifold blessings he has granted us—The general directs that the army remain in its present quarters, and that the chaplains perform divine service with their several corps and brigades—and earnestly exhorts, all officers and soldiers, whose absence is not indispensably necessary, to attend with reverence the solemnities of the day," Washington concluded.

"18th the weather still remains uncomfortable—this is Thanksgiving Day through the whole continent of America—but God knows we have very little to keep it with this being the third day we have been without flour or bread—& are living on a high uncultivated hill, in huts & tents laying on the cold ground, upon the whole I think all we have to be thankful for is that we are alive & not in the grave with many of our friends," Lt. Col. Henry Dearborn wrote of their food shortage.

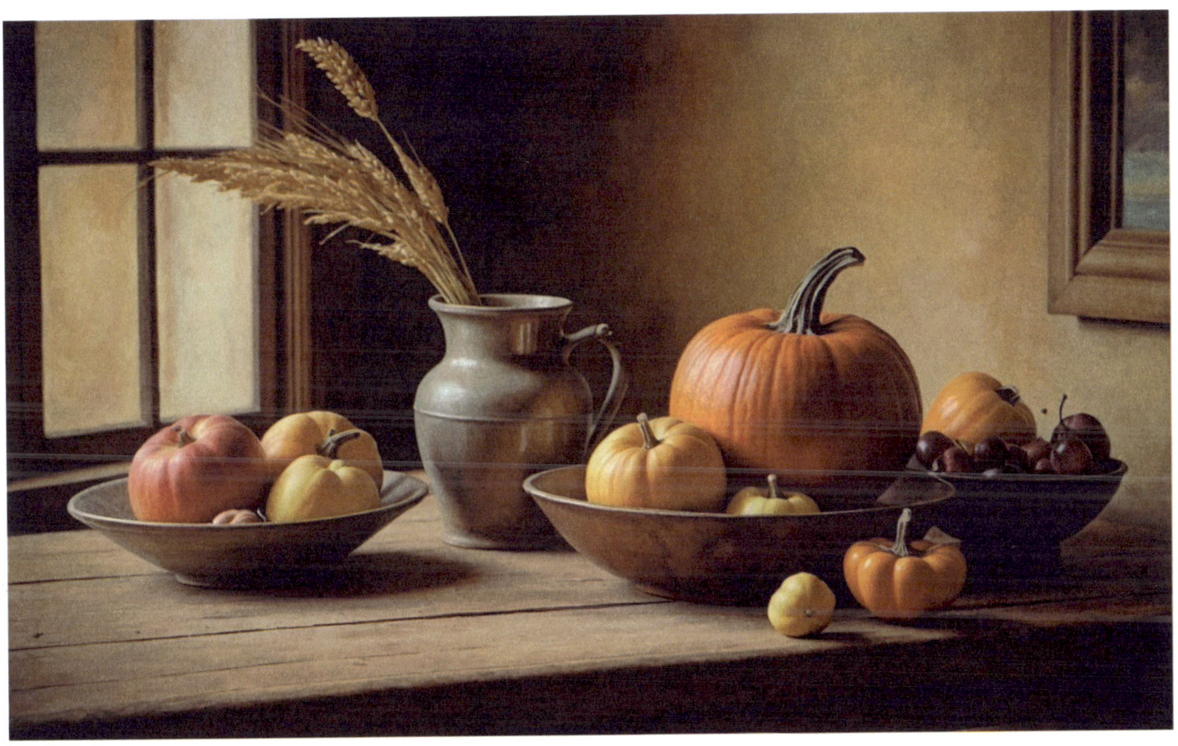

REDCOAT FRIVOLITY

"If Congress has not yet left Philadelphia, they ought to do it immediately without fail, for the enemy has the means of throwing a party this night into the city,"[113] Alexander Hamilton urgently wrote on September 18, 1778, to John Hancock, president of the Continental Congress, in Philadelphia. While on a secret mission from Washington to check their secret supplies at Valley Forge, the British had fired on Hamilton "One man was killed and another wounded. . . . I did all I could to prevent this but to no purpose." How did Hancock respond? He took action. "Whereupon, the members left the city." The Continental Congress fled to Lancaster, Pennsylvania.

On September 26, 1777, the British military marched into Philadelphia, where they occupied the nation's capital city for months. In the spring of 1778, they held a Meschianza, which was an elaborate party honoring one of their departing commanding officers, General Howe. From a floating parade of decorated ships to a jousting contest with costumed participants, the *Royal Pennsylvania Gazette* declared that the entertainment "far surpassed anything ... seen in this or perhaps any other country."[114]

"With the knights and squires leading in their favorite damsels" the party-goers enjoyed a ball, fireworks, and a banquet. "In short, the power of description are too languid to do justice to the whole of this singular entertainment, in which British taste was only aided by British magnificence."

Not everyone applauded the extravagance. "How insensible these people appear, while our land is so greatly desolated, and death and sore destruction has overtaken and impends over so many,"[115] a Philadelphia Quaker, Elizabeth Drinker, wrote in her diary.

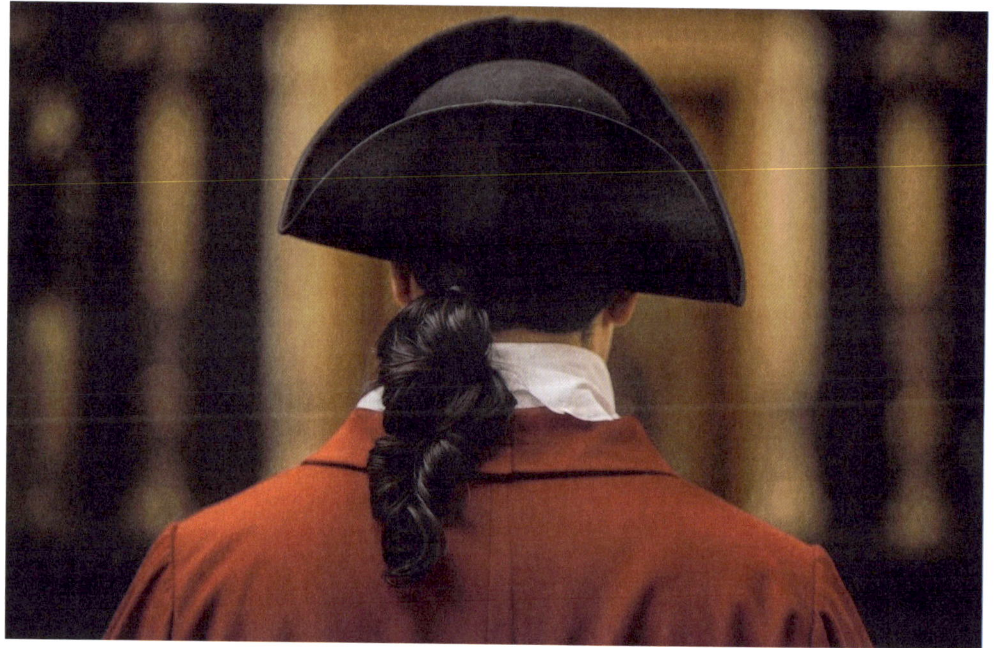

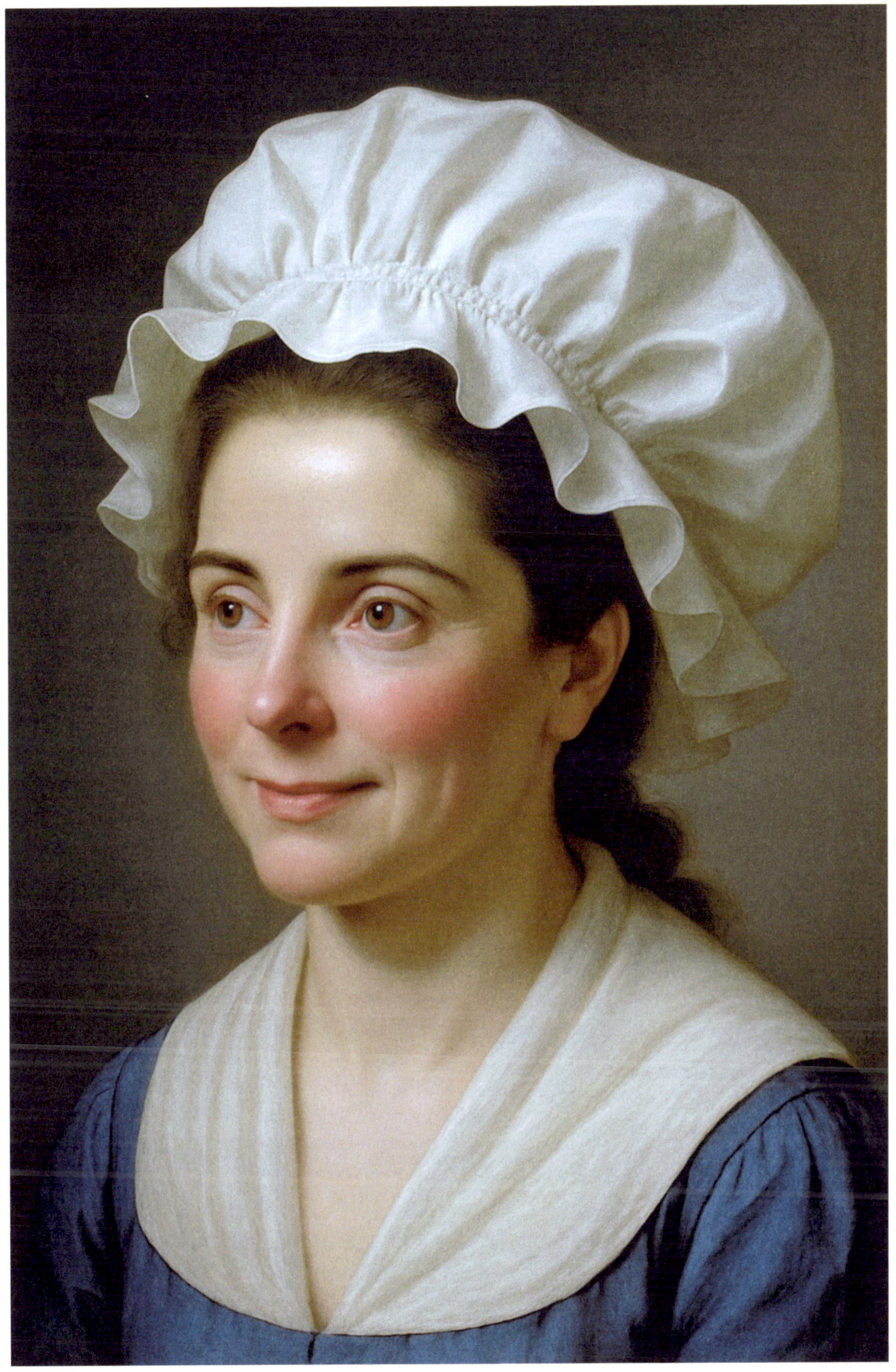

A rendered portrait of Lydia Darrah based on a rough sketch

A FREEZING FORCE FORGED IN THE VALLEY

Lydia Darrah, a pacifist Quaker woman, overheard the British plans of a surprise attack on George Washington's army. In addition to wearing plain clothing, Quakers often embraced anti-war and anti-slavery doctrines. Lydia was forced to allow the British to take over her Philadelphia home. Though several British officers ordered her to go to sleep, she'd crept into the hallway and listened to their surprise attack plans on Washington's troops at nearby White Marsh. Darrah then asked for a pass the next day to retrieve flour from a flour mill. After reaching the mill, she kept traveling until she reached Washington's advance guard at White Marsh. She told the Continentals soldiers about the British plans and returned to her home in Philadelphia. When the British launched their surprise attack, they found that the Continentals were ready for them. The British retreated back to Philadelphia.

Washington knew that his position at White Marsh was not secure.

"The General ardently wishes, it were now in his power, to conduct the troops into the best winter quarters—But where are these to be found? Should we retire to the interior parts of the state, we should find them crowded with virtuous citizens, who, sacrificing their all, have left Philadelphia and fled thither for protection. To their distresses humanity forbids us to add—This is not all, we should leave a vast extent of fertile country to be despoiled and ravaged by the enemy, from which they would draw vast supplies, and where many of our firm friends would be exposed to all the miseries of the most insulting and wanton depredation—A train of evils might be enumerated, but these will suffice."[116]

Where could he take his troops? He needed a location that was close enough to Philadelphia to keep an eye on the British but far enough away to prevent a surprise attack.

"These considerations make it indispensably necessary for the army to take such a position, as will enable it most effectually to prevent distress and to give the most extensive security; and in that position we must make ourselves the best shelter in our power."

He told them that they would have to build their camp at Valley Forge.

"With activity and diligence huts may be erected that will be warm and dry—In these the troops will be compact, more secure against surprises than if in a divided state and at hand to protect the country. These cogent reasons have determined the General to take post in the neighborhood of this camp; and influenced by them, he persuades himself, that the officers and soldiers, with one heart and one mind, will resolve to surmount every difficulty, with a fortitude and patience, becoming their profession, and the sacred cause in which they are engaged: He himself will share in the hardship, and partake of every inconvenience." Washington accurately predicted the hardship they would face.

"A general cry through the camp this evening among the soldiers—'No meat!—No meat!'—the distant vales echoed back the melancholy sound ... What have you for our dinners, boys?' 'Nothing but fire cake and water, Sir,' at night—'Gentlemen, the supper is ready.' What is your supper, lads? 'Fire cake and water, Sir,'" [117] Dr. Albigence Waldo wrote in his diary about Valley Forge, where he treated the sick.

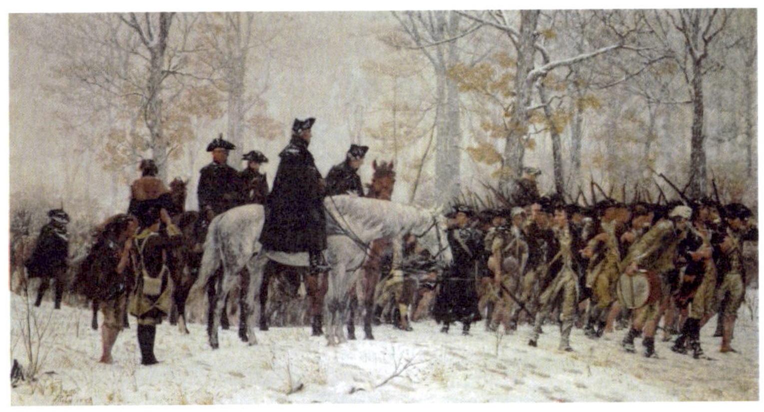

Marching to Valley Forge by Edward Percy Moran, Library of Congress

Fire cakes were tasteless pancakes made of a little flour and water cooked over a fire. Meat was scarce. Until they built their huts, the only way to keep warm was to continually burn campfires. Waldo was so irritated from the smoke that he feared his eyes were spoiled.

"But why do I talk of hunger and hard usage, when so many in the world have not even fire cake and water to eat," he wrote, counting his blessings as best he could. "Huts go on slowly—cold and smoke make us fret ... But mankind are always fretting, even if they have more than their proportion of the blessings of life. We are never easy—always repining at the Providence of an all wise and benevolent Being—blaming our country—or faulting our friends," he wrote.

The New Year brought him hope. "1778. January 1st.—New Year. I am alive. I am well. Huts go on briskly and our camp begins to appear like a spacious city," he wrote.

UNMASKING A CABAL

After General Gates won the Battle of Saratoga, General Washington sent Alexander Hamilton, who'd become one of his aid-de-camps several months earlier, to General Gates to find out why Gates had not sent him reinforcements as Washington had ordered. Though Hamilton pressed the issue several times, Gates continued to stall, which left Hamilton unsettled about Gates's respect for Washington. Something seemed afoot.

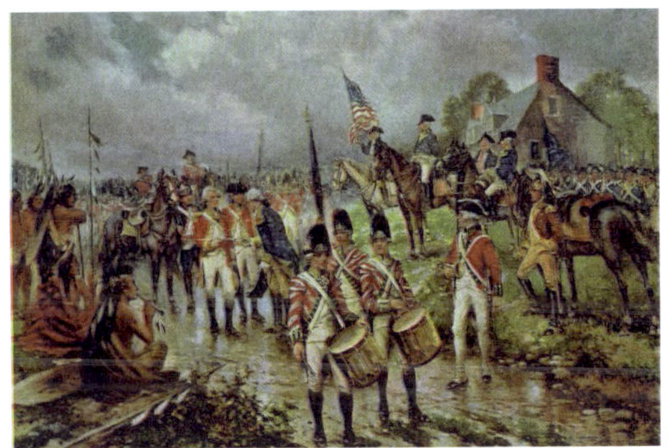

British surrender at Saratoga by Edward Percy Moran

Communication between General Gates and General Thomas Conway surfaced, as General Stirling informed Washington. General Gates had ordered his aid-de-camp, James Wilkinson, to travel to York, Pennsylvania, to give the Continental Congress the good news about Burgoyne's surrender. Along the way, Wilkinson stopped at Stirling's position in Reading, Pennsylvania and gave Stirling's aide-de-camp a copy of Conway's letter to Gates.

"Heaven has been determined to save your country; Or a weak general and bad counsellors would have ruined it," Conway had written to Gates after his victory at Saratoga.

Who was the weak general? Concluding that Conway was referring to General Washington, Stirling told Washington about the letter between Gates and Conway.

"Such wicked duplicity of conduct, I shall always think it my duty to detect,"[118] General Stirling wrote with disgust and indignation in a letter to Washington on November 3, 1777, from Reading, Pennsylvania. "The enclosed was communicated (an) idea of the state of politics and parties in this country."

How did Washington respond to this news that Conway, who was in camp with Washington, thought he was a weak general?

Washington took swift action. He wrote Conway a short, concise letter, without any emotion or requests. He simply notified Conway that he'd received this information. "Sir, a letter which I received last night, contained the following, paragraph. In a letter from General Conway to General Gates he says—'Heaven has been determined to save your country; or a weak general and bad counselors would have ruined it.' I am Sir, your humble servant."[119]

How did Conway respond? That same day, Conway wrote Washington a letter and defended himself. Declaring that he'd congratulated Gates and "spoke my mind freely, I found fault with several measures pursued in this army; but I will venture to say that in my whole letter the paragraph of which you are pleased to send me a copy cannot be found,"[120] he wrote, denying the authorship of the passage.

Congress soon learned of the Gates-Conway correspondence, which concerned Lafayette who wrote Washington about this growing enemy within. "I see plainly that America can defend herself if proper measures are taken. Now I begin to fear that she could be lost by herself and her own sons," Lafayette wrote on December 30, 1777. He doubted the integrity of General Conway, an English-speaker who'd trained in the French Army before serving in the Continental Army.

"There are open dissentions in Congress, parties who hate one another as much as the common enemy, stupid men who without knowing a single word about war undertake to judge you, to make ridiculous comparisons,"[121] Lafayette wrote. "They are infatuated with Gates without thinking of the different circumstances and believe that attacking is the only thing necessary to conquer. Those ideas are entertained in their minds by some jealous men and perhaps secret friends to the British government who want to push you in a moment of ill humor to some rash enterprise upon the lines or against a much stronger army."

Then Washington received a letter from Gates. "I conjure your Excellency, to give me all the assistance you can, in tracing out the author of the infidelity, which put extracts from General Conway's letters to me, into your hands. Those letters have been stealingly copied; but, which of them, when, or by whom, is to me, as yet, an unfathomable secret,"[122]

The phrase that stood out was "Conway's letters to me." Gates indicated there was more than one letter between him and Conway, which surprised Washington. What did Washington do? He confronted Gates in a letter. "I never knew that General Conway (who I viewed in the light of a stranger to you) was a correspondent of yours, much less did I suspect that I was the subject of your confidential letters."

If Gates and Conway were plotting to convince others, such as Congress, that Washington was weak and needed to be removed, the exposure of their letters stopped their cabal in its tracks. Called the Conway Cabal, the incident left Hamilton furious. "Since I saw you, I have discovered such convincing traits of the monster, that I cannot doubt its reality in the most extensive sense. I dare say, you have seen and heard enough to settle the matter, in your own mind,"[123] Hamilton fumed in a letter to his friend, George Clinton, in Poughkeepsie, New York, about this faction on February 13, 1778.

"I believe it unmasked its batteries too soon and begins to hide its head; but as I imagine it will only change the storm to a sap," he wrote, believing that the cabal was only thwarted for the moment. "Have you heard anything of Conway's history? He is one of the vermin bred in the entrails of this chimera dire, and there does not exist a more villainous calumniator and incendiary. He is gone to Albany on a certain expedition."

REVOLUTIONARY FAKE NEWS & PROPAGANDA

Though the phrase *fake news* is modern, the concept of disinformation is not new. Propaganda has been a war tactic for centuries. Misinformation is "false information that is spread, regardless of intent to mislead."[124] Disinformation is false information that someone spreads on purpose. Fake news can be both.

Around Valentine's Day in early 1778 at Valley Forge, a jaw-dropped George Washington read an article in the *Pennsylvania Ledger* that was published on December 24, 1777. "The printer has received from New York a few copies of an intercepted letter from General Washington to his lady [Martha Washington], dated June 24, 1776, which he is now selling at his shop in Market Street. The following is an extract."[125]

A disgusted Washington learned that this fake letter was circulating in New York taverns as a handbill, which is called a flyer in today's culture. The letter's most shocking statement was a passage that claimed Washington opposed independence on June 24, 1776, just days before July 4, 1776, when the Continental Congress announced the Declaration of Independence. The fake letter claimed: "The only true interest of both sides is reconciliation; nor can there be a point in the world clearer, than that both sides must be losers by war, in a manner which even peace will not soon compensate for. We must, at last, agree and be friends; for we cannot live without them, and they will not without us."

The letter was propaganda: "My attention is this moment called off to the discovery, or pretended discovery, of a most wild and daring plot. It is impossible, as yet, to develop the mystery in which it either is, or is not, supposed to be involved."

This letter suggested that Washington had launched a disinformation campaign, a war of lies. "No doubt it will make a good deal of noise in the country; and there are some who think it useful to have the minds of the people kept constantly on the fret by rumors of this sort." Though Washington knew that propaganda was a popular tactic in war, he also knew this attribution to him was as false as his dentures. "Thus much only I can find out with certainty, that it will be a fine field for a war of lies on both sides... But why should I tease you with tedious details of schemes and views which are perpetually varying?"

This June 24, 1776, letter to Martha and others like it were forgeries, literal fake news. "The enemy are governed by no principles that ought to actuate honest men – no wonder then that forgery should be amongst their other crimes – I have seen a letter published in a handbill at New York, and extracts of it republished in the Philadelphia paper, said to be from me to Mrs. Washington, not one word of which did I ever write,"[126] he wrote to his friend Richard Henry Lee, who was part of the Continental Congress.

This war of lies grew worse. There was more than one forged letter. In fact, there was a pamphlet full of letters. Failing to deny his authorship publicly during the Revolution, these forgeries were a nuisance for Washington until his last day as president of the United States in March 1797. As he entered retirement, he publicly denied his authorship of these letters by writing an opinion article that was published in multiple newspapers.

While these false letters circulated during the American Revolution at Valley Forge in 1778, Washington needed to train his army. In his General Orders on March 28, 1778, he announced that "Baron (von) Steuben, a lieutenant general in foreign service and a gentleman of great military experience" was appointed as inspector general of the army."[127]

"The importance of establishing a uniform system of useful maneuvers and regularity of discipline must be obvious, the deficiency of our army in these respects must be equally so," the orders explained of why obedience to von Steuben was essential. Fighting would begin in summer. "The time we shall probably have to introduce the necessary reformation is short," the orders concluded.

Establishing drill standards for the Continental Army, von Steuben taught his technique to one company of men. He showed them how to stand and march with precision. This company learned how to carry and use a bayonet and to quickly respond to orders, such as reforming lines in battle. This company then trained another company. The pattern continued until the entire army followed the same standards.

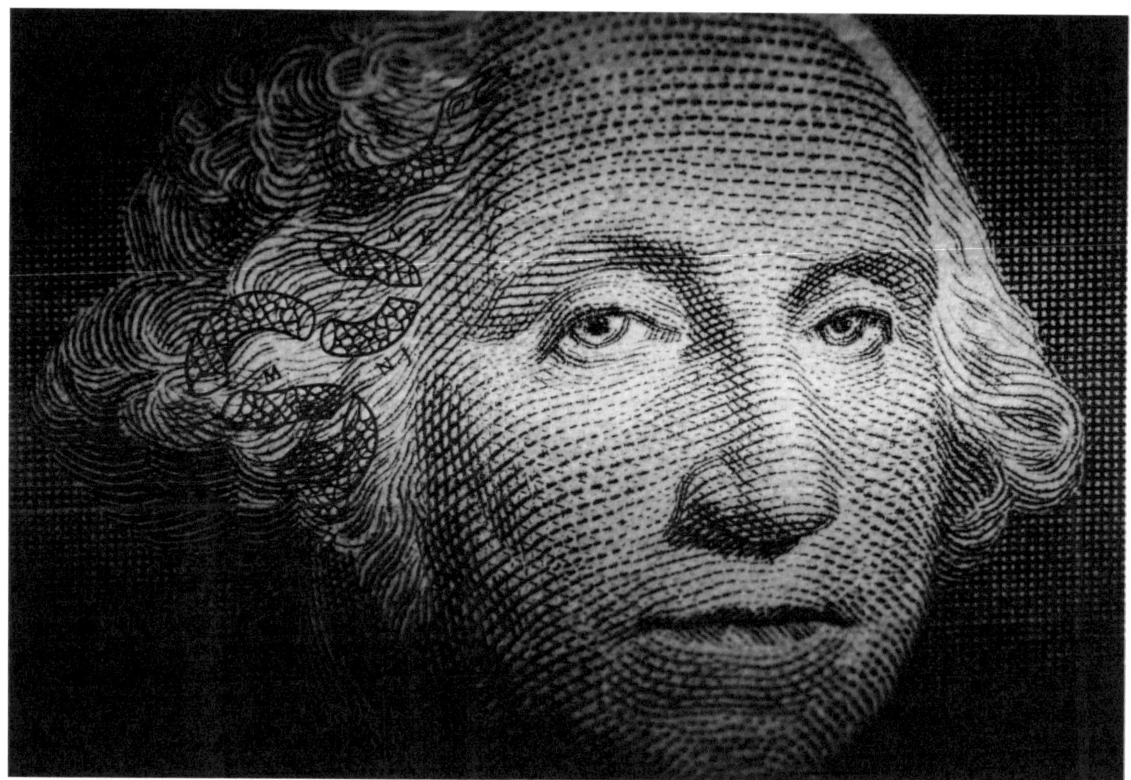

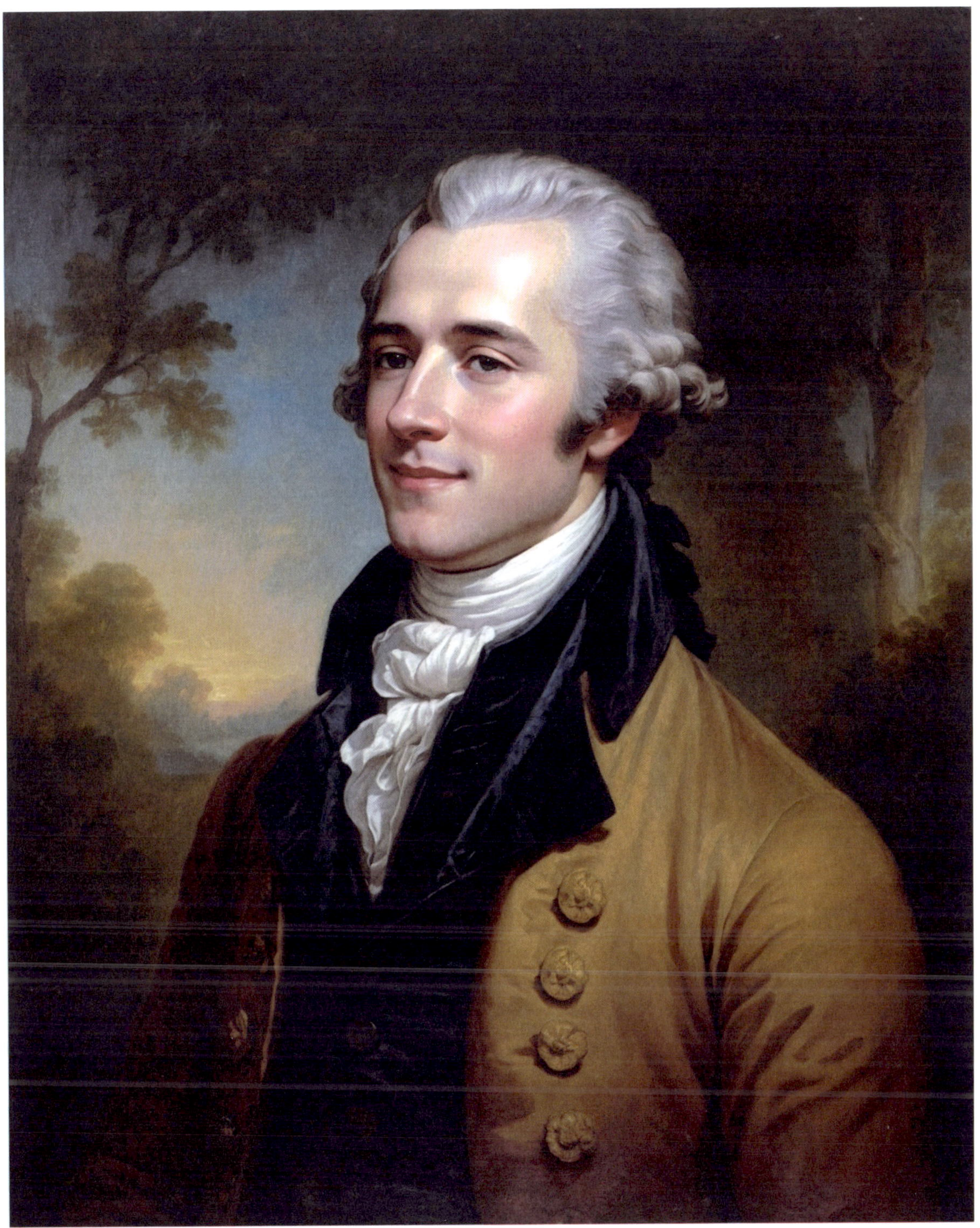

Alexander Hamilton adapted from several portraits

FRANKLIN IN THE ARMS OF FRANCE

As General Washington led his men at Valley Forge, he knew that Ben Franklin was calling upon the court of France to openly aid the American cause. "France yields us every aid we ask, and there are reasons to believe the period is not very distant, when she will take a more active part, by declaring war against the British Crown,"[128] Washington told his men in general orders on December 17, 1777.

Benjamin Franklin secured a treaty between the United States and France on February 6, 1778. He could hardly wait to rub the noses of his friends in England with the news of this alliance, especially to an English correspondent who'd recently written him.

"Your 'earnest caution and request, that nothing may ever persuade America to throw themselves into the arms of France; for that times may mend; and that an American must always be a stranger in France, but that Great Britain may for ages to come be their home,' marks the goodness of your heart, your regard for us, and love of your country,"[129] Franklin wrote to his English friend, David Hartley, on February 12, 1778, six days after the treaty with France was signed. Hartley was a physician who'd written a book comparing Franklin's electricity experiments to another scientist a few years earlier.

Though cordial, Franklin expressed his anger against England. "But when your nation is hiring all the cut throats it can collect of all countries and colors to destroy us, it is hard to persuade us not to ask and accept of aid, from any power that may be prevail'd with to grant it; and this only from the hope that tho' you now thirst for our blood and pursue us with fire and sword, you may in some future time treat us kindly. This is too much patience to be expected of us; indeed I think it is not in human nature."

Then, as if trying to make his friend jealous, he told Hartley about America's new friend. "The Americans are received and treated here in France with a cordiality, a respect and affection, they never experienced in England when they most deserved it," he wrote, referencing the dress down he'd received at London's Cockpit Tavern by the King's Privy Council in 1774.

He hinted that America and France were now allies. "And I cannot see why we may not upon an alliance hope for a continuance of it, at least of as much as the Swiss enjoy, with whom France has maintained a faithful friendship for 200 years past, and whose people appear to live here in as much esteem as the natives."

Then Franklin turned around Hartley's warning for the USA to stay out of the arms of France. "America has been forc'd and driven into the arms of France. She was a dutiful and virtuous daughter. A cruel mother-in-law turn'd her out of doors, defamed her, and sought her life. All the world knows her innocence and takes her part."

Hartley had written to Franklin to encourage him to pursue peace with England. Franklin now responded. "I know not whether a peace with us is desired in England. I rather think it is not at present, unless on the old impossible terms of submission and receiving pardon. Whenever you shall be disposed to make peace upon equal and reasonable terms you will find little difficulty if you get first an honest ministry," he wrote, referring to the current prime minister, the king and Parliament. "The present have all along acted so deceitfully and treacherously as well as inhumanly towards the Americans that I imagine the absolute want of all confidence in them will make a treaty at present between them and the Congress impracticable."

Washington did not learn of the French alliance until May 1778. "Give me leave dear Sir to congratulate you on the happy event of our treaty with France being so effectually concluded—Congress has ratified on their part and ordered the ratification to be delivered in due form,"[130] Richard Henry Lee wrote Washington on May 6. Lee had offered the resolution to declare independence at the Continental Congress in 1776. Congress would immediately announce the alliance to the public.

"The counsels of France have been governed in this affair by true magnanimity and sound policy ... Great Britain has its choice now of madness or meanness." Lee hoped this alliance would end the war with America because he thought that King George III would not want to be at war with both France and the United States. "England alone will pay for her wickedness and folly by the loss of North America." Hoping the news would "chalk out a plain and easy road to independence,"[131] Washington replied to Lee that "the favorable issue of our negotiations with France is a matter for heart felt joy."

THANKSGIVING IN MAY

General Washington was so thrilled to learn about the French alliance that he ordered his men to celebrate a day of Thanksgiving on May 6, 1778. He added this paragraph to his daily general orders: "It having pleased the Almighty ruler of the universe"[132] to defend the cause of the United States "by raising us up a powerful friend among the princes of the Earth to establish our liberty and independence." Washington set apart a day for gratefully acknowledging this "divine goodness" for the French alliance.

"The several brigades" were assembled. After hearing a thanksgiving message from their chaplains, the men performed celebratory rifle salutes and cannon blasts. The event culminated with a "discharge of thirteen cannon" followed by chants of "Huzza! 'Long Live the King of France' ... and long live the friendly European powers." The thanksgiving celebration ended by a final "discharge of thirteen pieces of artillery" followed by a "general running fire and Huzza! 'To the American states.'"

Major General Lord Stirling commanded the right while the Marquis de Lafayette, his loyal French officer, commanded the left. Washington ended this thanksgiving celebration by rewarding his men with rum.

FIRE AT MONMOUTH

How did the British military respond to the news of France's American alliance? Fearing an attack by the French fleet, they fled Philadelphia by land. When the Continental Army discovered that the British troops were marching through New Jersey, they launched an attack on British General Charles Cornwallis's troops on June 28, 1778, at the Battle of Monmouth.

Though General Charles Lee, who'd recently returned from British custody as a war

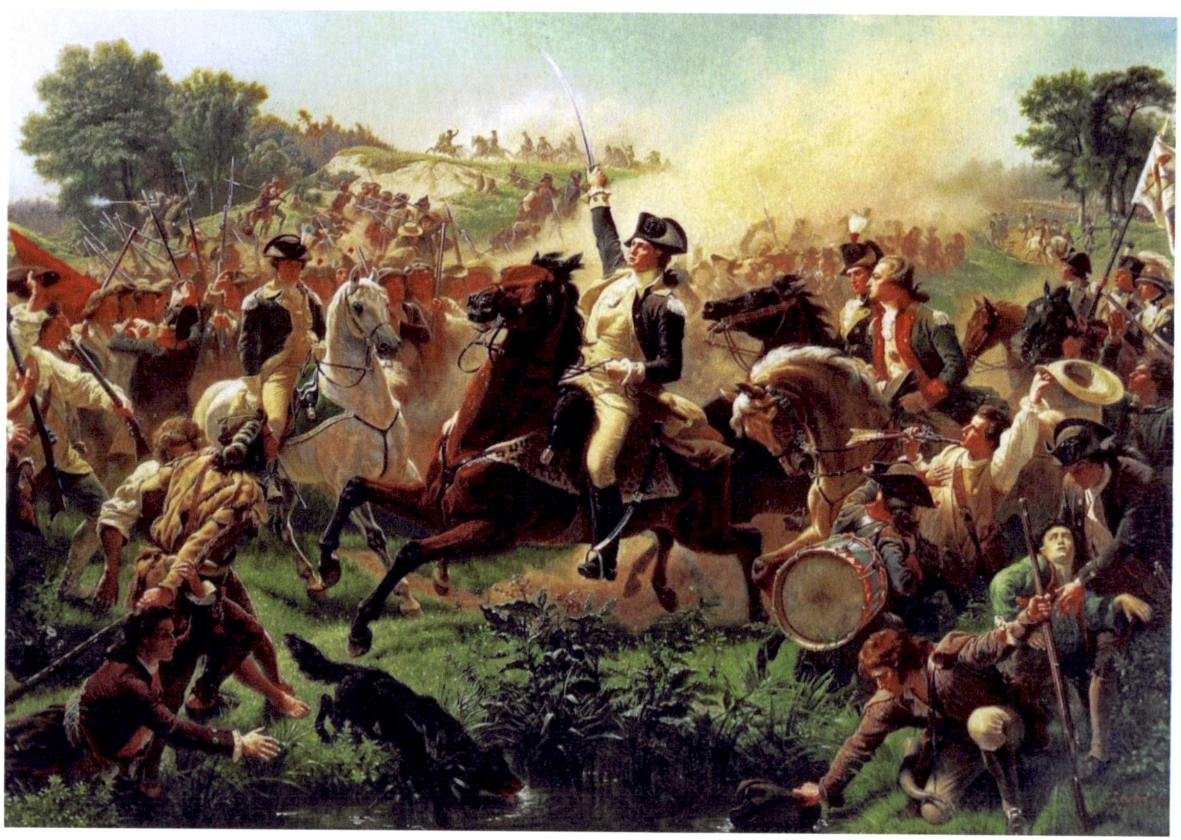

Washington Rallying the Troops at Monmouth by Emanuel Leutze

prisoner, disobeyed Washington's direct order, the Continental Army regrouped and engaged the enemy despite the heat and humidity. General Nathanael Greene's men repulsed an attack by Cornwallis. The battle see-sawed until fatigue from the brutal sun ended the engagement at sundown. The British slipped away overnight. The Battle of Monmouth proved the Continental Army's new prowess and discipline developed by Baron von Steuben at Valley Forge.

In an angry confrontation during the Battle of Monmouth, Washington arrested General Lee and court-martialed him." To Major General Charles Lee ... As soon as circumstances will permit, you shall have an opportunity, either of justifying yourself to the army, to Congress, to America, and to the world in general; or of convincing them that you were guilty of a breach of orders and of misbehavior before the enemy on the 28th instant in not attacking them as you had been directed and in making an unnecessary, disorderly, and shameful

Molly Pitcher firing a cannon a Battle of Monmouth by Edward Percy Moran, Library of Congress

retreat,"[133] Washington wrote to General Charles Lee on June 30, 1778.

Though Lee was dismissed from the army, Washington never knew just how traitorous Lee had been. While a prisoner of war, Lee had given the British a battle plan in March 1777. This document was discovered in a British general's papers in 1860, decades after Washington's death.

The Battle of Monmouth also gave America a new female hero: Molly Pitcher. Some believe that the legendary Molly Pitcher was a composite of several women who served as camp followers, nurses or disguised soldiers. Some believe Molly was Mary Hays. When her husband was injured at the Battle of Monmouth, Mary took his place at the cannon. She was called Molly Pitcher for hauling water from a spring to aid the men during the battle, which was fought in extreme heat.

THANKSGIVING AFTER MONMOUTH IN JUNE 1778

General Washington once again celebrated their success by calling for a time of thanksgiving after the Battle of Monmouth. "The men are to wash themselves this afternoon and appear as clean and decent as possible," he ordered on June 30, 1778. "Seven o'clock this evening is appointed that we may publicly unite in thanksgivings to the supreme disposer of human events for the victory which was obtained on Sunday over the flower of the British troops." Washington understood that giving thanks to God was good for the hearts and minds of his men.

NATIVE AND BLACK AMERICANS IN THE FIRST RHODE ISLAND REGIMENT–1778

Taking place on August 29, 1778, the Battle of Rhode Island was the first time the French Fleet participated in battle following France's official entry into the war. Led by Colonel Christopher Greene, the First Rhode Island regiment defended their home. This regiment included Black men, Native tribesmen as well as men with European ethnicities. Organized in 1775 by James Varnum, this regiment underwent several reorganizations but served throughout the war, from defending Boston in 1776 to the final battle in 1781.

Rhode Island's General Assembly voted in February 1778 to accept the enlistment of every able-bodied black, mulatto, or native man who chose to enlist of their own free will. If the man was enslaved, he received his freedom upon passing his first muster with Colonel Christopher Greene, a cousin of General Nathanael Greene.

From Heroes to Traitors—1779-80

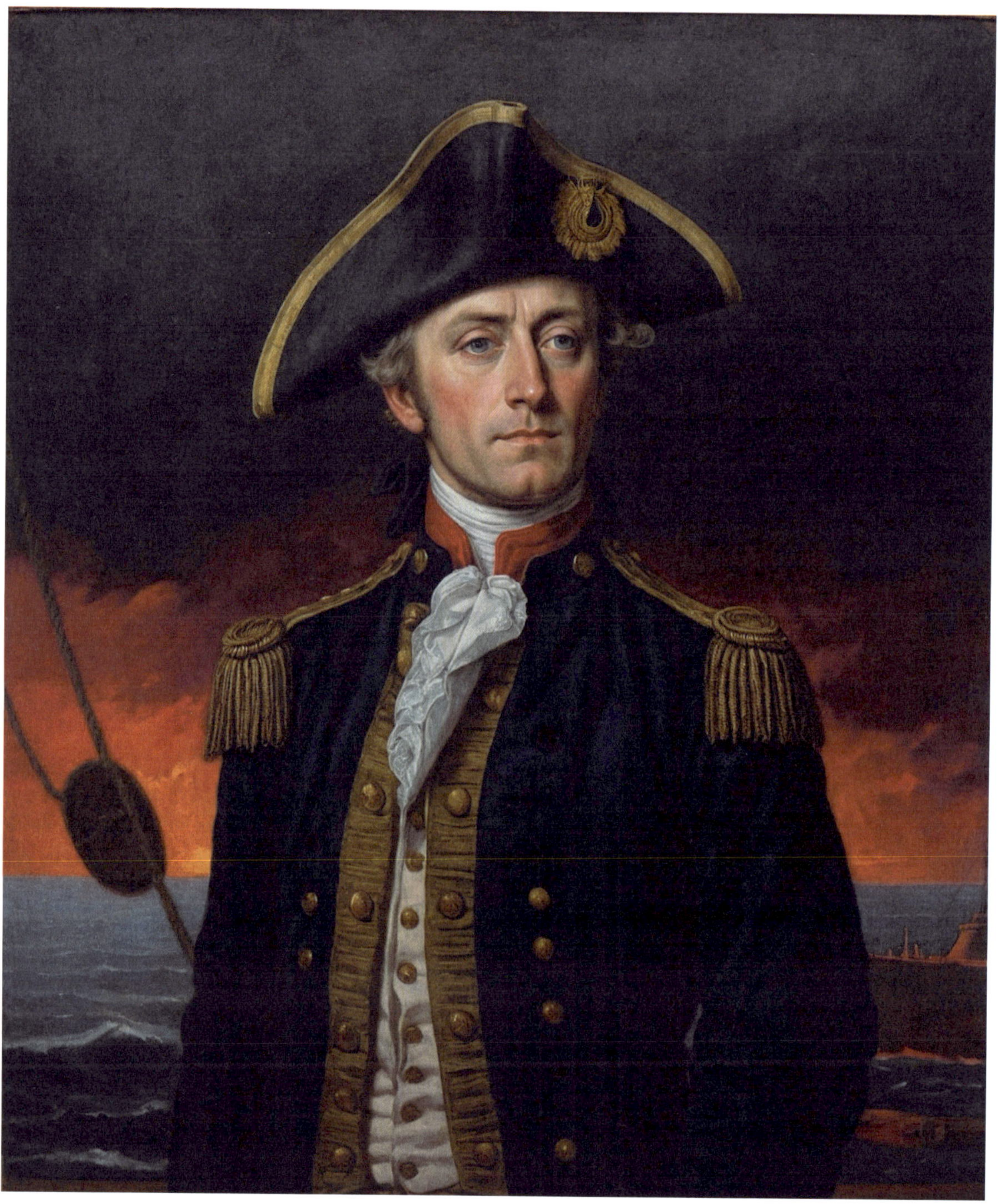

Captain John Paul Jones, America's first naval hero

"I HAVE NOT YET BEGUN TO FIGHT"

What motivated John Paul Jones to cry out some of the most famous words of the War of Independence? His flag, also called the colors, was missing from the main mast of his 42-gun ship, the *Bonhomme Richard,* not long after fighting began with the *Serapis*, a 44-gun British warship.

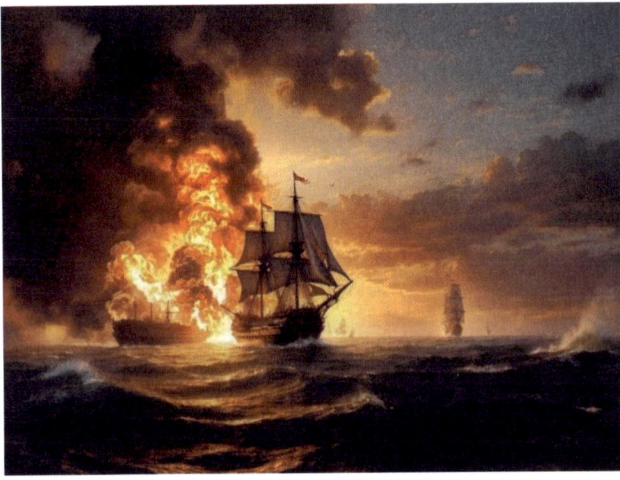

A modern rendering of the naval battle between John Paul Jones and his ship the Bonhomme Richard against the British Serapis

"Has your ship struck [your colors]?"[134] a *Serapis* crew member called shortly after the fighting began off England's North Sea on September 23, 1779. Wondering why the British asked if he was surrendering, Jones discovered that his flag on his mast was missing, which was a sign of surrender. He had not ordered it lowered. Instead cannon fire had blown it away or one of his men had removed it without his permission.

"Surrender? I have not yet begun to fight!" Jones defiantly replied. He later modestly described his now-famous words. "The English commodore asked me if I demanded quarter, and I having answered him in the most determined negative, they renewed the battle with double fury."[135]

Soon, the two ships became entangled as they rammed each other, separated, rammed again. Then Jones's men tied the ships together with rope. Jones realized that his ship, the *Bonhomme Richard*, named for Ben Franklin's *Poor Richard's Almanac*, was sinking.

"My situation was really deplorable; the *Bonhomme Richard* received various shot under water ... the leak gained on the pumps, and the fire increased much on board both ships ... My treacherous master-at-arms let loose all my prisoners without my knowledge, and my prospects became gloomy indeed," Jones recalled. He then ordered his men to sharp shoot the men on deck of the *Serapis.* This led the *Serapis to* surrender to Jones. Though his ship sank, Jones emerged the victor. He became the first American naval war hero for his valor, which became the definition of the color red in the flag. That fall in 1779, Congress did not forget to give thanks for Jones and his successful sea battle.

THE TREASON OF BENEDICT ARNOLD–1780

"TREASON of the blackest dye was yesterday discovered,"[136] George Washington's general orders proclaimed on September 26, 1780. "General Arnold, who commanded at West Point, lost to every sense of honor, of private and public obligation, was about to deliver up that important post into the hands of the enemy. Such an event must have given the American cause a dangerous, if not a fatal wound; but the treason has been timely discovered, to prevent the fatal misfortune."

Bitter and tempermental, General Benedict Arnold had often believed Congress had been too slow to promote him, which he took as a dishonor. After the British military evacuated Philadelphia in June 1778, Washington had placed General Arnold as the military governor in charge of Philadelphia. Arnold later faced 13 counts of corruption charges in a court martial that concluded in December 1779.

After Arnold was acquitted of the most serious charges and received a misdeanor reprimand, Washington offered Arnold a battle command. Arnold declined, citing his leg injury, and requested command of West Point instead. Bitter and angry, he secretly negotiated with the British to cross over and hand them West Point and possibly capture Washington. General Henry Clinton offered Arnold a large sum of money for West Point and 3,000 troops.

When Washington arrived at his planned meeting with Arnold at West Point on September 25, 1780, Arnold wasn't there. A messenger later arrived informing Washington that a British spy had been captured with papers in his boot that revealed Arnold's treason. Washington concluded that Arnold had learned of the spy's capture and fled before Washington's arrival. If Arnold's plan had gone as intended, Washington would have been captured by a British officer.

"The providential train of circumstances which led to it affords the most convincing proof that the liberties of America are the object of divine protection," Washington wrote of the miracle that they had discovered Arnold's treason.

"Great honor is due to the American Army that this is the first instance of treason of the kind where many were to be expected from the nature of the dispute—and nothing is so bright an ornament in the character of the American soldiers as their having been proof against all the arts and seduction of an insidious enemy."

"Arnold has made his escape to the enemy but Mr. André, the adjutant general to the British Army who came out as a spy to negotiate the business, is our prisoner." Had André been wearing a uniform when he was captured, he would not have been executed as a spy. Arnold fought for the British and lived in England after the war.

THE ACTION MOVES SOUTH

With the war at a stalemate in the north following the Battle of Monmouth in 1778, the British turned South, capturing Savannah in December 1778, and sieging Charleston in the spring of 1780. General Benjamin Lincoln, who led the Continental Army's Southern division, surrendered 2,500 men on May 12, 1780.

"It is the king's intention that an attack should be made against the Southern colonies with a view to the conquest and possession of Georgia and South Carolina."[137] Lord George Germain, British secretary of state, wrote to Sir Henry Clinton, British commander. The Congress appointed Nathanael Greene quartermaster general and promised that he could command troops in the future. After removing General Gates for the disastrous Battle of Camden, South Carolina in 1780, Washington replaced him with Greene.

With Greene in command, the Continental Army won the Battles of King's Mountain and Cowpens. Although the British won the Battle of Guilford Courthouse, British General Charles Cornwallis withdrew to replenish his force while Greene re-captured South Carolina's backcountry and isolated the British on the coast.

THE BEGINNING OF THE END

The turning point in the war in the South, the Battle of Cowpens took place on January 17, 1781, in South Carolina's back country, just months after General Gates had lost the Battle of Camden. General Nathanael Greene had sent General Daniel Morgan and his men to harass the British supply lines. With local militia joining him, Greene defeated the despised Lieutenant Colonel Banastre Tarleton and his men at a well-known crossroads and frontier pasture known as Cowpens.

Driving the British northward, General Greene then cost General Cornwallis 500 men at the Battle of Guilford Courthouse in North Carolina on March 15, 1781. Because Greene retreated, Cornwallis technically won but at a great cost.

WHICH YORK?

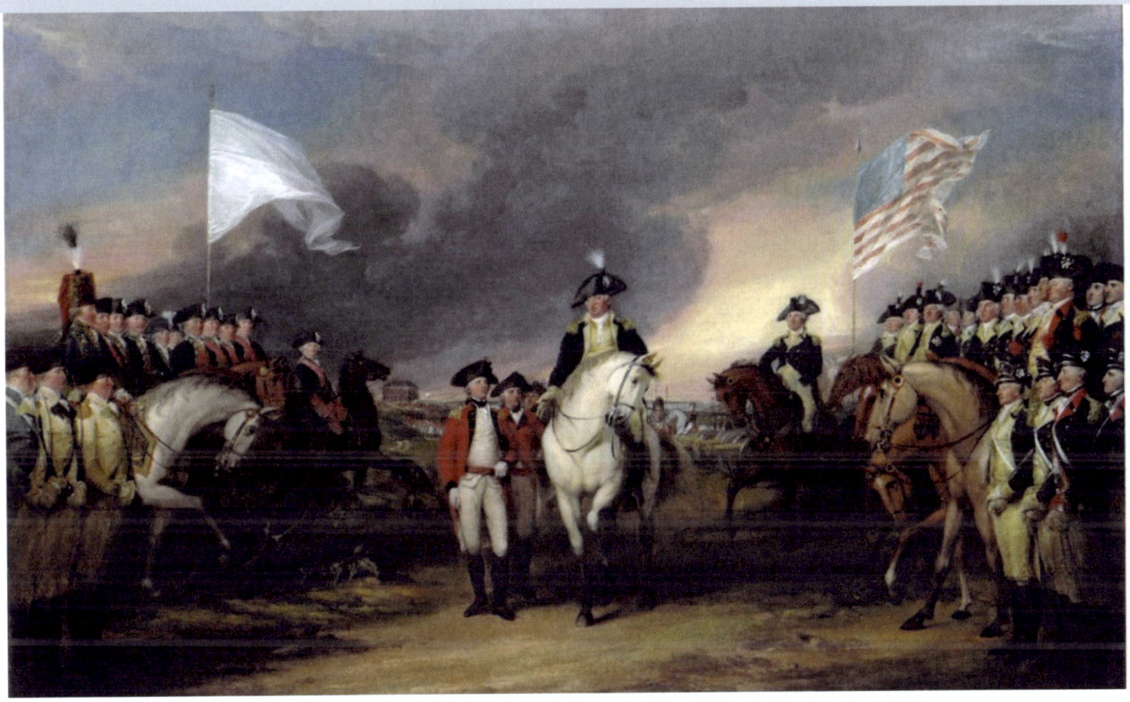

Surrender of Cornwallis at Yorktown by John Trumbull, public domain

With action in the northern states at a stalemate and the momentum turning in their favor in the tidewater of the Carolinas, George Washington considered his options in the summer of 1781. After losing New York City to the British military in 1776, General Washington wanted to defeat the British once and for all in New York City. To do so would have been a personal victory as much as a public triumph.

From his camp north of New York City at Dobbs Ferry, Washington and General Comte de Rochambeau, his French ally, evaluated their options. Lafayette, who tracked Lord Cornwallis's movements in Virginia, knew that New York was Washington's priority.

"Had not your attention been turned to New York, something with a fleet might be done in this quarter—But I see New York is the object and consequently I attend to your instructions ..."[138] General Lafayette wrote to Washington on August 6, 1781.

But Lafayette had his eye on a different York—Yorktown, Virginia. From his position on the Pawmunkey River, which joined another river to form the York River, Lafayette relied on the intelligence of spies. He knew that Cornwallis oversaw two light infantry battalions, two large regiments, and the Queen's Rangers.

"But instead of continuing his voyage up the bay, my Lord (Cornwallis) entered York River and landed at York(town) and Gloucester," Lafayette explained, noting that the British military had disembarked and taken possession of both sides of Virginia on the water at Gloucester and York.

Though Lafayette's intelligence reports from different spies had been fluctuating, he knew one thing for sure. The water separating Gloucester and Yorktown was narrow, which was perfect for a trap by ships. "Should a fleet come in at this moment, our affairs would take a very happy turn."

Five days later, Lafayette wrote Washington again. Lord Cornwallis wasn't going anywhere but his men were digging trenches and fortifications. This was a sign that he planned to stay at Yorktown for the winter.

"But to return to operations in Virginia, I will tell you, my dear General, that Lord Cornwallis is entrenching at York(town) and Gloucester. The sooner we disturb him the better,"[139] he wrote, noting that many of his men were sick. "But unless our maritime friends give us help, we cannot much venture below." As it turned out, Cornwallis wasn't going anywhere but was digging in for a longer stay at York. One of Lafayette's spies was a black man, a slave, named James Armistead, who worked as a servant for Cornwallis.

Lafayette wasn't the only one prodding Washington to turn his attention to Virginia's Chesapeake Bay. Washington responded to Lafayette on August 15 with surprising news. The French fleet led by Count de Grasse had left the Caribbean with at least 25 ships but de Grasse did not want to go as far north as New York because of hurricane season. "His destination is immediately for the Chesapeake,"[140] Washington wrote, ordering Lafayette to prevent Cornwallis's retreat by land. "You shall hear further from me as soon as I have concerted plans and formed dispositions for sending a reinforcement from hence," Washington wrote.

James Rivington, editor of New York's *Royal Gazette*, published the news on August 25, 1781, that Washington was abandoning his camp in New York and fleeing to New Jersey because the German emperor had allied himself with England.

"It is said that the French and rebels left their ground the day after Mr. Washington received the mortifying account of the (German) Emperor's alliance with his Majesty's old and natural friend, the court of Great Britain. We are assured (that) the French and rebel troops did not consort together as men determined either to secure the independence of America or realize Mr. Washington to be a dictator of it. In consequence of this great event, the French nation must withdraw all support from their new allies the rebels of this continent."[141]

While pretending to move their camp, in fact Washington and Rochambeau moved their combined forces to Yorktown, Virginia, which was the largest troop movement during the war. Years later, an American intelligence officer's report revealed that Rivington had given him a copy of the British Navy signal book at the same time of this publication. Rivington didn't just give Washington a signal book, but also gave him cover in his newspaper by making it look as if Washington was fleeing in a panic. This was a feint, a purposeful deceit to trick the enemy.

About this time, General Clinton, who commanded the British forces in New York, received a July 14 letter from Lord Germain, the British secretary of states for the colonies. Germain was thrilled that Washington was focused on New York. "I confess I am well pleased that they have fixed upon New York as the object to be attempted, as I have not the least doubt but that the troops you had remaining with you, after the ample reinforcements you so judiciously sent to the Chesapeake (with Lord Cornwallis), would be fully sufficient under your command to repel any force the enemy could bring against you."

The American and French armies of nearly 20,000 began the siege on September 28 to trap Cornwallis and his 9,000 men. With axes and spades, French engineers taught the Americans to build parallel trenches. Within range of the British by October 9, Washington launched their assault with cannon fire and barraged the British position for several days.

Under a moonlit night and armed with bayonets, Colonel Hamilton led a force of 400 light infantry on October 14 to assault British redout number 10. Climbing into the redoubt, they engaged in close range contact to land a stunning victory with few American casualties. At the same time, the French launched a similar assault against Cornwallis's redoubt number 9. After a British drummer boy beat a parley on October 17, Cornwallis surrendered two days later on October 19. Known today as the Siege or Battle of Yorktown, this was the last major battle of the American Revolution. Within a few months, peace negotiations between American and British diplomats began.

After the war, James Armistead, the slave who spied for Lafayette by working as a servant to Lord Cornwallis, sought what was owed to him for his service—his freedom. Because he was a spy, there wasn't a paper trail to prove his service. Lafayette's testimony on Armistead's behalf eventually led to his freedom, leading Armistead to change his name to James Lafayette.

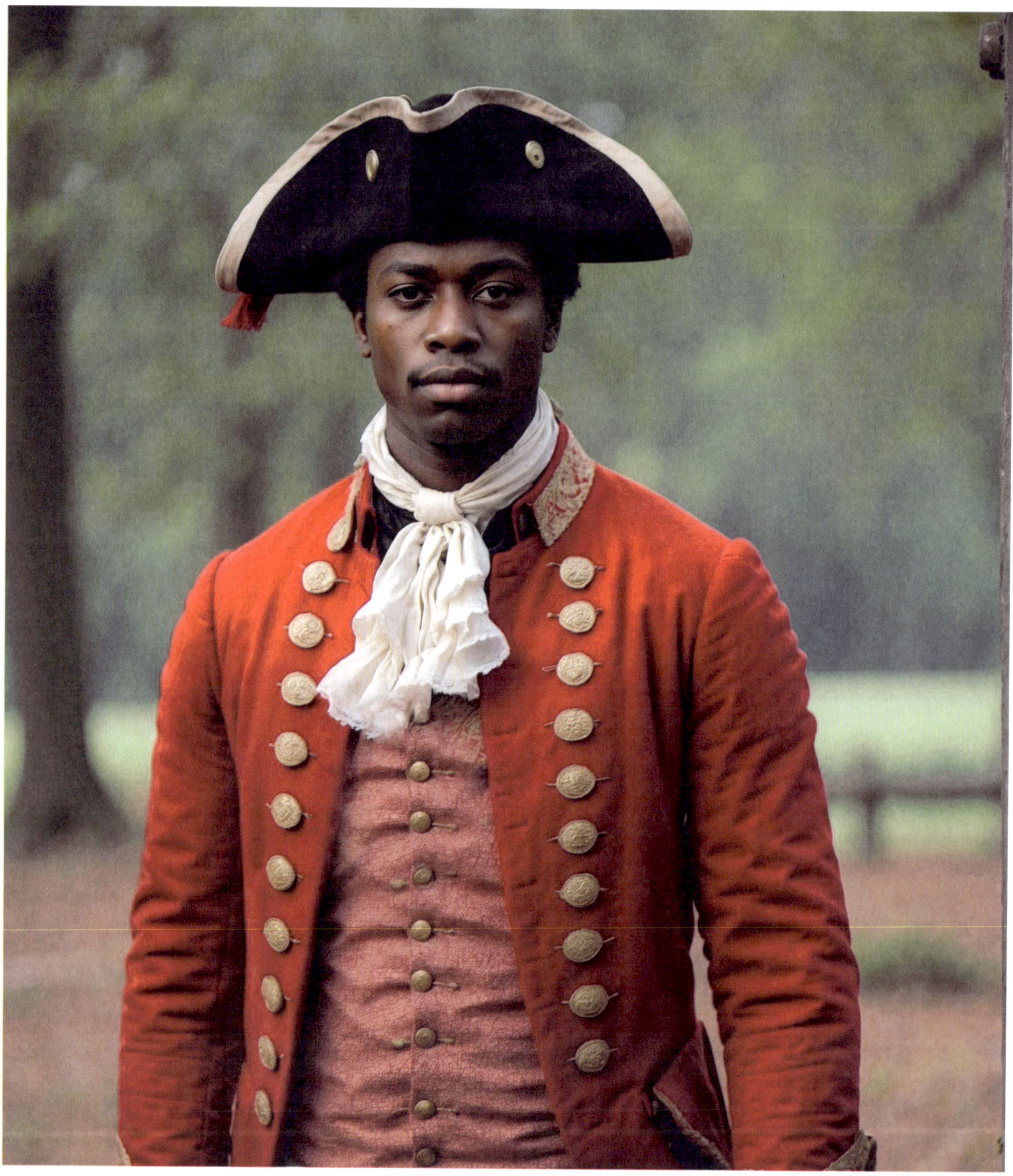

Hired by General Lafayette, James Armistead was a slave who acted as a servant to spy on British General Cornwallis. When he became free, he changed his last name to Lafayette.

IMPROVING PERSPECTIVE THROUGH THANKSGIVING

It affords me ineffable pleasure to present to your Excellency the thanks of the United States in Congress assembled, for the distinguished services you have rendered to your country, and particularly for the conquest of Lord Cornwallis and the British Garrisons of York(town) and Gloucester,"[142] Thomas McKean, the president of the Continental Congress, wrote to George Washington on October 31, 1781, after learning of the victory at Yorktown.

By this time, the war had been fought throughout the states. If the war had ended in 1778, it would've been viewed as a war in the north without much cost to the South. By 1781, however, major battles had been fought in the South, including the victory of Yorktown. Though McKean sent Washington an act of Congress expressing their appreciation, he struggled to adequately express his own emotions.

"Words fail me when I attempt to bestow my small tribute of thanks and praise to a character so eminent for wisdom, courage, and patriotism, and one who appears to be no less the favorite of heaven than of his country; I shall only therefore beg you to be assured, that you are held in the most grateful remembrance; and with a peculiar veneration, by all the wise and good in these United States."

He reflected on the miracle of Washington's service to his nation.

"That you may long possess this happiness; that you may be enabled speedily to annihilate the British power in America, which you have so effectually broken by this last capital blow; that you may be ever hailed the *Deliverer of your Country*, and enjoy every blessing Heaven can bestow, is (my) sincere and ardent prayer," McKean concluded.

NATIONAL THANKSGIVING–1781

Congress responded to the victory of Yorktown with the perspective of gratitude. The members issued a proclamation calling on Americans to set aside a day of prayer and thanksgiving. The Continental Congress and the American people showed that a great nation is first and foremost a grateful nation.

"Whereas it hath pleased the Almighty God, the Father of Mercies, remarkably to assist and support the United States of America, in their important struggle for liberty against the long-continued efforts of a powerful nation, it is the duty of all ranks to observe and thankfully acknowledge the interpositions of his Providence on their behalf."[143] The proclamation highlighted the reasons "in which the confederation of the United States has been completed." Victory was theirs.

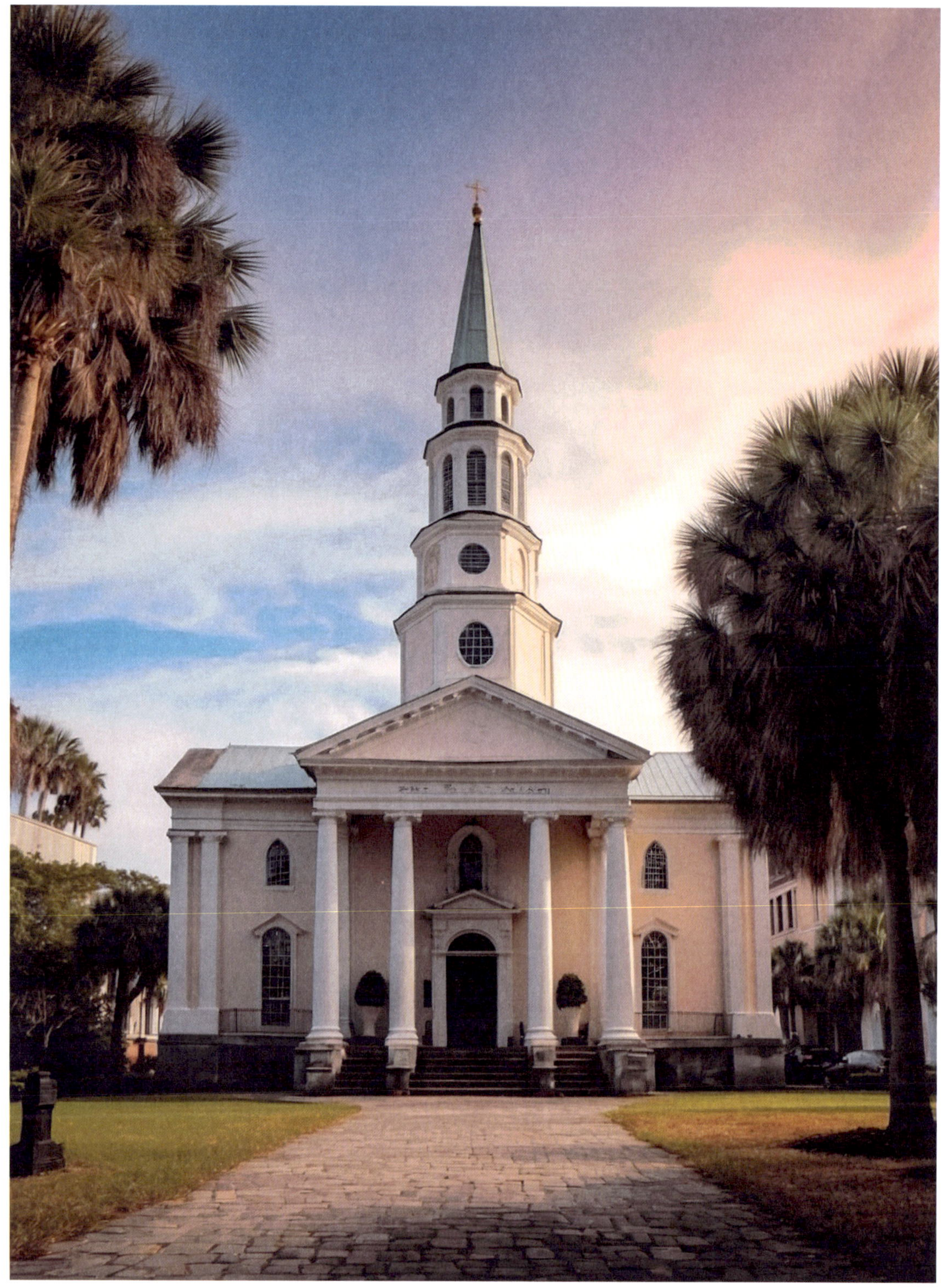

INDEPENDENCE & PEACE

THE GREAT SEAL OF THE UNITED STATES

Now that peace negotiations were underway in Europe after the Battle of Yorktown the previous fall, the Continental Congress had more time on their schedules. They had been so busy prosecuting the war in 1777 when they adopted the first official U.S. flag, they didn't have time to think too deeply about symbolism. In 1782 they took the time to reflect on the war and sacrifices of liberty. This led Congress to release the Great Seal of the United States on June 20, 1782.

The *Journal of the Continental Congress* from that day features a description of the Great Seal. In the center was a free-flying "American bald eagle" who held "an olive branch" in his right claw and a "bundle of thirteen arrows" in his left claw. In his beak, the eagle held a scroll "inscribed with this motto, 'E pluribus Unum,'" which means out of many, one.[144]

A red, white, and blue shield adorned the eagle's breast. Explaining that the shield reflected the colors of the U.S. flag, Congress assigned virtues to the nation's colors. Red symbolized hardiness and valor. White reflected purity and innocence. Washington had told his men they were fighting for the innocent women and children in their lives. The color blue was symbolized by the virtues of vigilance, perseverance, and justice. By 1782, they knew many heroes and heroines who embodied those virtues. They honored them through the seal's and flag's symbolism.

AMERICAN INDEPENDENCE–A STANDING MIRACLE

"It only remains for the Commander in Chief to address himself once more, and that for the last time, to the armies of the United States ... and to bid them an affectionate—a long farewell,"[145] Washington wrote in his farewell address to his army on November 2, 1783.

"But before the Commander in Chief takes his final leave of those he holds most dear, he wishes to indulge himself a few moments in calling to mind a slight review of the past."

"A contemplation of the complete attainment (at a period earlier than could have been expected) of the object for which we contended, against so formidable a power, cannot but inspire us with astonishment and gratitude—The disadvantageous circumstances on our part, under which the war was undertaken, can never be forgotten."

"The singular interpositions of Providence in our feeble condition were such, as could scarcely escape the attention of the most unobserving, while the unparalleled perseverance of the armies of the United States, through almost every possible suffering and discouragement, for the space of eight long years, was little short of a standing miracle."

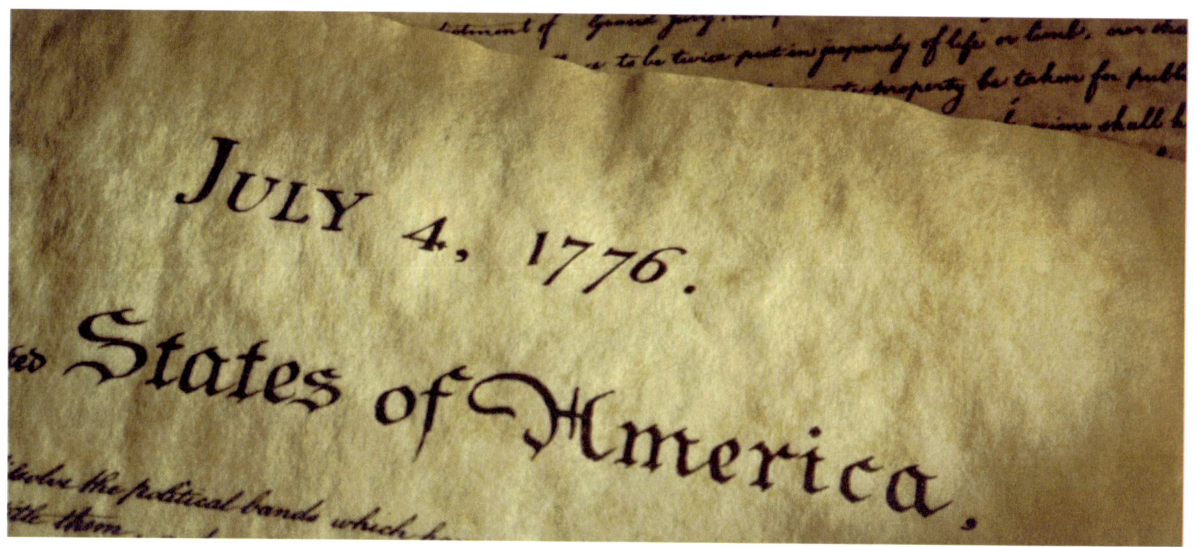

The Declaration of Independence ©Shutterstock

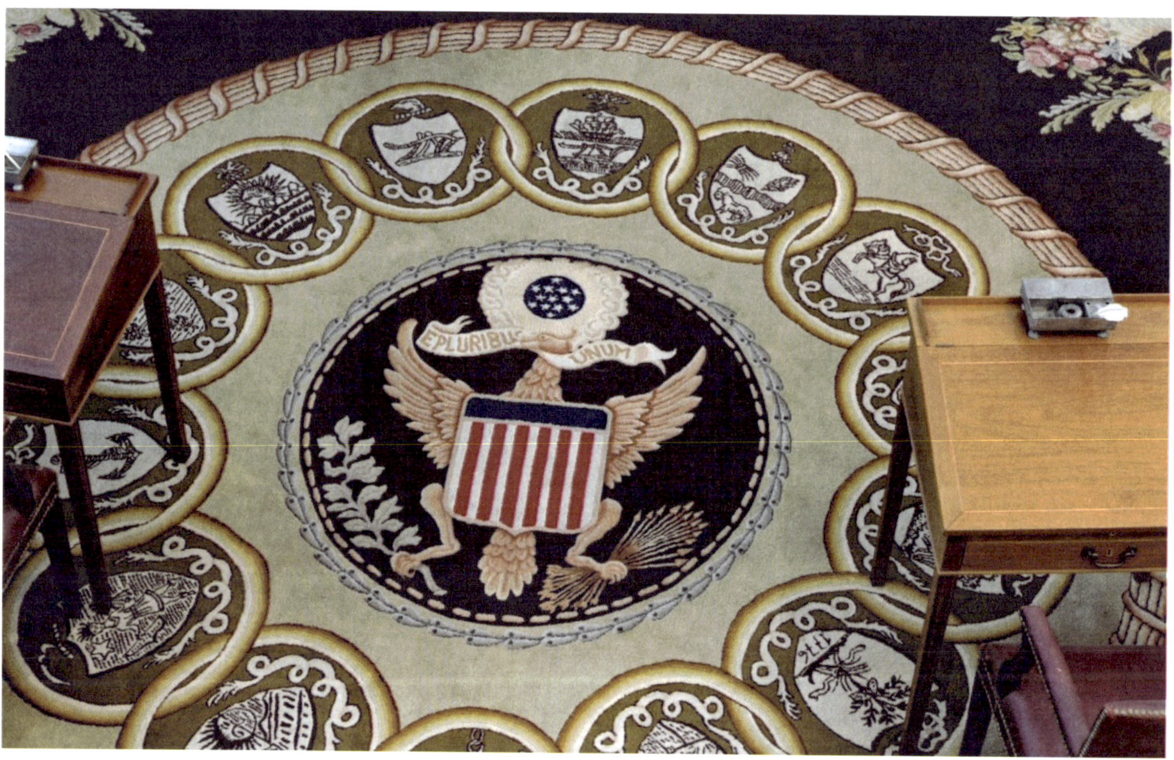

The Great Seal is the center of a carpet in the U.S. Capitol, public domain, National Parks Service.

ARTICLES OF CONFEDERATION

"The building up a Great Empire, which was only hinted at by my correspondent, may now I suppose be realized even by the unbelievers. Yet will not ten thousand difficulties arise in the formation of it?"[146] Abigail Adams asked in late 1775. "The reins of government have been so long slackened, that I fear the people will not quietly submit to those restraints which are necessary for the peace, and security, of the community; if we separate from Britain, what code of laws will be established[?]"

Separating from England was one thing, but what form of government would replace it was anyone's guess. Abigail's questions reflected the worry of the populace.

"How shall we be governed so as to retain our liberties? Can any government be free which is not administered by general stated laws? Who shall frame these laws? Who will give them force and energy? 'Tis true your resolution[s] as a body have hitherto had the force of laws. But will they continue to have?"

After forming a committee in 1776, the Continental Congress sent the Articles of Confederation to the states for ratification in 1777. Conflicts over land between Maryland and Virginia slowed the ratification process, which was completed March 1, 1781 after Maryland's final ratification. America's new states had come together under an agreed upon governance document. Would it work? After the war ended, many had their answer.

THE U.S. CONSTITUTION

Three years after the peace treaty was signed in 1783, the thirteen sovereign, independent states struggled. "Your sentiments, that our affairs are drawing rapidly to a crisis, accord with my own. What the event will be is also beyond the reach of my foresight. We have errors to correct. We have probably had too good an opinion of human nature in forming our confederation,"[147] the retired George Washington wrote to John Jay in August 1786 about the crisis created by the Articles of Confederation, which made Congress too weak to govern the United States.

"I do not conceive we can exist long as a nation, without having lodged somewhere a power which will pervade the whole union in as energetic a manner, as the authority of the different state governments extends over the several states."

Washington knew that many were afraid to give Congress national authority over matters of trade, currency, and other issues between the states.

"What then is to be done? Things cannot go on in the same train forever. It is much to be feared, as you observe, that the better kind of people being disgusted with the circumstances will have their minds prepared for any revolution whatever. We are apt to run from one extreme into another. To anticipate and prevent disastrous contingencies would be the part of wisdom and patriotism," Washington wondered.

"What astonishing changes a few years are capable of producing! I am told that even respectable characters speak of a monarchical form of government without horror. From thinking proceeds speaking, thence to acting is often but a single step," he wrote, concerned about going backwards instead of forward.

"But how irrevocable and tremendous! What a triumph for the advocates of despotism to find that we are incapable of governing ourselves, and that systems founded on the basis of equal liberty are merely ideal and fallacious! Would to God that wise measures may be taken in time to avert the consequences we have but too much reason to apprehend," Washington wrote, without naming what wise measures he thought could be taken to solve the problems with the Articles of Confederation. He wanted to help but could only do so with the call of the people.

"Retired as I am from the world, I frankly acknowledge I cannot feel myself an unconcerned spectator. Yet having happily assisted in bringing the ship into port and having been fairly discharged; it is not my business to embark again on a sea of troubles. Nor could it be expected that my sentiments and opinions would have much weight on the minds of my countrymen—they have been neglected, tho' given as a last legacy in the most solemn manner."

A few leaders from five states first met informally in Annapolis, Maryland in September 1786. Then they called for an official convention to meet in Philadelphia to amend the Articles of Confederation. Delegates from each state, including Benjamin Franklin from Pennsylvania, began arriving in May 1787 and met until September 1787 at Philadelphia's Independence Hall. Overseen by Washington, who insisted on a media blackout, they debated intensely over the difficult issues dividing the states, including the power of small states verses large states. Realizing they could not easily amend the Articles, the delegates opted for a new constitution instead, largely drawn from James Madison's Virginia Plan. This decision turned the Philadelphia Convention into the Constitutional Convention.

With individual states retaining many powers, the delegates established a stronger federal government among three co-equal branches—legislative, executive, and judicial. They further divided the power of Congress into two bodies, the House of Representatives and the Senate. Division of power was the key to unity and to prevent an easy overthrow or coup of the federal government. On September 17, 1787, the convention approved the new United States Constitution and sent it to the 13 states for ratification.

THE FEDERALIST PAPERS–THE FIRST POLITICAL CAMPAIGN

Alexander Hamilton knew that many people, including the governor of New York, opposed replacing the Articles of Confederation with the new Constitution. "The constitution proposed has in this state warm friends and warm enemies. The first impressions everywhere are in its favor; but the artillery of its opponents makes some impression. The event cannot yet be foreseen. The enclosed is the first number of a series of papers to be written in its defense,"[148] Hamilton alerted Washington of his campaign to win public support for the U.S. Constitution.

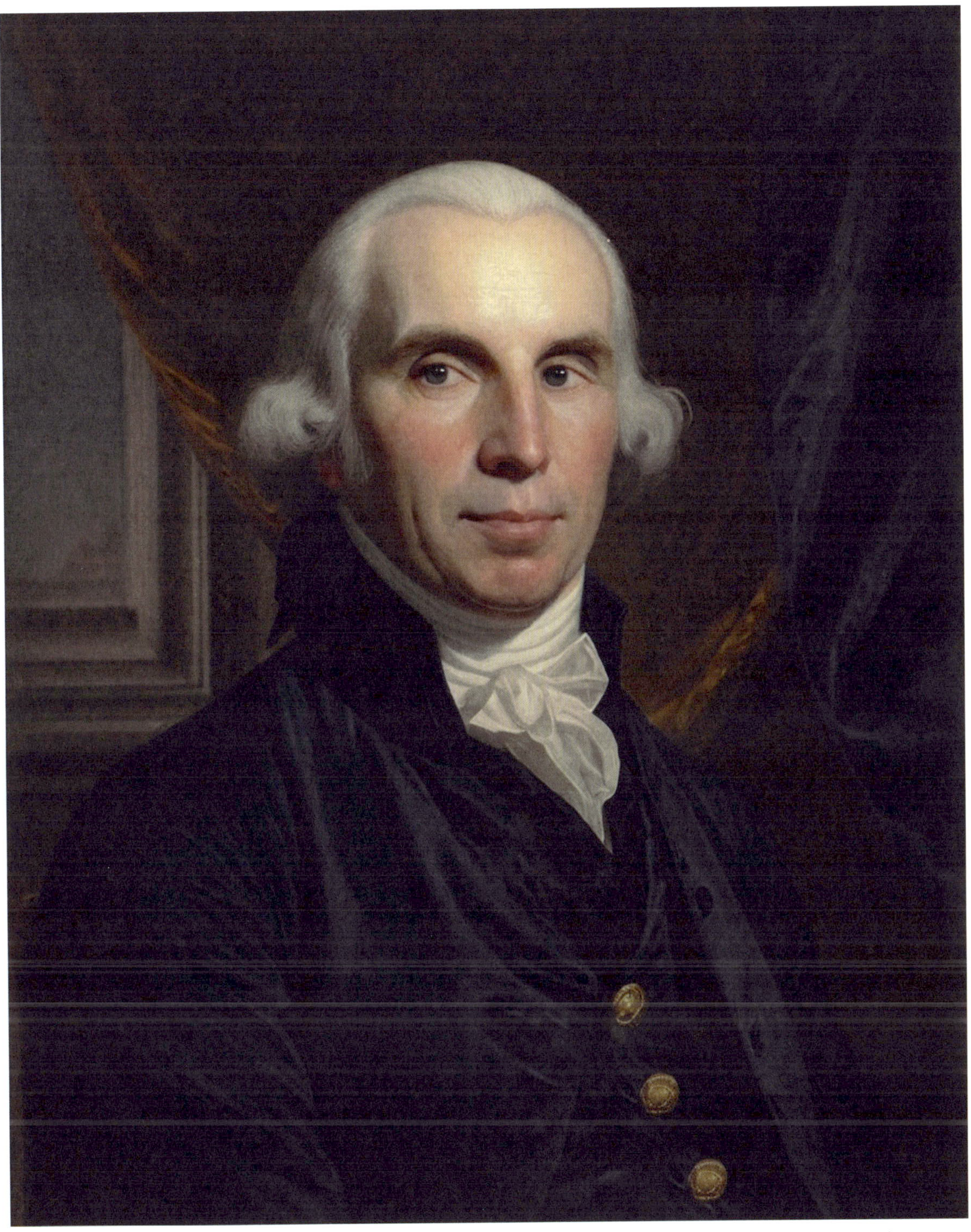

A modern rendering of James Madison, father of the U.S. Constitution, from a public domain painting

Hamilton, John Jay, and James Madison responded to division over the proposed Constitution by writing newspaper articles explaining the reasoning behind the new Constitution and advocating that the people ratify it. This public relations campaign was the first of its kind in the new United States of America. Known today as the *Federalist Papers*, these 85 essays provided important information for adopting the new Constitution. Today, they help Americans understand the framers' intentions.

Sending Washington the first essay, Hamilton, Jay, and Madison published the *Federalist Papers* using the pseudonym *Publius*. "I thank you for the pamphlet, and for the gazette contained in your letter ... For the remaining numbers of Publius, I shall acknowledge myself obliged, as I am persuaded the subject will be well handled by the author," Washington wrote encouragingly to Hamilton after reading the first Federalist essay.[149]

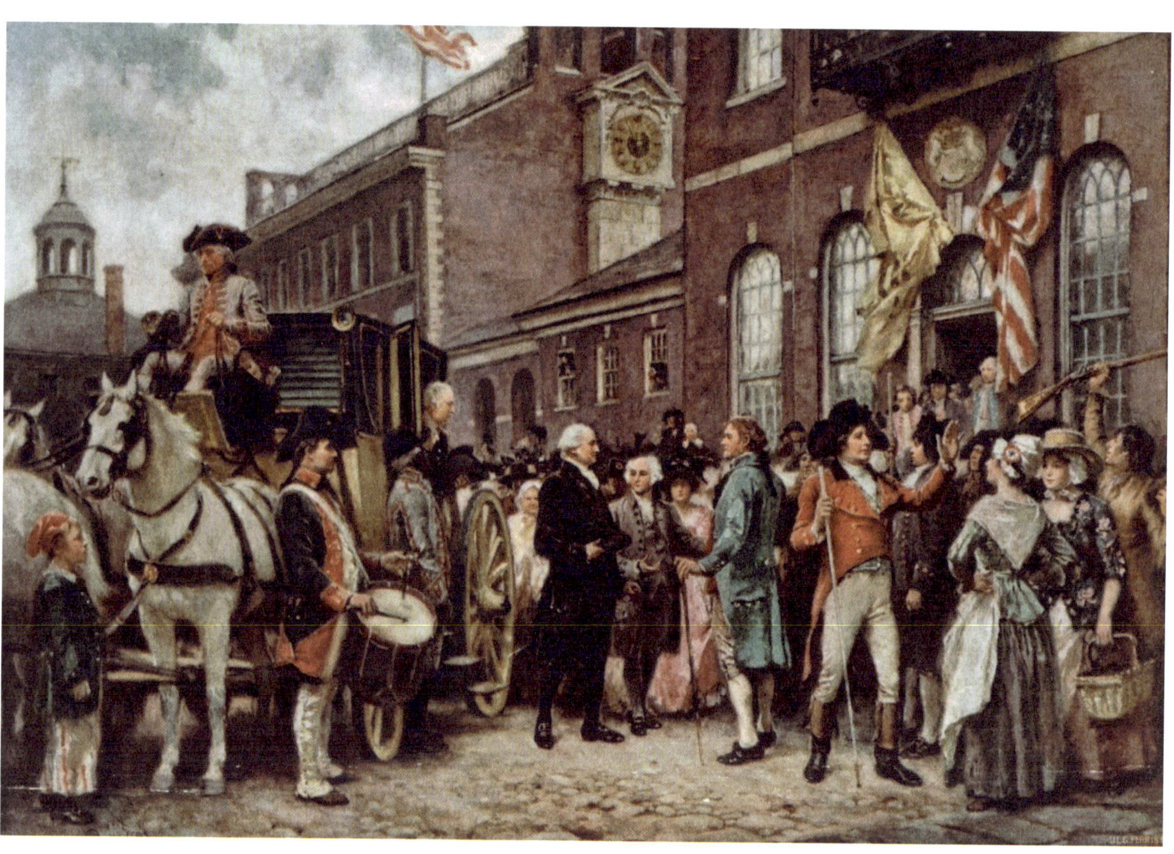

George Washington's Inauguration at Philadelphia in 1793 by Jean Leon Gerome Ferris, Library of Congress

THE BILL OF RIGHTS & THE FIRST AMENDMENT: FROM THIRD TO FIRST

When George Washington became America's first president in 1789, two states had not re-joined the union under the new U.S. Constitution: North Carolina and Rhode Island. A major stumbling block for many people in these states, and other antifederalists who opposed the Constitution, was the Constitution's lack of a Bill of Rights. Without recommending any specifics in his inaugural address, Washington asked Congress to propose amendments to the Constitution that would maintain unity and preserve individual rights.

This led Congressman James Madison (who had helped Washington to write his inaugural address) to call on Congress to pass amendments to the Constitution. Madison had studied the discussions of the Constitutional ratifying conventions from the different states and identified hundreds of possible amendments, some of which fell into similar categories of freedom. After analyzing these possibilities, Congress settled on twelve amendments to be ratified by the people through their state legislatures.

The original first two amendments focused not on the rights of the people but on Congress's power, specifically its apportionment power and salary. Not surprisingly, these two amendments failed to be ratified by three-quarters of the states.

The people's rejection of the first two amendments elevated the Third Amendment into the First Amendment. The First Amendment and the other nine amendments became law on December 15, 1791, when Virginia's General Assembly became the final state needed to ratify the Bill of Rights.

"Congress shall make no law respecting an establishment of religion, or prohibiting the free exercise thereof; or abridging the freedom of speech, or of the press; or the right of the people peaceably to assemble, and to petition the Government for a redress of grievances," the First Amendment to the U.S. Constitution declares.

Perspective-taking sometimes involves change. After taking stock of a situation, the people's perspective played a role in elevating their rights of freedom of religion, speech, the press, and the rights to protest and petition their government. If it had been left to Congress, today's First Amendment would be the third. Instead, the people prevailed.

PART III: PERSPECTIVE-TAKING ESSAYS

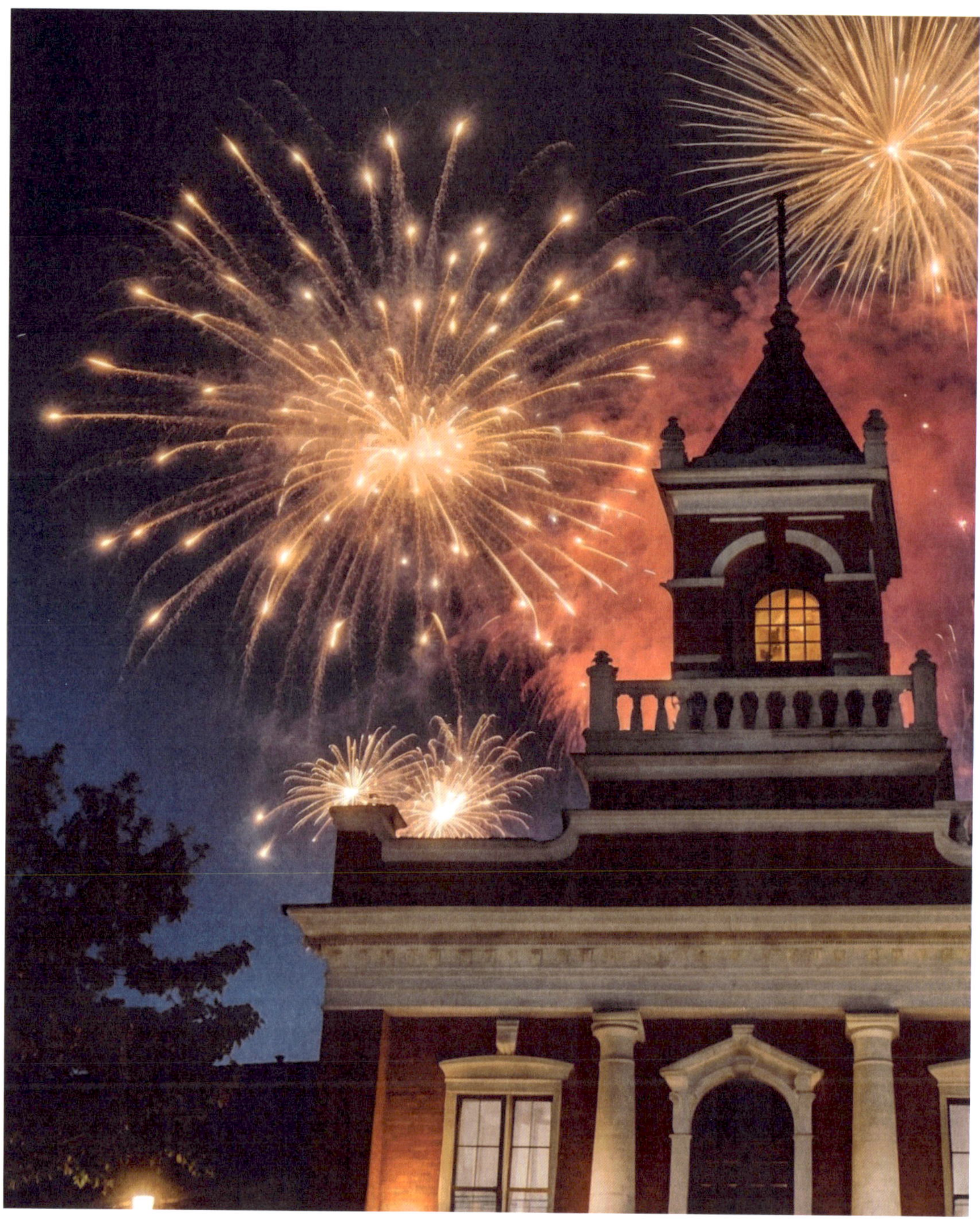

LOVE OF COUNTRY IS ESSENTIAL FOR SURVIVAL

Passing love of country to the next generation has long been a cultural priority in the United States. In fact, the person who most motivated Americans to declare independence from England concluded that patriotic education would be the key to America's future survival and success.

"This ardent love of one's country is most essential to the preservation of all Republican governments, the inspiring therefore the minds of youth in the first dawn of reason, with this passion ought to be the principal view of education,"[150] this influencer observed.

Who wrote this? Was it Thomas Jefferson, who passed along this advice: "I hope so much from the patriotism of all, that they will make all smaller motives give way to the greater importance of the general welfare,"[151] Thomas Jefferson wrote.

Was it George Washington, who believed that unity was crucial to preserving freedom? "In this sense it is, that your Union ought to be considered as a main prop of your liberty, and that the love of the one ought to endear to you the preservation of the other,"[152] President Washington declared in his 1796 Farewell Address.

Washington understood that patriotism was a choice. He knew that being an American was more important than any other identity, whether immigrant or natural born. Jefferson, Adams, and Washington could have written the above introductory quote, but they didn't. Their mutual enemy did.

King George III was the author of this statement: "This ardent love of one's country is most essential to the preservation of all Republican governments, the inspiring therefore the minds of youth in the first dawn of reason, with this passion ought to be the principal view of education."[153]

The British monarch defeated by Washington and deemed a tyrant by Jefferson in the Declaration understood that patriotism and unity would preserve his enemy, America. "Therefore, the principle of a Republican education will be virtue; of that in monarchy, honor; in despotic states fear," the king observed.

Where did King George write this? Digitized and released a few years ago by British archivists under the direction of his third great-granddaughter Queen Elizabeth II, King George III's private writings included this undated quote in a section where he described different types of governments. The tone of the quote implies that he wrote this sentiment in a more reflective mindset, perhaps when he was being tutored on governments as a student or decades later after the American Revolution.

The point is that America's fiercest enemy—the tyrant who implemented martial law and denied Americans jury trials among many other atrocities—figured out that the key to America's survival was to pass on a love of country to each new generation through education. If this tyrant could understand the importance of unity and patriotism to America's future as a secure and independent nation, then surely there is hope that those lured and blinded by today's divisive and destructive ideologies, which are fracturing

American culture as if on purpose from an enemy, can see things from a different perspective—a freedom-for-all perspective.

President Ronald Reagan reminded Californians in his gubernatorial inaugural address that: "Freedom is a fragile thing and it's never more than one generation away from extinction. It is not ours by way of inheritance; it must be fought for and defended constantly by each generation, for it comes only once to a people. And those in world history who have known freedom and then lost it have never known it again."[154]

The keys to maintaining a love of country among the people are 1. Fostering a healthy perspective on America's history through the universal virtue of gratitude for survival and greatness. 2. Forgiving longsuffering injustices. 3. Determining to learn from the sins and mistakes of the past so they are not repeated. 4. Believing that a person's current identity and future destiny are not defined by their ancestors' social status and 5. Passing along America's freedoms to the next generation through ethical and cultural means.

MEMORIALS–PERSPECTIVE-TAKING OPPORTUNITIES

"These stones are to be a memorial to the people of Israel forever." Joshua 4:7

Disease has destroyed ten men for us, where the sword of the enemy has killed one," John Adams had written after seeing Philadelphia's mass grave in April 1777. "I have spent an hour, this morning, in the congregation of the dead. I took a walk into the Potter's Field, a burying ground between the new stone prison, and the hospital, and I never in my whole life was affected with so much melancholy."[155]

"The graves of the soldiers, who have been buried, in this ground, from the hospital and bettering house, during the course of the last summer, fall, and winter, dead of the small pox, and camp diseases, are enough to make the heart of stone to melt away." Adams had concluded that the lack of food, clothing, and soap, had led to death by disease.

Adams was correct. More men died of disease than were killed on the battlefield. The numbers tell the story: 6,800 men were killed in action for the cause of American independence. Another 17,000 soldiers died of disease.

Today, the potter's field that Adams visited is known as Washington Square, where Philadelphia's Tomb of the Unknown Revolutionary War Soldier is located. Anthropologists found the unmarked graves of several Revolutionary War soldiers on the square several months before the memorial was dedicated in 1957.

"The plaque behind the tomb bears the memorial's theme: 'Freedom is a light for which many men have died in darkness.'"[156] The memorial also says: "Beneath this stone rests a soldier of Washington's army who died to give you liberty." Memorials like this one give modern Americans a chance to remember those known and unknown soldiers who died to both give us liberty and to keep us free, especially on Memorial Day and Veterans Day.

Today, extremists seek to destroy monuments with a fervor similar to the radicals in the French Revolution that decapitated Notre Dame's iconic statues, including ones that had come from the Holy Land. Similarly, the Soviets destroyed statues and art when they came to power in Russia in 1917. In recent years, lawless agitators have destroyed or damaged monuments in the United States through vandalism. Other radical activists have put pressure on government leaders to destroy statues and memorials by removing them.

In 2019, a committee reporting to Washington, D.C., Mayor Muriel Bowser recommended removing, relocating, or contextualizing monuments to historical figures that did not conform to their definitions of societal diversity. Seeking to impose today's cultural standards on historical figures, they identified four dozen D.C. sites for removal, including the Washington Monument, Jefferson Memorial, and Benjamin Franklin Statue. This led to backlash that slowed the measure.

Since the founders, Americans have benefited from the toil of civil rights activists who sought a more perfect union. Americans today have the benefit of standing on the shoulders of not just Revolutionary War soldiers, but also the soldiers of the Civil War, two World Wars, wars in Korea, Vietnam, Iraq, and Afghanistan. Millions have put their lives on the line for the belief that all men and women are created equal, endowed by a Creator with inalienable rights. Is it fair to impugn those who risked their lives for a future they could not see but hoped would be better and more just? No. Memorials provide opportunities to put history into perspective, allowing to compare and contrast, to appreciate progress.

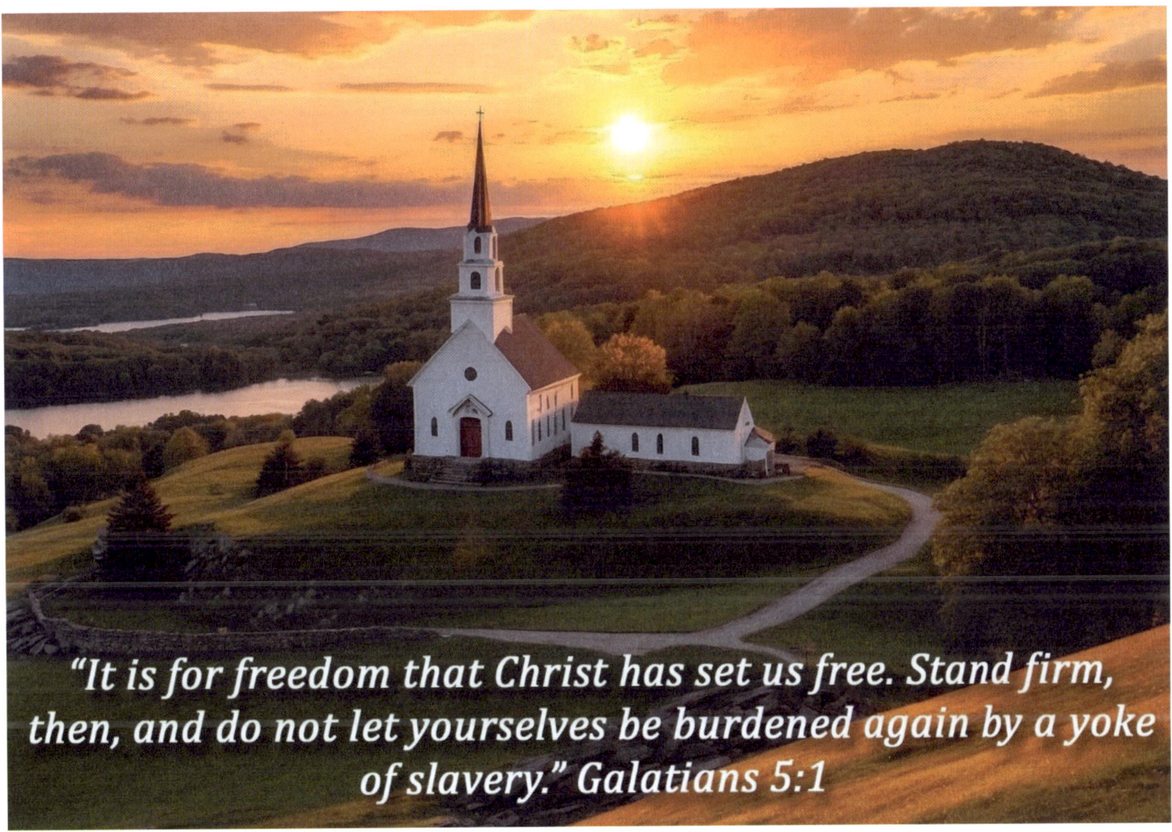

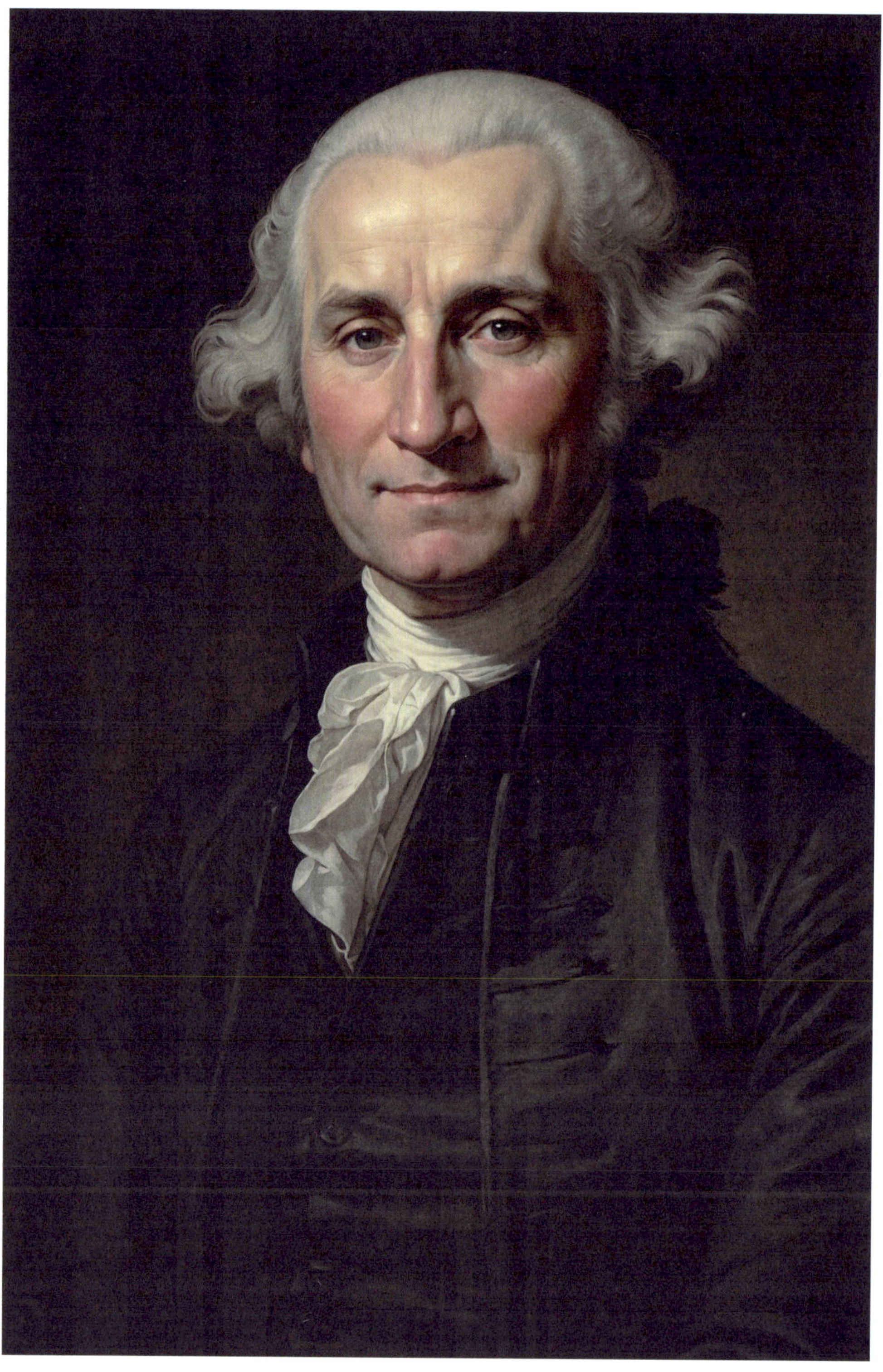

A modern rendering of George Washington as president based on several previous portraits

WASHINGTON'S PERSPECTIVE ON HISTORY

Though his first inaugural address is the shortest on record, George Washington was candid about how he viewed his new role as the first president of the United States. He didn't consider himself qualified to be the chief executive of a civil office but had left retirement to accept the position of president out of his love for his country.

More than anything else in his first inaugural address—from declining his salary to promising to show no favors by region or party—Washington offered perspectives that are relevant today. The first president revealed to the American people that he had gratitude to God for the nation's founding. He could not let his inauguration slip by without acknowledging Providence. Invoking a benediction from the "Almighty Being who rules over the universe, who presides in the councils of nations, and whose providential aids can supply every human defect,"[157] Washington asked for blessings on the new government and the people of the United States.

Though six years had passed since the war ended, he had not forgotten the nation's miraculous founding. At his inauguration, he proved that he held a healthy perspective on the past and wanted Americans to have the same perspective.

"No people can be bound to acknowledge and adore the invisible hand, which conducts the affairs of men more than the people of the United States. Every step, by which they have advanced to the character of an independent nation, seems to have been distinguished by some token of providential agency," George Washington said in his first Inaugural Address. After the crisis of the Articles of Confederation, he also considered the coming together of the Constitution to be miraculous. Most nations had not voluntarily united in this way.

"And in the important revolution just accomplished in the system of their united government, the tranquil deliberations and voluntary consent of so many distinct communities from which the event has resulted, cannot be compared with the means by which most governments have been established, without some return of pious gratitude along with a humble anticipation of the future blessings," he said.

Washington believed that reflecting with gratitude was the best way to start the new government. "Since we ought to be no less persuaded that the propitious smiles of Heaven, can never be expected on a nation that disregards the eternal rules of order and right, which Heaven itself has ordained: And since the preservation of the sacred fire of liberty, and the destiny of the Republican model of Government, are justly considered as deeply, perhaps as finally staked, on the experiment entrusted to the hands of the American people." America would continue to need God's blessings, with each generation sharing the responsibility for passing on liberty to the future. To do so would require a balanced, optimistic perspective.

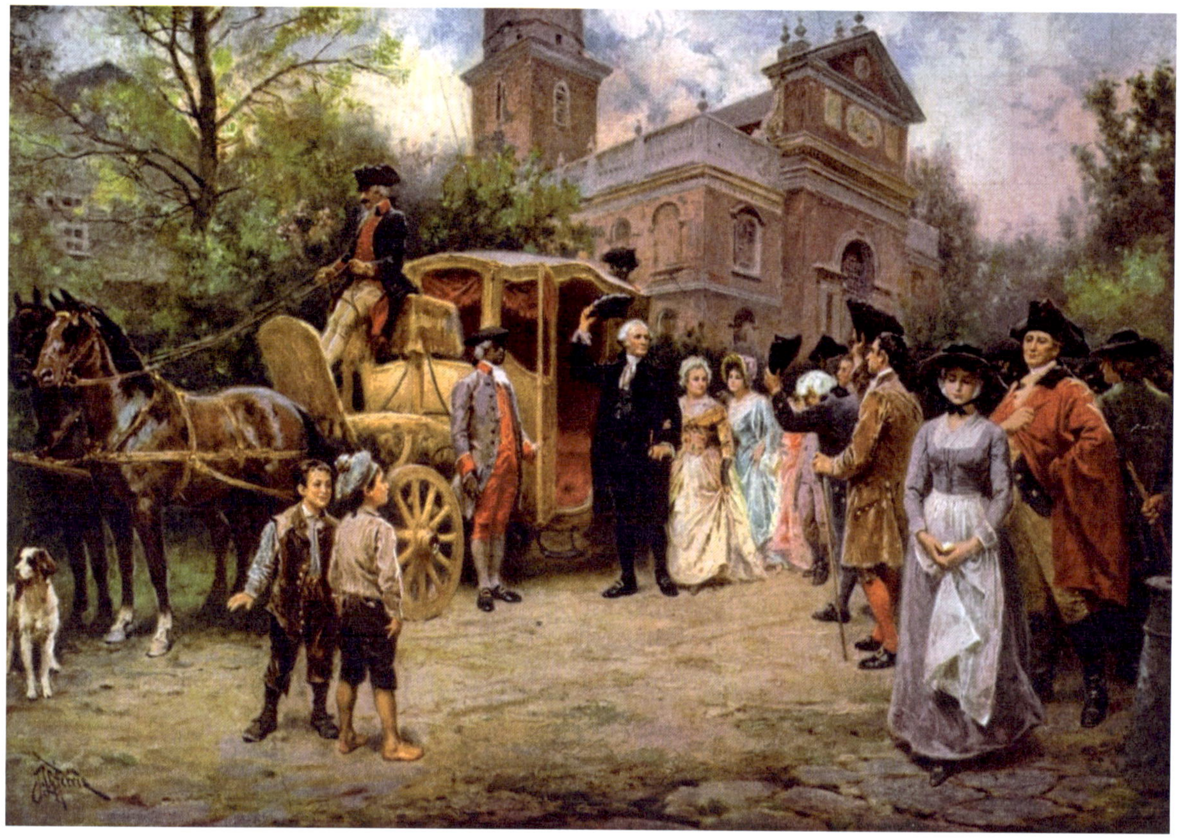

George Washington at church, Jean Leon Gerome Ferris, Library of Congress

THE FIRST THANKSGIVING UNDER THE CONSTITUTION

Giving thanks proved to be the primary method for Americans to maintain a healthy, humble perspective on their personal lives and public life during the nation's founding and early years. Abraham Lincoln is rightfully credited with establishing the annual national holiday of Thanksgiving starting in 1863, which was the same year he freed slaves in the Emancipation Proclamation. President Washington twice called on all Americans to set aside a day for thanksgiving during his two terms in office.

From the nation's capital of New York, in his 1789 Thanksgiving proclamation, he once again emphasized God's hand in their history, particularly the Almighty's Providence during the war for independence. He also gave thanks for the unity formed by the U.S. Constitution, civil and religious freedom, and hope for the future.

Washington sent the proclamation to all of the states' governors so they could also issue their own documents. Though the proclamation is dated October 3, 1789, the day for public thanksgiving was Thursday, November 26, 1789.

STANDING FOR THE FLAG

In recent years, Americans have witnessed many sports figures and others castigate the U.S. flag and America's national anthem. Hence, they refuse to stand for them in order to promote a radical political agenda. When two sports teams compete, they play in fierce opposition to each other. Standing for the national anthem before a football or baseball game has long been the only two minutes of unity between the opposing teams. Not only does standing for the flag and its anthem promote unity as Americans at sporting events, but it also promotes good sportsmanship.

This problem has also manifested itself in certain media outlets. In June 2021 just a few days before Flag Day, a journalist for a major media outlet claimed that she was "disturbed"[158] to see "dozens of American flags" over the weekend on Long Island. "I think that as long as they see Americanness as the same as one with whiteness, this is going to continue."

Whether pledging allegiance to the U.S. flag or singing "The Star-Spangled Banner," Americans need these moments of unity to bring them together despite their political and cultural differences. Standing together united under the national anthem and saluting the U.S. flag have been acts of unity for centuries.

When the Continental Congress issued the first flag under the United States of America on June 14, 1777, they emphasized the union of the states. Thirty-seven years later in August 1814, the White House and U.S. Capitol were in ashes after the British military burned the public buildings in Washington D.C. In the immediate aftermath of this act of terror, many Americans understandably feared that another flag, Britain's Union Jack, would soon fly over all of America again. The United States was in danger of collapse.

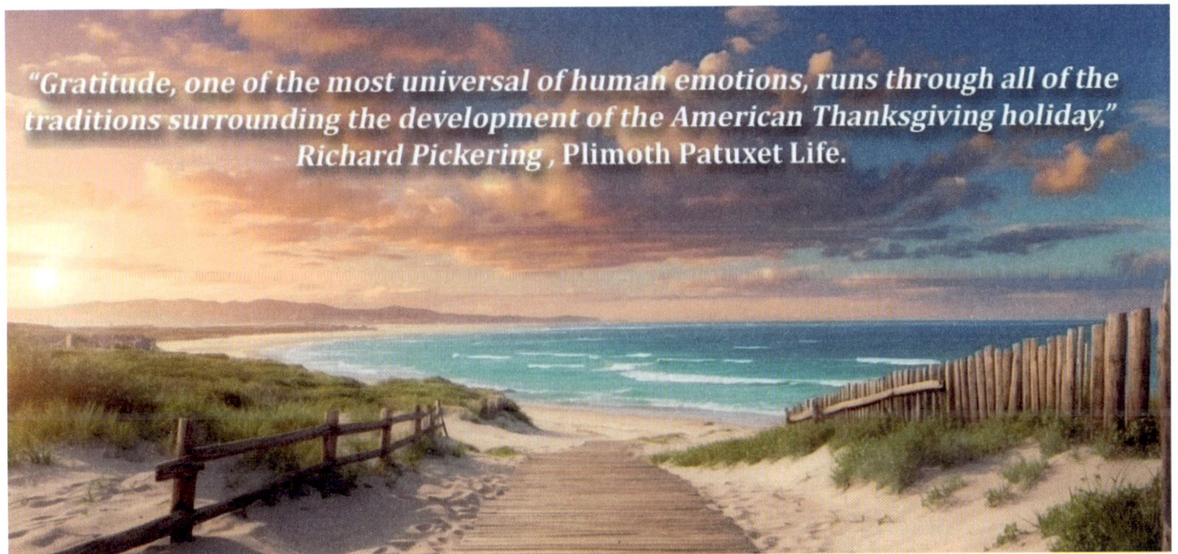

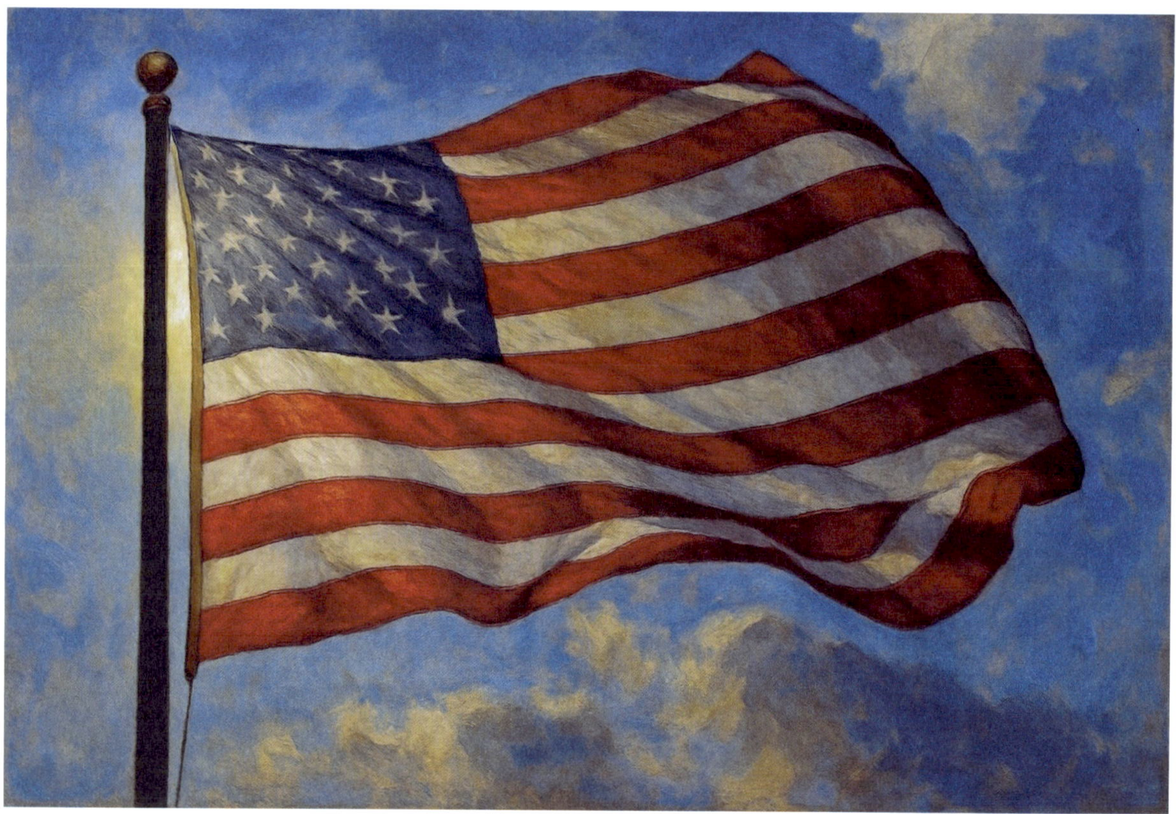

Three weeks after the sacking of Washington, a Maryland attorney named Francis Scott Key was detained on a British military ship in Baltimore's harbor. He witnessed the British soldiers as they hurled rockets at Fort McHenry all day and all night. Patriots had sunk their own boats in the harbor to prevent the larger British ships from getting close enough to destroy the fort. As dawn broke on the morning of September 14, 1814, Key saw the U.S. flag flying victoriously over Fort McHenry and heard the sound of silence instead of the rhythm of bombs. The British attack was over and America, not Britain, had won.

Overflowing with relief that his nation was not conquered, Key wrote lyrics for a new song. Today, we call this song *The Star-Spangled Banner*, which became the national anthem and begins this way:

O say can you see by the dawn's early light
What so proudly we hail'd at the twilight's last gleaming
Whose broad stripes and bright stars through the perilous fight
O'er the ramparts we watch'd were so gallantly streaming?

Without specifying the Battle of Fort McHenry, the majority of the lyrics fit the context of the War of 1812. They are also universal, which means they resonate with subsequent battles and patriotic moments.

In recent years, the rarely sung third verse has given many understandable reasons to pause. *No refuge could save the hireling and slave, from the terror of flight or the gloom of the grave.* Without knowing the history of the War of 1812, many modern-day Americans are confused and angered by this seemingly inhumane sentence.

This line was written seven months after the British military issued a proclamation that promised slaves that if they risked the *terror of flight*, they could receive their freedom from the British but only if they agreed to first serve in the British military against the United States. Francis Scott Key believed the risk of the *gloom of the grave* by serving on the front lines was not a true refuge for slaves. After coming face to face with the illiberal British days before he wrote these lyrics, he didn't think the enemy, the British military, was a genuine refuge for slaves.

He was not alone. Charles Ball, a free Black man from Baltimore boarded one of the British ships holding slaves who had become British soldiers. He was so disgusted with the haughtiness of the British military against Americans that he left. Ball loved America, not Britain. Volunteering to fight with the American military, Ball was injured at the Battle of Bladensburg on August 24, 1814.

One reason that Americans lack historical context about the national anthem is that most school textbooks give scant attention to the War of 1812. Students read one or two pages about America's second war for independence. Yet, the War of 1812 solidified the sovereignty of the United States. Before this war, America was a country in name only in the eyes of Europeans. British sea captains would deny U.S. citizenship, kidnap American sailors and force them into the British Navy. This captivity, which abolitionist John Quincy Adams called another form of slavery, was the moral cause of the War of 1812. John Quincy calculated that British captains had kidnapped 9,000 American sailors between Washington's presidency in 1789 and 1812.

One reason *The Star-Spangled Banner* became the national anthem is because the majority of the national anthem's lyrics have a universal quality about them, especially in the first verse, that apply to many sacrificial moments in America. The third verse's lyrics are not universal and don't transcend generations. The idea of our flag remaining after battle resonated in the Civil War, World War I, World War II, and after the terrorist attacks of September 11, 2001.

And the rocket's red glare, the bombs bursting in air,
Gave proof through the night that our flag was still there,
O say does that star-spangled banner yet wave
O'er the land of the free and the home of the brave?

Americans, regardless of their skin color, ethnicity, religion, class or gender, have many reasons to stand together to salute the flag and sing their anthem.

FIVE REASONS TO STAND FOR THE FLAG

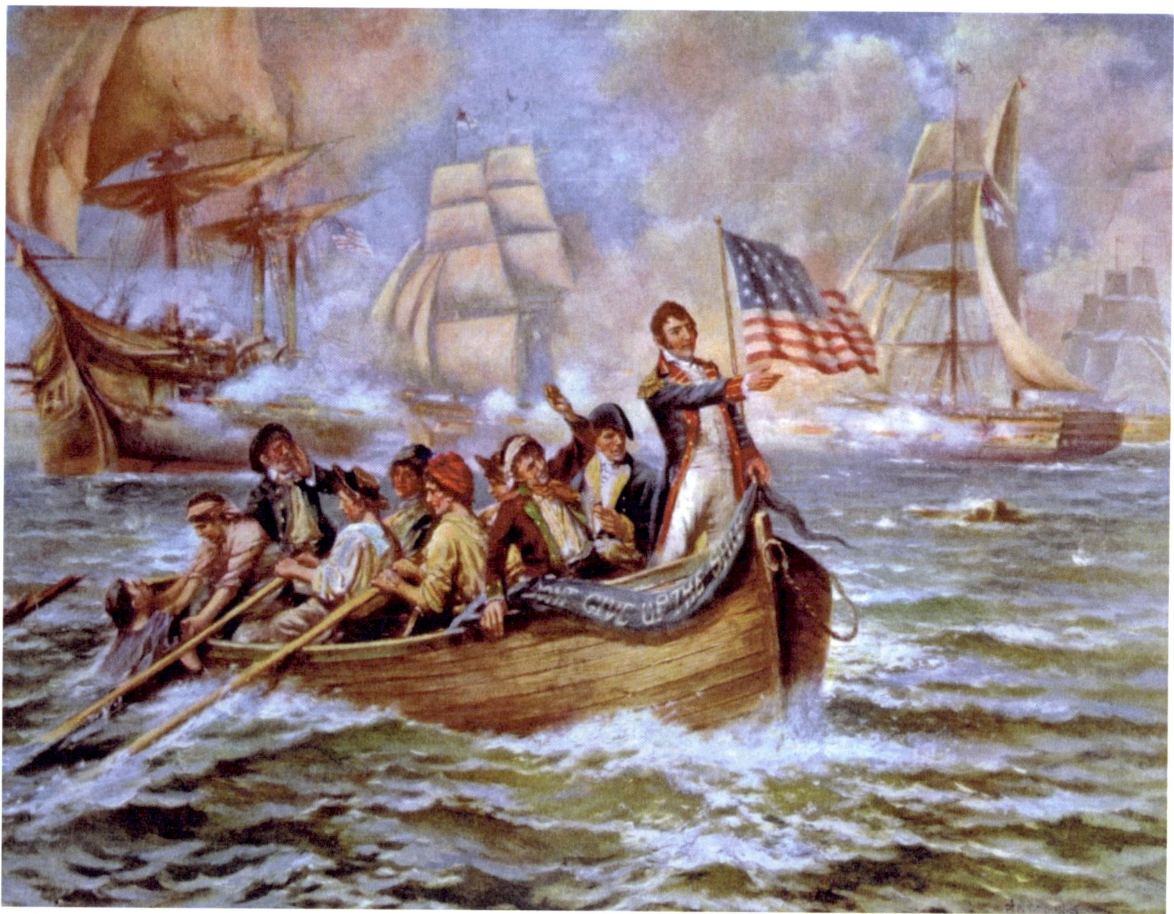

Oliver Hazard Perry in a boat after the War of 1812's Battle of Lake Erie by Edward Percy Moran

1. **Americans stand for the flag, not to please ourselves but to honor those who died and paid the ultimate sacrifice for our freedom.** More than 1.2 million Americans[159] have died because of wars throughout the centuries. When we stand for the flag and sing the anthem, we stand for all members of the armed services, including one who showed bravery at Fort McHenry, the battle that inspired the national anthem. A runaway slave who'd voluntarily joined the 38th U.S. Infantry, William Williams's leg was blown off at the Battle of Fort McHenry. He later died from his injuries.[160]

2. **Americans stand for the flag and sing the anthem to focus on what unites us, not on what divides us. This unity is what it means to be an American.**

"The name of AMERICAN, which belongs to you, in your national capacity, must always exalt the just pride of patriotism, more than any appellation derived from local discriminations. With slight shades of difference, you have the same religion, manners, habits, and political principles. You have in a common cause fought and triumphed together—the independence and liberty you possess are the work of joint councils, and joint efforts—of common dangers, sufferings and successes,"[161] George Washington, declared in his Farewell Address to Americans in 1796. The same is true today. More than our love for a sports team, our home state or our political affiliations, the name *American* deserves our highest respect. Standing is the ultimate display of sportsmanship.

3. Americans stand for the flag not to pledge allegiance to a specific president, but to honor the reality that we have an elected president and not a lifetime king. When we stand, we honor the fact that our country elects our leaders. We honor the fact that our nation has had dozens of presidents, not a handful of lifetime kings. We also honor our flag because it reflects a division of power. Represented by the flag's stars, 50 different states are united under a federal government.

4. Americans stand to salute the principle of justice. Justice is one of the definitions for the color blue in our flag. Patriotism is not pride in any pain from our nation's past or past injustices, especially slavery. Rather, patriotism is pride in the principles that paved the way for change, that put justice into practice, whether that change was trading tyrannical royalty for representation in 1776, exchanging enslavement for emancipation in 1863, or dissolving discrimination in the 1960s.

5. Americans stand for the flag not for our generation but to set an example for the next generation. "If we do not advocate a love of country to our children and the generations to come, then why would our children grow up to fight for their countries, the founding principles and moral truths?"[162] First Lady Melania Trump asked in a speech to the United Nations. Passing along patriotism is crucial to America's future survival. The color of white in the flag symbolizes the purity and innocence of our children.

When we stand, we are hopeful for our children's future, that thy will embrace the principles of patriotism and live out its moral truths of justice, perseverance, and courage. We stand for the flag and anthem so our children can stand for the flag and anthem in the years to come. We stand for the flag so it will outlive us, a symbol of the continuance of the United States.

CORRUPTION'S ANTIDOTE–INTEGRITY

Why did George Washington give up his government salary when he became president in 1789? Avoiding even the appearance of corruption, he didn't want to appear to be beholden to anyone for his income, including Congress that appropriated his salary. Washington also sought to reassure Americans that the United States government was not going to be corrupt under his administration. He had a worthy partner on the same wavelength in Vice President John Adams.

President Washington knew that one of the main problems Americans had faced in the lead up to the American Revolution was corruption. They had witnessed their colonial governments corrupted by the king's money. Prior to King George III's implementation of new laws, their colonial legislative bodies had paid the salaries of their colonial governors.

Then the king made the governors dependent on him for their salaries. Hence, the colonial governors owed their sole allegiance to King George III, not to the people. Under this corrupted government system, the people could not hold their governors accountable.

"What opportunities then shall we in this province have to demand and obtain the redress of grievances, if our governors and judges and other officers and magistrates are to be supported by the ministry, without the gifts of the people?"[163] John Adams had asked in 1772.

He'd questioned "the independency of the governor, his salary granted by the crown, out of a revenue extorted from this people… The instruction to the governor, not to consent to any tax bill unless certain crown officers are exempted." He had noted that the British Americans had no ability to stop this power because they were not represented in Parliament. The problem had worsened when the king had dissolved the General Court, which had been the colonial governing body of Massachusetts, and had replaced the governor with a military general, who implemented martial law.

Judges had also become dependent on the crown for their salaries, which had motivated them to rule against the colonists. In customs courts, judges had heard cases where defendants, such as ship owners, were accused of smuggling. If the defendants lost, their confiscated cargo or ships were sold. The system had been further corrupted when judges received a cut of these sales or were bribed.

"Is not the natural and necessary tendency of these innovations, to introduce dark intrigues, insincerity, simulation, bribery, and perjury, among custom house officers, merchants, masters, mariners, and their servants?" Adams observed about this judicial corruption. Adams had a strong grasp of human nature. During the revolution, he'd clearly understood that when the world seems upside down, corruption is often the culprit.

"But when a government becomes totally corrupted, the system of God Almighty in the government of the world and the rules of all good government upon earth will be reversed. … Virtue, integrity and ability will become the objects of the malice, hatred and revenge of the men in power … In such times you will see a governor … whose welfare he was under every moral obligation to study and promote, ruin and destroy the people." John Adams wrote in 1772.

He understood that corruption could also happen to society's humanitarians, such as physicians and preachers.

"… You will see a philanthrop(ist)—for propagating as many lies and slanders against his country as ever fell from the pen of a sycophant—rewarded … The consequence of this will be that the iron rod of power will be stretched out vs. the poor people …"

He believed that the corruption and despotism they had faced in the Revolutionary War had come from a combination of the king and aristocracy scheming together to crush them.

Also witnessing corruption and understanding the temptations of humanity, President Washington had never forgotten that Benedict Arnold had first been corrupted while serving as a military governor of Philadelphia before he'd committed treason against America. Arnold had shown that financial corruption was a continuum of behavior that had led to increasingly damaging or dangerous crimes, such as treason.

Prior to his election as president, Washington had written the Marquis de Lafayette in 1788 about the new Constitution and how to protect America against corruption. Thomas

Jefferson and Lafayette had believed the Constitution should limit the number of years that a president could serve. They believed that term limits would lower the risk of corruption.

Washington had shared Lafayette's and Jefferson's concerns about what would happen if a president were to become corrupt, especially from foreign actors. Washington believed that a president who was under "bribery and undue influence" would be "in the last stage of corrupted morals and political depravity."[164]

Though he'd shared their concerns about bribery, Washington disagreed with their solution because he knew that a president could be corrupted prior to taking office or during office. Washington addressed Lafayette's and Jefferson's concerns about the lack of term limits on presidents. Leading by example, he stepped down from office after two terms despite predictions by newspaper editors and others that he would serve 20 years or more until he died in office.

Washington's example lasted until President Franklin Roosevelt exceeded two terms when he won a third term in 1940 and a fourth in 1944. The American people responded in 1951 when they ratified the 22nd Amendment to the Constitution to limit a president's terms to two.

The founders knew that all types and levels of government could be corrupted. "Liberty, under every conceivable form of government is always in danger. It is so even under a simple, or perfect democracy, more so under a mixed government, like the republic of Rome, and still more so under a limited monarchy," Washington wrote.

Why is liberty under threat no matter the form of government? Because ambition is intoxicating. "Ambition is one of the more ungovernable passions of the human heart. The love of power, is insatiable and uncontrollable ... There is danger from all men. The only maxim of a free government, ought to be to trust no man living, with power to endanger the public liberty. ... Be upon your guard then, my countrymen," Adams wrote.[165]

Both Washington and Adams had concluded that ambition could corrupt any system if not checked. Washington was concerned that political parties would lead to a "spirit of revenge ... and mischief"[166] and to "frightful despotism." He warned Americans that political parties could lead to unnecessary "jealousies and false alarms, kindles the animosity of one part against another, foments occasionally riot and insurrection. It opens the door to foreign influence and corruption, which find a facilitated access to the government itself through the channels of party passions."

Adams also feared cultural corruption. "As long as knowledge and virtue are diffused generally among the body of a nation, it is impossible they should be enslaved. This can be brought to pass only by debasing their understandings or by corrupting their hearts."

What did he mean by knowledge being diffused? He meant education and the media. As long as Americans were being educated in how to think critically to discover truth and sort fact from fiction and as long as they received accurate, truthful information about their government and world from newspapers, their understanding could not be debased.

What were their solutions to corruption? Power sharing. The founders created the three equal branches of the federal government (executive, legislative and judicial) and the three levels of government (federal, state and local) to minimize the potential for corruption by diffusing government power.

Integrity would also have to be a priority of both leaders and the people for America to survive. "I hold the maxim no less applicable to public than to private affairs, that honesty is always the best policy," Washington had explained in his 1796 Farewell Address. The people must hold government officials, newspaper publishers, educators, and others accountable.

Adams had warned that a statesman can "scatter ruin and destruction in his path who by deceiving a nation can render despotism desirable in their eyes and make himself popular in undoing." In addition to integrity, courage was a bulwark against tyranny, the end result of corruption.

While not seeking to mandate a specific religion or undermine the First Amendment, Adams nonetheless believed that "religion and virtue are the only foundations; not only of republicanism and of all free government: but of social felicity under all governments and in all the combinations of human society."

THE FIRST DIVERSITY STRUGGLE–FAITH DIVIDED

Understanding history is not about applying modern standards or modern law retroactively to historical figures. To develop a healthier perspective of our past, we must first understand how past Americans viewed their lives, their circumstances, and how they changed their beliefs and conclusions. Instead of trying to impose diversity on the past, we should ask better questions such as: How would our nation's Founders have defined diversity? What injustices did they face?

"The revolution was in the minds and hearts of the people, a change in their religious sentiments, of their duties and obligations,"[167] John Adams reflected in 1818, decades after the American Revolution. "This radical change in the principles, opinions, sentiments and affection of the people, was the real American Revolution."

European history overflowed with stories of persecution of Protestants, Catholics, and Jews. Catholic English monarchs had persecuted Protestants while Protestant English monarchs had persecuted Catholics. Jews had been persecuted regardless of who was in power, especially through the inquisitions in Spain and Portugal. Thousands from all these groups came to America for religious freedom as a result. Puritans came to Massachusetts, while Catholics chartered Maryland. More than half of the 13 colonies were established under the Anglican Church. Quakers in Pennsylvania welcomed all, which made Philadelphia a rare safe haven for Jews, as was Rhode Island.

> *"The colonies had grown up under constitutions of government, so different, there was so great a variety of religions, they were composed of so many different nations, their customs, manners and habits had so little resemblance," Adams wrote of Americans' diversity.*

"Their knowledge of each other so imperfect, that to unite them in the same principles in theory and the same system of action was certainly a very difficult enterprise." In 1774, the Continental Congress wanted to have a member of the clergy speak to them but they were divided on whom to choose "because we were so divided in religious sentiments, some

Episcopalians, some Quakers, some Anabaptists, some Presbyterians and some Congregationalists, so that we could not join in the same act of worship,"[168] Adams explained.

With such diversity and division in their minds, how did Congress solve this problem? "Mr. (Samuel) Adams arose and said he was no bigot, and could hear a prayer from a gentleman of piety and virtue, who was at the same time a friend to his country."

That year, Virginia's British authorities imprisoned five Baptists ministers for preaching without a license from the Church of England. This led James Madison and Thomas Jefferson to call for the free exercise of religion. Adams agreed, concluding, "if Parliament could tax us, they could establish the Church of England ... and prohibit all other churches."[169]

Religious intolerance was sometimes on public display. Boston was known for celebrating Guy Fawkes Day, an anti-Catholic British holiday where disguised gang members paraded the Pope like a puppet in effigy, broke windows, and went door-to-door soliciting money. This Halloween-like event celebrated the capture of Guy Fawkes, a Catholic, who failed to blow up a Protestant king and Parliament in 1605.

When George Washington sent an expedition to Canada in 1775, he explicitly told his men to tolerate different religious views. He wanted their discipline to be as obvious as their courage and valor. That discipline included religious tolerance. He asked them "to avoid all disrespect or contempt of the religion of the country and its ceremonies—prudence, policy, and a true Christian spirit will lead us to look with compassion" without insulting them. Washington knew that most of his army were Protestants while many Canadians were Catholics. "While we are contending for our own liberty, we should be very cautious of violating the rights of conscience in others; ever considering that God alone is the judge of the hearts of men and to him only in this case they are answerable," Washington instructed on September 14, 1775.[170]

Despite past injustices and current differences, the Founders united Americans into one nation. Seeking to protect their God-given rights, they enshrined freedom of religion in the Bill of Rights. They overcame their diversity to unite. They had enough confidence in their Judeo-Christian beliefs that they were willing to let their faith be free. They embraced the freedom to choose faith. In contrast, the French Revolution's radicals in the 1790s adopted the opposite philosophy. Instead of uniting French Catholics with French Protestants, they replaced God with man when they took over Notre Dame Cathedral and turned it into an atheist temple of reason. Like today's radicals, they also decapitated iconic statues.

Although America's first diversity struggle was over religion, Americans can still be united *Under God* regardless of their religious beliefs because they can join together in the commitment that America's freedom of religion allows Christians, Jews, Muslims, Buddhists, Hindus, and others to practice their faith. Freedom of religion under God is part of America's national identity with a cultural bent of Judeo-Christian roots.

Understanding our national identity requires a better, wider, deeper, and more tolerant view of our history. We benefit by not viewing the founders as monolithic but by considering how they viewed themselves, their commonalities, and their differences. More importantly, we benefit when we remember what they overcame to unite in a representative government. We benefit when we celebrate a shared commitment to upholding the best of America. We benefit when we learn from the past and lean into the people, places, and events that show the greatness of America's story and identity.

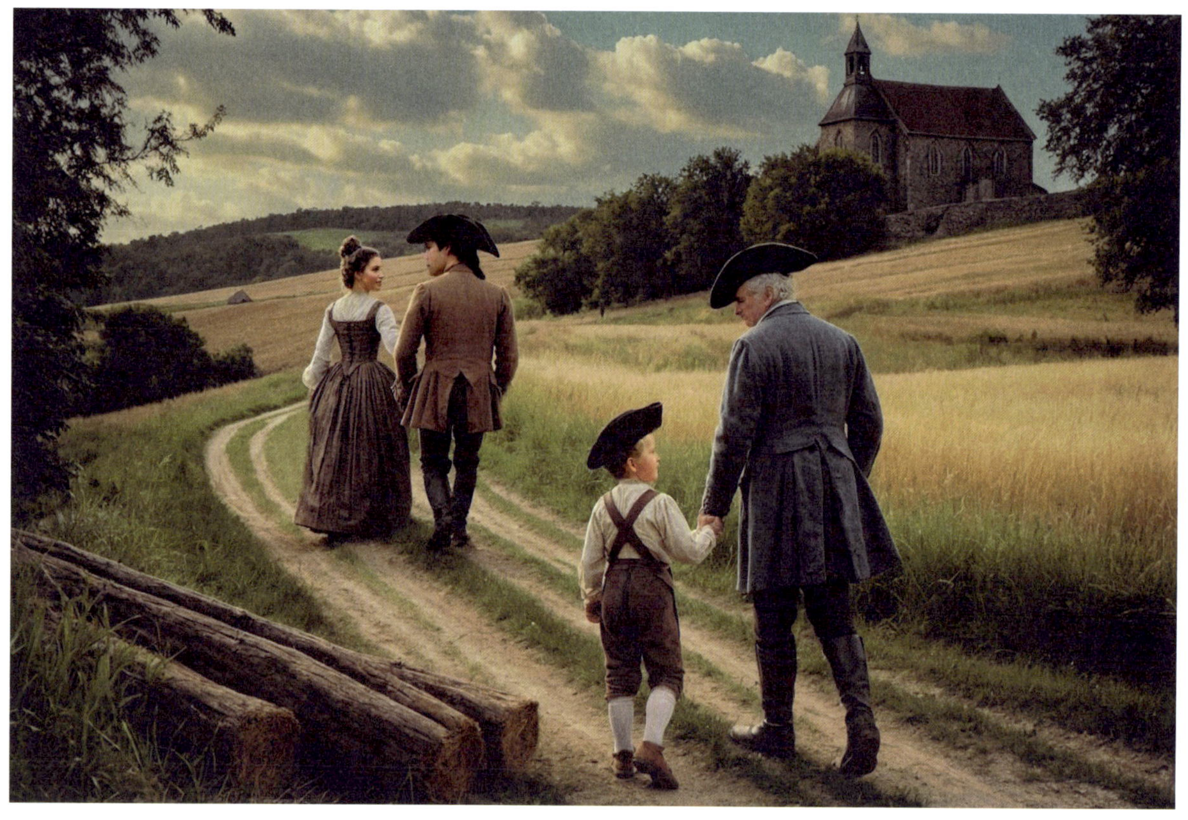

A modern rendition of the public domain painting *Sunday Morning* by Jennie Augusta Brownscombe

THE END OF AMERICA'S REVOLUTION WAS THE START OF THE ABOLITION MOVEMENT TO END SLAVERY

"The fundamental [1619] claim that the Revolutionary War was fought to preserve slavery simply does not correspond with the facts, too conclusively for the point to be dismissed as mere hair-splitting. The issue is not differing interpretations of history, but an outright misinterpretation of it,"[171] scholar John McWhorter wrote for 1776 Unites in response to one of the key fallacies of the 1619 Project of the *New York Times*. McWhorter's essay was called "We Cannot Allow '1619' to Dumb Down America in the Name of a Crusade."

"For one, note the suspension of disbelief we are expected to maintain. Supposedly the Founding Fathers were trying to protect slavery, despite never actually making such a goal clear for the historical record, and at a time when there would have been no shame in doing so," McWhorter observed.

McWhorter is correct. In fact, throwing off political slavery by England was a primary motivator to fight for independence. Original letters, writings, and sermons from the nation's founding generation are filled with anti-slavery, pro-freedom discourse. These writings planted the seeds of abolishing African slavery that bore fruit as emancipation during the Civil War.

"We have no choice left to us, but to submit to absolute slavery and despotism, or as freemen to stand in our own defense, and endeavor a noble resistance ... every reasonable method of reconciliation has been tried in vain,"[172] Baptist minister David Jones declared in his 1775 sermon, *Defensive War in a Just War Sinless*.

Jones, who served as a chaplain to the Continental Army, looked to Galatians 5:1, as did many pro-patriot pastors, for guidance. "Stand fast therefore in the liberty wherewith Christ hath made us free. And be not entangled again with the yoke of bondage."

"Our addresses to our king have been treated with neglect or contempt," Jones declared. The king's tyranny had enslaved all Americans as subjects and not free people.

"The time is now near at hand which must probably determine, whether Americans are to be, freemen, or slaves; whether they are to have any property they can call their own; whether their houses, and farms, are to be pillaged and destroyed, and they consigned to a state of wretchedness from which no human efforts will probably deliver them,"[173] Washington told his soldiers in New York on July 2, 1776.

John Adams had contemplated the universality of all humanity regardless of their traits. He believed that all people were rational and had God-given natural rights.

"Here we should spread before us a map of man—view him in different soils and climates, in different nations and countries, under different religions and customs, in barbarity and civility, in a state of ignorance and enlightened with knowledge, in slavery and in freedom, in infancy and age. He will be found, a rational, sensible and social animal, in all. The instinct of nature impels him to society, and society causes the necessity of government,"[174] Adams wrote, underscoring the commonality of all human beings.

The first antislavery petition from a religious group was published by Quakers in 1688 in Germantown, Pennsylvania. Years later, the first anti-slavery pamphlet, *The Selling of Joseph* by Samuel Sewall, was first published in Massachusetts in 1700. Despite these petitions, public policy about slavery did not change. Slavery remained legal in each of the original thirteen colonies. Before the war, there was no forcing function in the law or culture to legally end slavery throughout the 13 original states.

When the American Revolution came along, it sowed the seeds of abolition through new political rhetoric, spiritual priorities, and the hope of the Declaration of Independence. Many Americans saw themselves as enslaved by Great Britain. This metaphor opened the door for many to see the hypocrisy and injustice of enslaving Africans.

"By the 1770s, black New Englanders, thousands of whom were Revolutionary War veterans, had begun sending petitions to northern state legislatures demanding an end to slavery. These, essentially, worked,"[175] African-American scholar Wilfred Reilly wrote for 1776 Unites in an essay called "Slavery Does Not Define the Black American Experience."

Reilly is correct. After all, when Prince Hall and several fellow slaves petitioned Massachusetts to end slavery in January 1777—a few months after the Declaration of Independence— they referenced the new principles espoused in the current political debate. "Every principle from which America has acted in the course of their unhappy difficulties with Great Briton pleads stronger than a thousand arguments in favors of your petitioners."

Hall used language from the Declaration of Independence in his declaration. "The petition of a great number of blacks detained in a state of slavery in the bowels of a free and Christian country humbly showeth that your petitioners apprehend that they have in common with all other men a natural and unalienable right to that freedom which the great parent of the universe hath bestowed equally on all mankind."[176]

Slavery remained legal in each of the states until the end of the American Revolution, when a Massachusetts judge declared slavery illegal in Massachusetts in 1783 under the state constitution. Along with other cases, this was in response to a lawsuit from Elizabeth Freeman, who sued for her freedom and won.

"By the 1790s, 10 states and territories, containing more than 50 percent of the free population of the new nation — Maine, New Hampshire, Vermont, Massachusetts, Rhode Island, Connecticut, New York, Pennsylvania, the North-West Territory, and the Indiana Territory — were free land by law. And, the anti-slavery upswell continued apace,"[177] Reilly explained. Some states banned slavery outright while others gradually abolished it over a designated time frame.

Other examples of this upswell included Phillis Wheatley's poetry, which was sold to raise money for abolition in 1791. An advertisement in the *Massachusetts Spy* in July 1791, noted that the posthumous sale of Wheatley's poems, included ones never-before-published, would add "a weight in the scale of human rights."[178] Wheatley herself defined race in spiritual terms, calling America: "The land of freedom's heaven-defended race!"

Likewise, Ben Franklin's last request of Congress before his death was to call on Congress to end slavery. As a young man, he had advertised antislavery Quaker pamphlets. Becoming a public abolitionist advocate after the adoption of the U.S. Constitution, his February 1790 petition called on Congress to "devise means for removing the inconsistency from the character of the American people,"[179] and to "promote mercy and justice toward this distressed race."

The tide turned slowly in Northern states until the issue of slavery became a standoff with Southern states, which led to the Civil War that ultimately abolished slavery. Abraham Lincoln issued the Emancipation Proclamation that freed slaves while Congress and the people adopted the thirteen to fifteen Amendments to the Constitution. The Civil War finished the job of abolition that the Revolutionary War had started. The cost of the Civil War was high. According to the Department of Veterans Affairs, deaths in battle combined with deaths in theater of war totaled 498,332.

Freed slaves and slaves who fought in the War for Independence should be remembered for their heroism first, not their societal status. Soldiers with African ancestry put their lives on the line as much as their fellow soldiers with European ancestry. These heroes are sources of pride for all, not victims.

"While acknowledging that slavery and discrimination are part of our nation's history, we believe that America should not be defined solely by this 'birth defect' and that black Americans should not be portrayed as perpetual helpless victims,"[180] 1776 Unites founder Robert L. Woodson, Sr. explained in his essay *The Crucial Voice of '1776.'*

History isn't always what it seems. It is more nuanced, incremental, and complicated than the Marxist, all-or-nothing purity approach demonstrated by mobs who topple statues. This headline-only approach to history fails to ask questions like this: How did George Washington transform from being born into a slave-owning family to emancipating slaves in his will, which was published in newspapers throughout the nation after his death? What were the steps that made this transformation possible?

Washington struggled with slavery, particularly near the end of his life. Sprinkled throughout his life were moments that challenged the world he'd been born into. From corresponding with Phillis Wheatley in 1776 to meeting anti-slavery proponents such as John Laurens, Washington discovered different opinions. He listened to the counsel of the Marquis de Lafayette, who opposed slavery.

"I never mean ... to possess another slave by purchase: it being among my first wishes to see some plan adopted by the legislature by which slavery in the country may be abolished by slow, sure, and imperceptible degrees,"[181] Washington wrote in 1786.

When he returned to Mount Vernon after his presidency, he made small changes, such as ending the practice of separating slave families. He came to view slavery as his primary greatest regret.

At age 67, he placed an abolition clause in his will for freeing the 123 slaves under his direct care. "This bold decision marked the culmination of two decades of introspection and inner conflict for Washington, as his views on slavery changed gradually but dramatically," Mount Vernon historians explain today in Washington's Changing Views on Slavery. He died on December 14, 1799, a little more than two months before his sixty-eighth birthday. When his will was published in newspapers around the nation, Americans learned of his counter-cultural decision to free his slaves.

Some say history repeats itself while others claim it rhymes. What rhymes with slavery today? Human trafficking and forced labor? Forced medical mandates? Segregating people by their skin color or medical status?

"When the popular power becomes grasping, and eager after augmentation, or for amplification, beyond its proper weight, or line, it becomes as dangerous as any other,"[182] John Adams wrote, recognizing that tyranny could come in different forms.

"Liberty, under every conceivable form of government is always in danger. It is so even under a simple, or perfect Democracy, more so under a mixed government, like the Republic of Rome, and still more so under a limited monarchy ... There is danger from all men. The only maxim of a free government, ought to be to trust no man living, with power to endanger the public liberty."

Adams believed that dispersed power and integrity were the antidotes to oppression, a wise observation for our times. "Be upon your guard then, my countrymen ... Liberty depends upon an exact balance, a nice counterpoise of all the powers of the state."

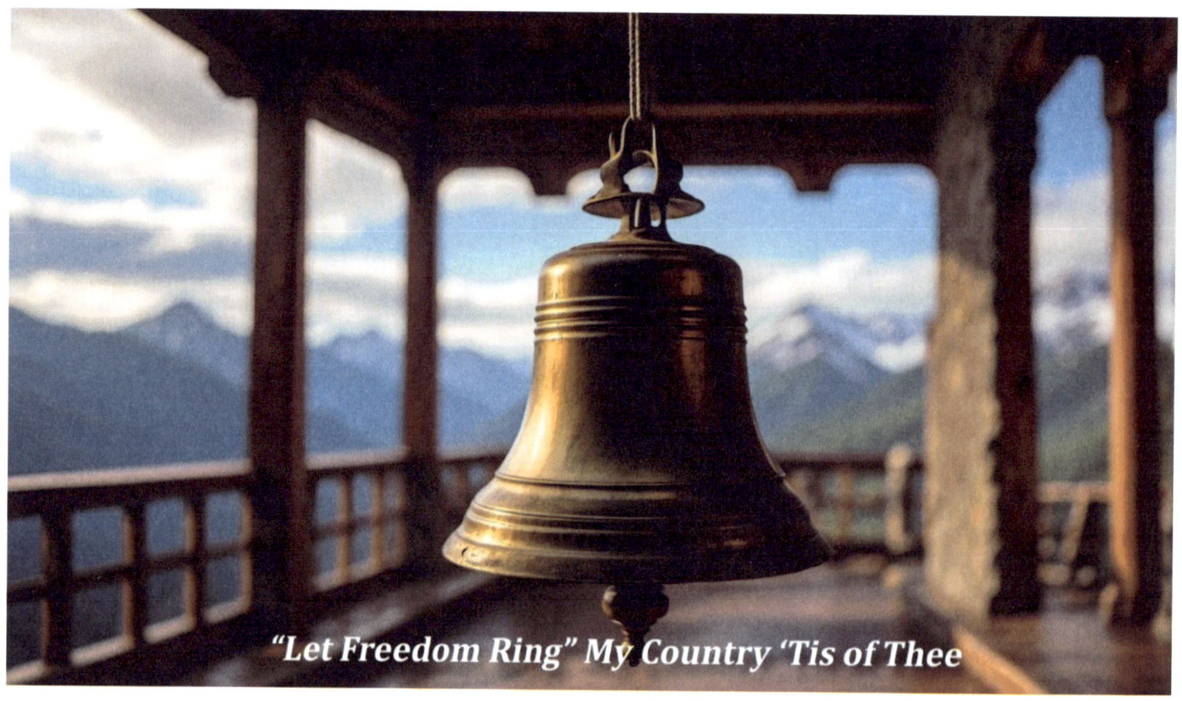

"Let Freedom Ring" My Country 'Tis of Thee

HOW THE DECLARATION OF INDEPENDENCE INSPIRED OUR GREATEST CIVIL RIGHTS MOVEMENTS

In addition to planting the seeds that ended slavery during the Civil War, the Declaration of Independence inspired our greatest civil rights movements. The first women's rights conference was held in Seneca Falls, New York, in 1848. Elizabeth Cady Stanton modelled the women's Declaration of Sentiments after the Declaration of Independence and asserted "that all men and women are created equal." Women's rights advocates held numerous conferences in the decade leading to the Civil War. Sojourner Truth, a former slave, abolitionist, and women's voting rights advocate, gave a memorable speech to a conference in Ohio.

After the Civil War, abolitionist and suffragist Susan B. Anthony continued to tap the Declaration's powerful rhetorical logic and emotional appeal.

"'Governments derive their just powers from the consent of the governed.' This is the fundamental principle of democracy," [183] Anthony proclaimed, borrowing another phrase from the Declaration. Anthony and Elizabeth Cady Stanton believed it was time to put the Declaration into practice for all Americans, which they conveyed in a speech to the Equal Rights Association after the Civil War.

"The Scripture declaration is, 'So God created man in his own image, male and female created he them,' and all divine legislation

throughout the realm of nature recognizes the perfect equality of the two conditions; for male and female are but different conditions. Neither color nor sex is ever discharged from obedience to law, natural or moral, written or unwritten. The commandments thou shalt not steal, or kill, or commit adultery, recognize no sex; and hence we believe that all human legislation which is at variance with the divine code, is essentially unrighteous and unjust ..."

"Women and colored men are loyal, liberty-loving citizens, and we cannot believe that sex or complexion should be any ground for civil or political degradation. Against such outrage on the very name of a republic we do and ever must protest; and is not our protest against this tyranny of 'taxation without representation' as just as that thundered from Bunker Hill, when our Revolutionary fathers fired the shot which shook the world?

"We respectfully and earnestly pray that, in restoring the foundations of our nationality, all discriminations on account of sex or race may be removed; and that our government may be republican in fact as well as form; A GOVERNMENT BY THE PEOPLE, AND THE WHOLE PEOPLE; FOR THE PEOPLE, AND THE WHOLE PEOPLE."

The abolition and women's suffrage movements came to fruition through the 13th, 14th, 15th, and 19th Amendments to the Constitution. These amendments abolished slavery, declared freed slaves to be U.S. citizens, protected voting rights for black men, and eventually protected voting rights for all women.

The Declaration of Independence also inspired Ida B. Wells-Barnett, a former slave, journalist, suffragist, and anti-lynching activist. "The flower of the 19th century civilization for the American people was the abolition of slavery and the enfranchisement of all manhood. Here at last was squaring of practice with precept, with true democracy, with the Declaration of Independence and with the Golden Rule,"[184] Wells-Barnett wrote.

The Declaration's aspirational core philosophy influenced the Civil Rights movement of the 1960s because it was not fully realized for black Americans. "But 100 years later, the life of the Negro is still sadly crippled by the manacles of segregation and the chains of discrimination,"[185] Martin Luther King, Jr. declared in his 1963 "I Have a Dream" speech. King looked to the Declaration of Independence as he spoke to thousands on the National Mall in Washington, D.C.

"When the architects of our republic wrote the magnificent words of the Constitution and the Declaration of Independence, they were signing a promissory note to which every

American was to fall heir," King proclaimed. "This note was a promise that all men—yes, black men as well as white men—would be guaranteed the unalienable rights of life, liberty, and the pursuit of happiness."

While concluding that America had defaulted on that promissory note for black Americans through Jim Crow laws, King didn't believe that America was morally bankrupt. He still had faith in its founding promise. Because of King and civil rights advocates, Congress passed the Civil Rights Acts of the 1960s to tear down "Jim Crow" laws.

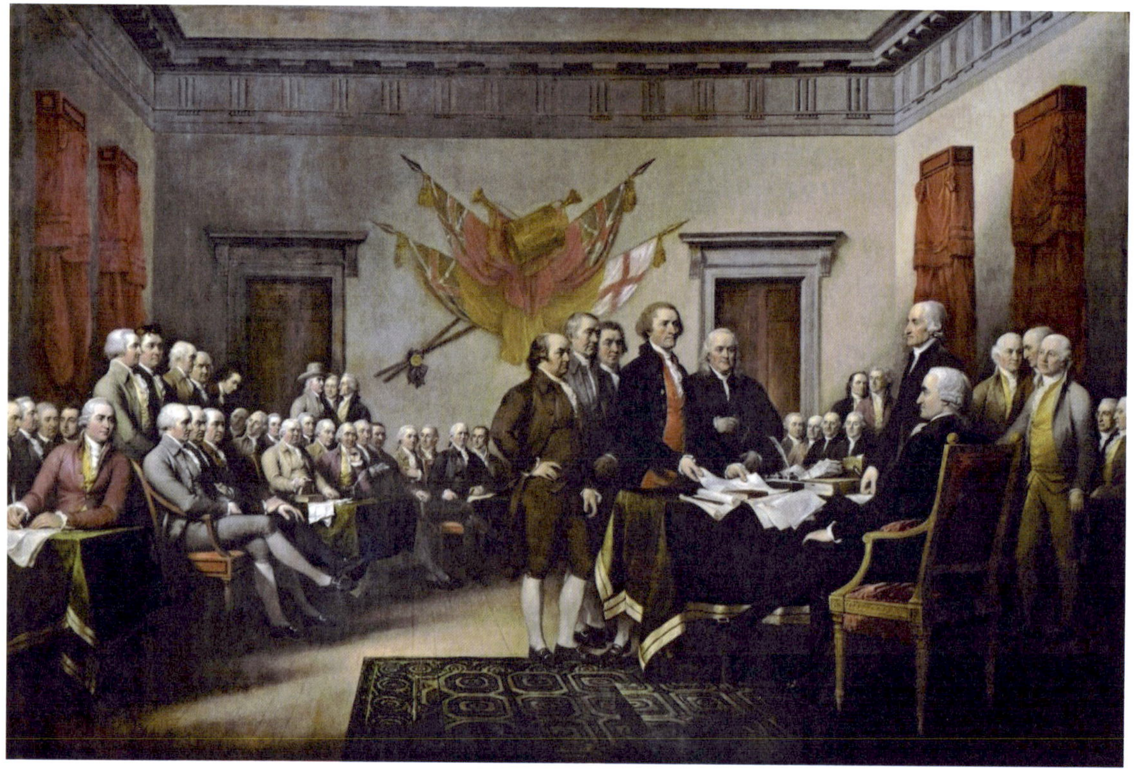

The Declaration of Independence by John Trumbull, public domain

FROM GRIEVANCE TO GRATITUDE

As this book has uncovered, giving thanks to God was an important part of American culture during its founding. Gratitude was part of private prayer and regular worship. Public days of thanks, which often included repentance, were also special observances for important events, such as the victory of the Battle of Saratoga and the victory at Yorktown.

From Ben Franklin's personal liturgy of thanks to Washington's thanksgiving proclamations, the founders practiced gratitude during the War for Independence and the early Republic spanning to the War of 1812. Despite their grievances, gratitude gave them a virtue to help them process and overcome the king's tyranny.

Gratitude also provides a lens to appreciate the accomplishments of those who sacrificed for freedom and enables us to give thanks for the good in our past, have forgiveness for the sins of others in the past, and strengthens us to face the future. Perhaps British novelist Jane Austen put it best when she wrote: "Think only of the past as its remembrance gives you pleasure." America's 250th anniversary on July 4, 2026 is the culmination of celebrating the good and great in America's overarching story. It's the ultimate act of gratitude and a symbol of justice for all. America's 250th gives hope for the future and the nation's next 250 years.

ORIGINAL DOCUMENTS

Featured in this section are a few original Thanksgiving documents. Download more here at no charge.

https://janecook.com/shop/original-documents-in-a-great-and-grateful-nation/

EDWARD WINSLOW, MAYFLOWER PILGRIM, 1621

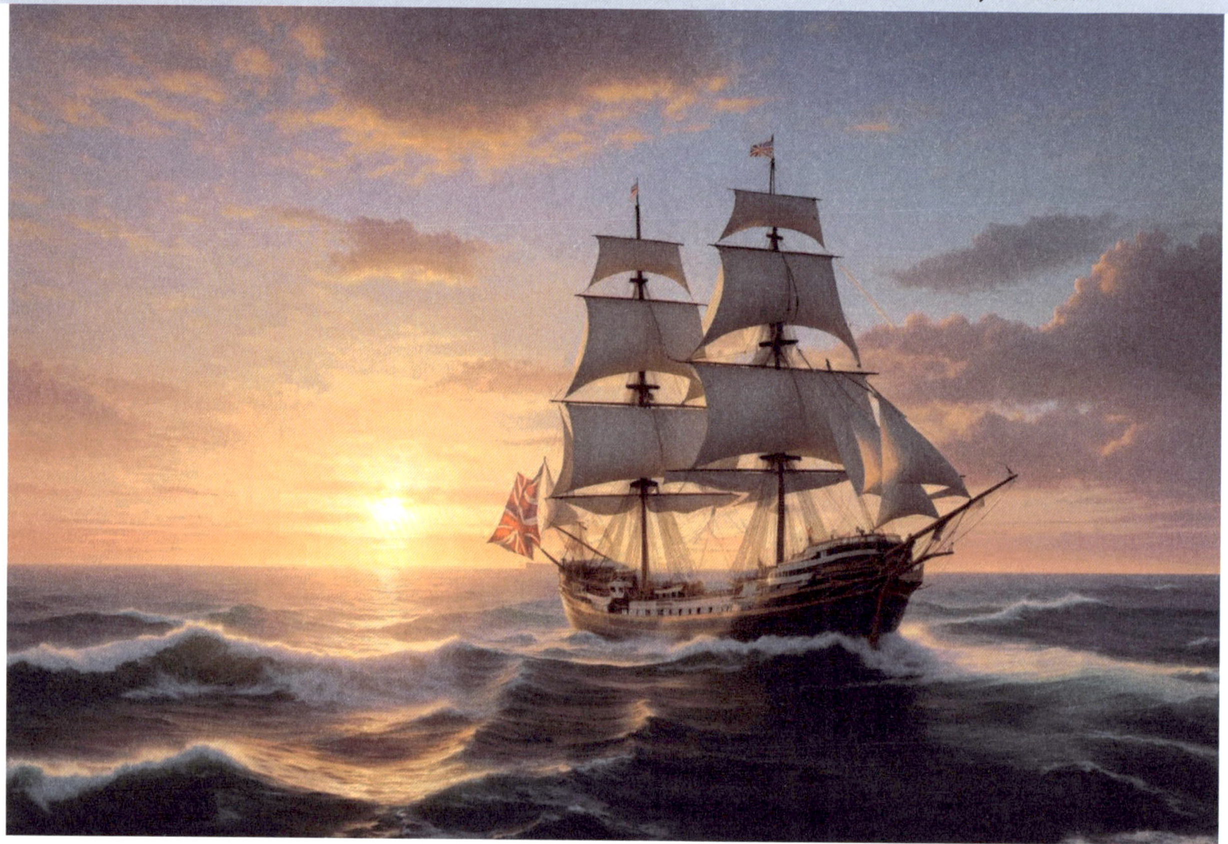

"Our harvest being gotten in, our governor sent four men on fowling, that so we might after a special manner rejoice together after we had gathered the fruit of our labors. They four in one day killed as much fowl as, with a little help beside, served the company almost a week. At which time, among other recreations, we exercised our arms, many of the Indians coming amongst us, and among the rest their greatest king Massasoit, with some ninety men, whom for three days we entertained and feasted, and they went out and killed five deer, which they brought to the plantation and bestowed upon our governor, and upon the captain, and others. And although it be not always so plentiful as it was at this time with us, yet by the goodness of God, we are so far from want that we often wish you partakers of our plenty," Edward Winslow, 1621.

NATIONAL THANKSGIVING–1781

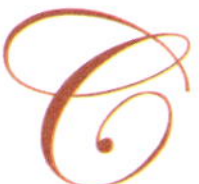ongress issued a proclamation for a day of prayer and thanksgiving after the Battle of Yorktown in 1781. The Continental Congress and the American people showed that a great nation was first and foremost a grateful nation.

"Whereas it hath pleased the Almighty God, the Father of Mercies, remarkably to assist and support the United States of America, in their important struggle for liberty against the long-continued efforts of a powerful nation, it is the duty of all ranks to observe and thankfully acknowledge the interpositions of his Providence on their behalf. Through the whole of the contest, from its first rise to this time, the influence of Divine Providence may be clearly perceived in many signal instances, of which we mention but a few:

—In revealing the councils of our enemies, when the discoveries were seasonable and important and the means seemingly inadequate and fortuitous;

—In preserving and even improving the union of the several states on the breach of which our enemies placed their greatest dependence;

—In increasing the number and adding to the zeal and attachment of the friends of liberty;

—In granting remarkable deliverances, and blessing us with the most signal success, when affairs seemed to have the most discouraging appearance;

—In raising up for us a most powerful and generous ally, in one of the first of the European powers;

—In confounding the councils of our enemies, and suffering them to pursue such measures as have most directly contributed to frustrate their own desires and expectations;

—Above all, in making their extreme cruelty to the inhabitants of these states, when in their power, and their devastation of property, the very means of cementing our union, and adding vigor to every effort against them.

And as we cannot help leading the good people of these states to a retrospect on the events which have taken place since the beginning of the war, so we recommend, in a particular manner, to their observations, the goodness of God in a year now drawing to a conclusion;

—In which the confederation of the United States has been completed;

—In which there have been so many instances of prowess and success in our armies, particularly in the southern states, where, notwithstanding the difficulties with which they had to struggle, they have recovered the whole country which the enemy had overrun, leaving them only a post or two on or near the sea;

—In which we have been so powerfully and effectually assisted by our allies, while in all the conjunct operations the most perfect harmony has subsisted in the allied army;

—In which there has been so plentiful a harvest, and so great abundance of the fruits of the earth of every kind, as not only enables us easily to supply the ones of our army, but give comfort and happiness to the whole people;

—And, in which after the success of our allies by sea, a general of the first rank, with his whole army, has been captured by the allied forces, under the direction of our Commander-in-chief.

It is therefore recommended to the several states to set apart the 13th day of December next, to be religiously observed as a day of THANKSGIVING and PRAYER:

—That all the people may assemble on that day, with grateful hearts to celebrate the praises of our gracious benefactor;

—To confess our manifold sins;

—To offer up our most fervent supplications to the God of all Grace, that it may please him to pardon our offenses, and incline our hearts for the future to keep all his laws;

—To comfort and relieve our brethren who are in distress or captivity;

—To prosper our husbandman, and gives success to all engaged in lawful commerce;

—To impart wisdom and integrity to our counselors, judgment and fortitude to our officers and soldiers;

—To protect and prosper our illustrious ally, and favor our united exertions for the Speedy establishment of a safe, honorable, and lasting peace;

—To bless all seminaries of learning and cause the knowledge of God to cover the Earth, as the waters cover the seas.

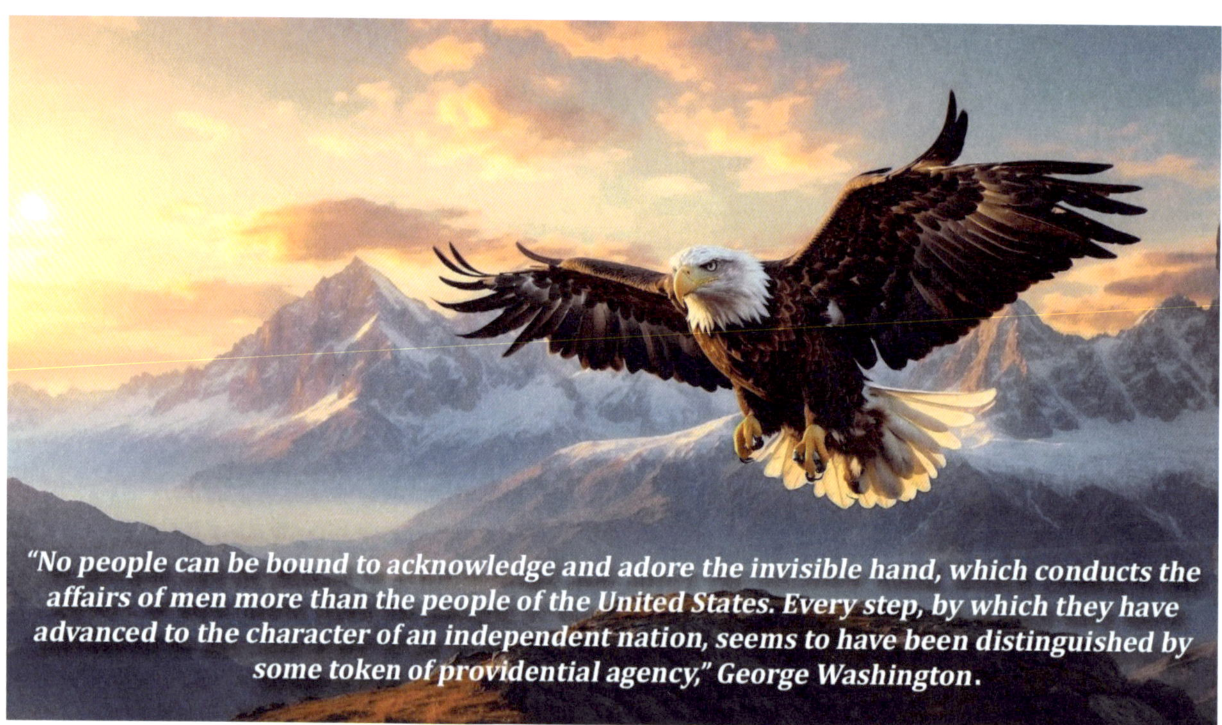

THANKSGIVING PROCLAMATION, OCTOBER 3,1789

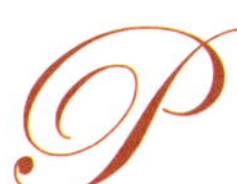

President George Washington issued the first Thanksgiving proclamation under the U.S. Constitution.

Thanksgiving Proclamation, New York, 3 October 1789
By the President of the United States of America, a Proclamation.

Whereas it is the duty of all Nations to acknowledge the providence of Almighty God, to obey his will, to be grateful for his benefits, and humbly to implore his protection and favor—and whereas both Houses of Congress have by their joint Committee requested me "to recommend to the People of the United States a day of public thanksgiving and prayer to be observed by acknowledging with grateful hearts the many signal favors of Almighty God especially by affording them an opportunity peaceably to establish a form of government for their safety and happiness."

Now therefore I do recommend and assign Thursday the 26th day of November next to be devoted by the People of these States to the service of that great and glorious Being, who is the beneficent Author of all the good that was, that is, or that will be—That we may then all unite in rendering unto him our sincere and humble thanks—for his kind care and protection of the People of this Country previous to their becoming a Nation—for the signal and manifold mercies, and the favorable interpositions of his Providence which we experienced in the course and conclusion of the late war—for the great degree of tranquility, union, and plenty, which we have since enjoyed—for the peaceable and rational manner, in which we have been enabled to establish constitutions of government for our safety and happiness, and particularly the national One now lately instituted—for the civil and religious liberty with which we are blessed; and the means we have of acquiring and diffusing useful knowledge; and in general for all the great and various favors which he hath been pleased to confer upon us.

And also that we may then unite in most humbly offering our prayers and supplications to the great Lord and Ruler of Nations and beseech him to pardon our national and other transgressions—to enable us all, whether in public or private stations, to perform our several and relative duties properly and punctually—to render our national government a blessing to all the people, by constantly being a Government of wise, just, and constitutional laws, discreetly and faithfully executed and obeyed—to protect and guide all Sovereigns and Nations (especially such as have shewn kindness unto us) and to bless them with good government, peace, and concord—To promote the knowledge and practice of true religion and virtue, and the increase of science among them and us—and generally to grant unto all Mankind such a degree of temporal prosperity as he alone knows to be best.

Given under my hand at the City of New-York the third day of October in the year of our Lord 1789. Go: Washington

ABOUT THE AUTHOR

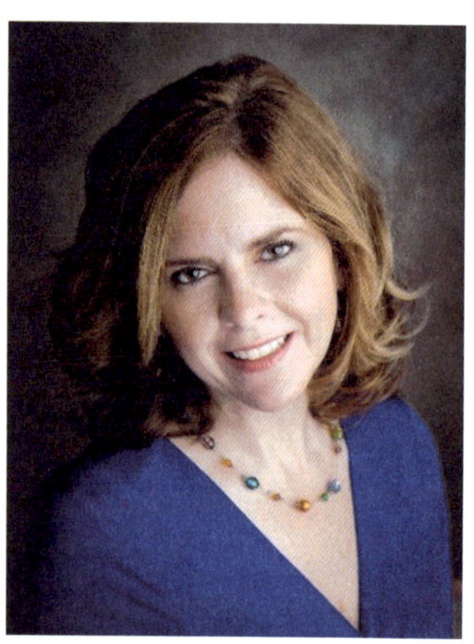

Jane Hampton Cook's passion is igniting patriotism and making American history relevant to modern life, news, current events, politics, and faith. She is an award-winning screenwriter and author of 20 books, including *War of Lies: When George Washington Was the Target and Propaganda Was the Crime* and *Stories of Faith & Courage from the Revolutionary War*. Jane has written books and recorded videos about the American Revolution for America's 250th anniversary. She has written award-winning screenplay adaptations for two of her books. SAVING WASHINGTON placed third in ScreenCraft's 2018 drama screenwriting competition and AMERICAN PHOENIX was a top ten winner in ISA's Emerging Screenwriters contest in 2020.

A national media commentator and former White House webmaster, Jane has been a frequent guest on many networks, such as the Fox News Channel, SKY News, C-SPAN, BBC, WMAL, and many independent outlets. Jane is an on-camera scholar in a 2025 docudrama called THE AMERICAN MIRACLE. She has been a cast member and on-camera storyteller for several documentaries, including an episode about women's voting rights for Fox Nation's WHAT MADE AMERICA GREAT hosted by Brian Kilmeade, and THE FIRST AMERI9CAN about George Washington hosted by Newt and Callista Gingrich.

Jane received a bachelor's degree from Baylor University and a master's degree from Texas A&M University. Jane lives with her husband and their sons in a Washington D.C. suburb, Centreville, Virginia. www.janecook.com.

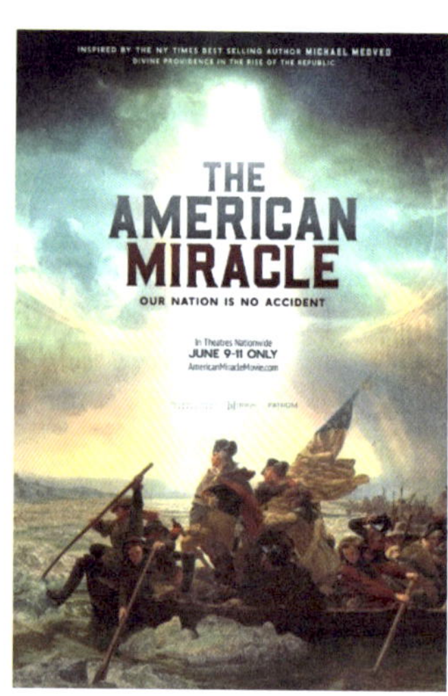

FILMS and DOCUMENTARIES

- THE AMERICAN MIRACLE hosted by Michael Medved
- Fox Nation's WHAT MADE AMERICA GREAT: THE WOMEN'S VOTE hosted by Brian Kilmeade
- THE FIRST AMERICAN Gingrich Productions,
- REDISCOVERING GOD IN AMERICA, II
- OUR SACRED HONOR
- History Channel's UNITED STUFF OF AMERICA
- Award-winning screenplays about John Quincy and Louisa Adams called AMERICAN PHOENIX and James and Dolley Madison called WHITE HOUSE PHOENIX

JANE HAMPTON COOK'S BOOKS

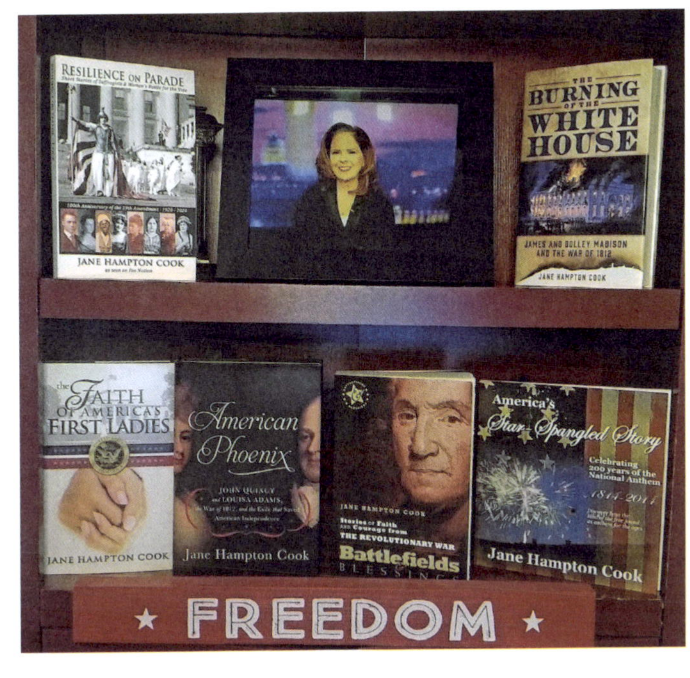

- *The Submarine & the Spies: Friendship & Vigilance in the American Revolution*
- *War of Lies: When George Washington Was the Target & Propaganda Was the Crime*
- *Resilience on Parade: Short Stories of Suffragists & Women's Battle for the Vote*
- *The Burning of the White House: James & Dolley Madison & the War of 1812*
- *American Phoenix: John Quincy & Louisa Adams (War of 1812)*
- *America's Star-Spangled Story*
- *Stories of Faith & Courage from the Revolutionary War*
- *Stories of Faith & Courage from the War in Iraq & Afghanistan*
- *The Faith of America's First Ladies*

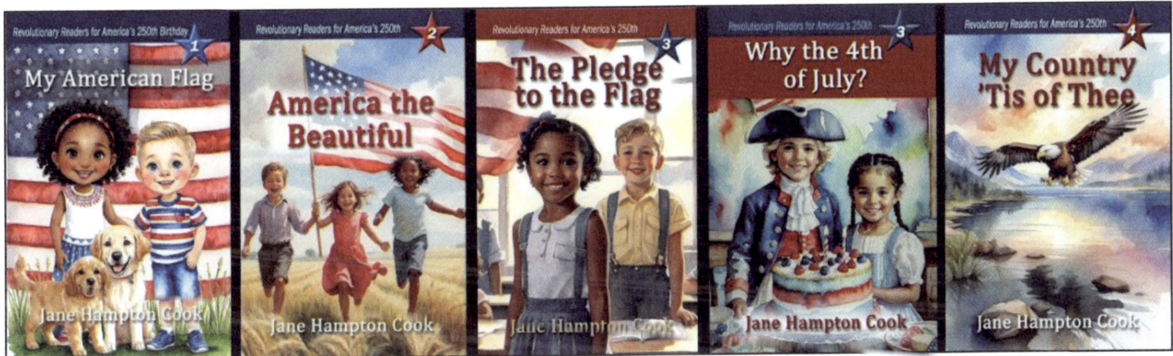

CHILDREN'S BOOKS

- *Revolutionary Readers for America's 250th:*
- *My American Flag*
- *America the Beautiful*
- *The Pledge to the Flag*
- *My Country 'Tis of Thee*
- *What's True about the Red, White, and Blue?*
- *Why the 4th of July?*
- *First Fireworks for Independence: Virginia's Gift to America*
- *What Does the President Look Like?, B is for Baylor, and Maggie Houston*

ENDNOTES

---

[1] Victor Davis Hanson, "The Ungracious and Their Demonization of the Past," January 9, 2022,*News-Herald*, accessed February 10, 2022, https://www.news-herald.com/2022/01/09/hanson-the-ungracious-and-their-demonization-of-the-past/.

[2] President Donald J. Trump, Mount Rushmore, July 3, 2020, accessed January 10, 2022, https://rumble.com/vjpp29-donald-trump-at-mount-rushmore-event-july-3-2020.html.

[3] Richard Pickering, "Seasons of Gratitude," in *The Thanksgiving Edition* of *Plimoth Patuxet Life*, 2021, 28, https://plimoth.org/.

[4] "Trump Honors Victims of Communism at White House ahead of Berlin Wall Anniversary," November 8, 2019, Fox News, accessed February 8, 2022, https://video.foxnews.com/v/6101891462001#sp=show-clips.

[5] Donald Trump, "Trump announces '1776 Commission' to promote 'patriotic education,'" September 17, 2020, accessed January 10, 2022, https://www.fox46.com/news/national-news/trump-announces-1776-commission-to-promote-patriotic-education/.

[6] Donald Trump, First Baptist Church Dallas, December 2021, author transcribed from video.

[7] Andrew Mark Miller, "Thanksgiving canceled? Liberals who say America's holiday promotes genocide and White supremacy," Fox News, November 25, 2021, *FoxNews.com*, https://www.foxnews.com/politics/liberals-slam-thanksgiving-holiday-that-promotes-genocide-white-supremacy.

[8] Richard Pickering, "Seasons of Gratitude."

[9] "Thanksgiving," *Salem Gazette*, November 25, 1813, (Salem, Massachusetts), 3, accessed February 8, 2022, https://www.genealogybank.com/.

[10] Edward Winslow, *Thanksgiving,* Plimoth Patuxet Museums, accessed February 8, 2022, https://www.plimoth.org/learn/just-kids/homework-help/thanksgiving/thanksgiving-history.

[11] *Jewish Messenger*, November 20, 1863, GenealogyBank.com

[12] First Landing https://vachristian.org/appeal-to-heaven-a-re-dedication-of-america-back-to-god/

[13] "First Thanksgiving in America Was Decreed for Town of Berkley on James [River]," *Richmond News Leader*, April 3, 1931, Berkley Plantation, accessed February 8, 2022, http://www.berkeleyplantation.com/first-thanksgiving.html

[14] "Did Florida Host the First Thanksgiving?" *History*, accessed February 8, 2022, https://www.history.com/news/did-florida-host-the-first-thanksgiving.

[15] "Francisco Vasquez de Coronado on the Texas Plains (Atlas Number 5381002048) Historical Marker — Atlas Number 5381002048," Texas Historic Sites Atlas, accessed February 8, 2022, https://atlas.thc.state.tx.us/.

[16] Pedro Reyes Castañeda, *The Journey of Coronado: 1540-1542,* (New York: A.S. Barnes & Company) 1904, 73.

[17] Kate LaPrad with contributions from Nanepashemet, Jim Baker and Richard Pickering, "Seasons of Gratitude," in *The Thanksgiving Edition* of Plimoth Patuxet Life, 2021, 11, https://plimoth.org/.

[18] George Washington, Farewell Address to the Army, November 2, 1783, accessed January 10, 2022, https://founders.archives.gov/documents/Washington/99-01-02-12012.

[19] George Washington to John Augustine Washington, July 18 1755, *Founders Online*, accessed January 10, 2022, https://founders.archives.gov/documents/Washington/02-01-02-0169

[20] Samuel Davies, Footnote from a sermon, August 17, 1755, *Founders Online*, accessed January 10, 2022, https://founders.archives.gov/documents/Washington/03-12-02-0109

[21] George Washington Parke Custis, *Recollections & Private Memoirs of Washington*, (Philadelphia: JW Bradley, 1861) 314-5.

[22] Join or Die, *Pennsylvania Gazette*, May 9, 1754, GenealogyBank.com, accessed January 12, 2022,

[23] Ben Franklin, "Apology for Printers," June 10, 1731, *Founders Online,* accessed January 12, 2022, https://founders.archives.gov/documents/Franklin/01-01-02-0061.

[24] Ben Franklin, Silence Dogood No, 8, *New England Courant*, July 9, 1722, *Founders Online*, accessed January 12, 2022, https://founders.archives.gov/documents/Franklin/01-01-02-0015.

[25] Colonial Society of New England, New England Courant Bibliographical Notes, accessed January 12, 2022, https://www.colonialsociety.org/publications/301/bibliographical-notes-new-england-courant.

[26] Benjamin Franklin, Articles of Belief and Acts of Religion, November 20, 1728, https://founders.archives.gov/documents/Franklin/01-01-02-0032.

[27] The King's Speech on Opening the Session' in 'Hansard' November 18, 1760, col. 942

[28] George Washington, Letter to Francis Dandridge, September 20, 1765, *Founders Online*, accessed January 14, 2022, https://founders.archives.gov/documents/Washington/02-07-02-0250

[29] John Hancock, *John Hancock, His Book, (Boston: Lee and Shepard Publishers, 1898,)* 71.

[30] Samuel Adams, *The Writings of Samuel Adams* Vol. 1, 1764-69, ed, Harry Alonzo Cushing (New York: G.P. Putnam, 1904), accessed January 12, 2022, https://archive.org/details/writitngssamadam01adamrich/page/n5/mode/2up.

[31] John Adams, Diary, December 28, 1765, *Founders Online*, accessed February 2, 2022, https://founders.archives.gov/documents/Adams/01-01-02-0009-0005-0011.

[32]Samuel Ward Proclamation, *Newport Mercury*, November 18, 1765, (Newport, Rhode Island), *Genealogy Bank*, accessed February 4, 1765, https://www.genealogybank.com/.

[33] Isaac Touro, *Newport Mercury*, December 2, 1765.

[34] Abigail Adams, Letter to Mary Smith Cranch, July 15, 1766, *Founders Online,* accessed February 2, 2022, https://founders.archives.gov/documents/Adams/04-01-02-0043.

[35] John Adams, Diary, July 24, 1766, *Founders Online,* accessed February 2, 2022, https://founders.archives.gov/documents/Adams/01-01-02-0010-0006-0002.

[36] From John Adams to François Adriaan Van der Kemp, 30 November 1810, accessed October 30, 2023. https://founders.archives.gov/documents/Adams/99-02-02-5577.

[37] John Adams, First Residence in Boston, 1768, Founders Online, accessed January 10, 2022, https://founders.archives.gov/documents/Adams/01-03-02-0016-0014.

[38] Abram English Brown, *John Hancock: His Book*. Boston: Lee and Shepard Publishers, 1898, p. 141.

[39] Benjamin Franklin to Dennys Deberdt, August 31, 1768, https://founders.archives.gov/documents/Franklin/01-15-02-0112, accessed April 28, 2022,

[40] "On Thursday," *Boston Evening Post*, October 3, 1768, 3, *Genealogy Bank*, accessed January 14, 2022, https://www.genealogybank.com/.

[41] Extract of a Letter from a Gentleman in Boston, to His Friend in This City, Dated March 7, 1770, *The Pennsylvania Chronicle*, Monday, Mar 19, 1770. Philadelphia, PA. https://www.genealogybank.com/nbshare/AC01111014165929282711698629778

[42] John Adams, Draft of a Newspaper Communication, August? 1770, *Founders Online*, accessed January 12, 2022, https://founders.archives.gov/documents/Adams/01-01-02-0014-0005-0005.

[43] *The New-York Gazette*, December 13, 1773 New York, NY, p. 1.

[44] George Washington to Bryan Fairfax, July 20, 1775, *Founders Only,* accessed October 30, 2023, https://founders.archives.gov/documents/Washington/02-10-02-0081.

[45] Thomas Hutchinson, Letter to ——, January 20, 1769, *Founders Online,* accessed January 12, 2022, https://founders.archives.gov/documents/Franklin/01-20-02-0282-0007.

[46] George Washington to Bryan Fairfax, July 20, 1775, Founders Only, accessed October 30, 2023, https://founders.archives.gov/documents/Washington/02-10-02-0081.

[47] Abigail Adams to Edward Dilly, May 22, 1775. Founders online, access April 28, 2024, https://founders.archives.gov/documents/Adams/04-01-02-0135

[48] Abigail Adams, Letter to John Adams, June 18, 1775, *Founders Online,* accessed January 16, 2022, https://founders.archives.gov/documents/Adams/04-01-02-0150.

[49] George Washington, General Orders, November 18, 1775, *Founders Online,* accessed February 12, 2022, https://founders.archives.gov/documents/Washington/03-02-02-0362,

[50] "Poor Tom's a-cold," *Pennsylvania Evening Post*, January 1, 1776 (Philadelphia, PA), *Genealogy Bank*, accessed January 12, 2022, https://www.genealogybank.com/.

[51] *Pennsylvania Evening Post*, January 13, 1776, (Philadelphia, PA), 26, accessed January 13, 2022, *Genealogy Bank*, https://www.genealogybank.com/.

[52] *New England Chronicle*, March 21, 1776, (Cambridge, MA), 4, accessed January 13, 2022, *Genealogy Bank*, https://www.genealogybank.com/.

[53] George Washington, Letter to Joseph Reed, January 31, 1776, *Founders Archives,* accessed January 13, 2022,https://founders.archives.gov/documents/Washington/03-03-02-0163.

[54] George Washington, Letter to Joseph Reed, April 1, 1776, *Founders Archives,* accessed January 13, 2022, https://founders.archives.gov/documents/Washington/03-04-02-0009.

[55] *New England Chronicle*, March 21, 1776, (Cambridge, MA), 4, *Genealogy Bank*, accessed January 13, 2022, https://www.genealogybank.com/nbshare/AC0111101416592928271164125 1395.

[56] George Washington, Letter to Joseph Reed, February 10, 1776, Founders Online, accessed January 13, 2022, https://founders.archives.gov/documents/Washington/03-03-02-0209.

[57] Phillis Wheatley, "On The Death of Mr. Snider Murder'd By Richardson," accessed January 13, 2022, http://www.phillis-wheatley.org/on-the-death-of-mr-snider-murderd-by-richardson/.

[58] Phillis Wheatley, Letter to George Washington, October 26, 1775, *Founders Online*, accessed January 13, 2022, https://founders.archives.gov/documents/Washington/03-02-02-0222-0002.

[59] George Washington to Phillis Wheatley, February 28, 1776, *Founders Online*, accessed January 13, 2022, https://founders.archives.gov/documents/Washington/03-03-02-0281.

[60] Henry Knox, Letter to George Washington, December 17, 1775, *Founders Online*, accessed January 10, 2022, https://founders.archives.gov/documents/Washington/03-02-02-0521-0001.

[61] "Extract of a letter from an officer on board the *Philip and Mary* transport in Boston Harbor dated March 23," *Massachusetts Spy*, August 28, 1776, (Worcester, Massachusetts) 2, *Genealogy Bank,* accessed January 13, 2022, https://www.genealogybank.com/.

[62] Abigail Adams, Letter to John Adams, March 31, 1776, *Founders Online,* accessed January 13, 2022, https://founders.archives.gov/documents/Adams/04-01-02-0241.

[63] Abigail Adams, Letter to John Adams, March 31, 1776, *Founders Online,* accessed January 13, 2022, https://founders.archives.gov/documents/Adams/04-01-02-0241.

[64] John Adams, Letter to James Warren, April 20, 1776, *Founders Online,* accessed January 13, 2022, https://founders.archives.gov/documents/Adams/06-04-02-0048.

[65] Charles Chauncy, "A Letter to a Friend, Containing Remarks Opt Certain Passages in a Sermon Preached by . . . John Lord Bishop of Landaff, Boston, 1767," 44–50 passim in *American History Contemporaries*, ed., Albert Bushnell Hart, (New York: MacMillan Co., 1897), 418–20.

[66] Abigail Adams, Letter to John Adams, November 27, 1775, *Founders Online,* accessed January 13, 2022, https://founders.archives.gov/documents/Adams/04-01-02-0218.

[67] Charles Inglis, *The True Interest of America Impartially Stated, in Certain Strictures on a Pamphlet Intitled Common Sense*, (Philadelphia: James Humphreys, 1776) 32.

[68] John Adams, Letter to Abigail Adams, May 17, 1776, *Founders Online*, accessed January 13, 2022, https://founders.archives.gov/documents/Adams/04-01-02-0266.

[69] Abigail Adams, Letter to John Adams, November 27, 1775, *Founders Online*, accessed January 13, 2022, https://founders.archives.gov/documents/Adams/04-01-02-0218.

[70] John Adams, Letter to Abigail Adams, May 17, 1776.

[71] "Galatians 5:1," (KJV), *Bible Gateway,* accessed January 24, 2022, https://www.biblegateway.com/.

[72] Simeon Howard, *"Election Sermon 1773"* in *American Political Writing During the Founding Era: 1760-1805*, Vol. 1, eds., Charles S. Hyneman and Donald S. Lutz, accessed January 13, 2022, https://oll.libertyfund.org/title/lutz-american-political-writing-during-the-founding-era-1760-1805-vol-1.

[73] John Adams, Letter to Abigail Adams, May 17, 1776.

[74] "In Convention Present 112 Members (in Virginia) Wednesday, May 15, 1776," *The Pennsylvania Ledger*, June 1, 1776, *Genealogy Bank*, accessed January 17, 2022, https://www.genealogybank.com/nbshare/AC0111101416592928271164304 5718.

[75] John Adams, Letter to Abigail Adams, July 3, 1776, *Founders Online*, accessed January 13, 2022, https://founders.archives.gov/documents/Adams/04-02-02-0016.

[76] Abigail Adams to John Adams December 10, 1775, Founders Online, accessed April 28, 2024, https://founders.archives.gov/documents/Adams/04-01-02-0221

[77] John Adams, Letter to Thomas Pickering, August 22, 1822, *Founders Online*, accessed January 13, 2022, https://founders.archives.gov/documents/Adams/99-02-02-7674.

[78] Thomas Jefferson, Letter to Samuel Adams Wells, May 12, 1819, *Founders Online*, accessed January 18, 2022, https://founders.archives.gov/documents/Jefferson/03-14-02-0281.

[79] John Adams, Letter to Thomas Pickering, August 22, 1822, *Founders Online*, accessed January 18, 2022, https://founders.archives.gov/documents/Adams/99-02-02-7674.

[80] Thomas Jefferson, Original Draught of the Declaration of Independence, June 11-July 4, 1776, accessed January 18, 2022, https://founders.archives.gov/documents/Jefferson/01-01-02-0176-0004.

[81] John Adams, Letter to Thomas Pickering, August 22, 1822, Founders Online, accessed January 18, 2022, https://founders.archives.gov/documents/Adams/99-02-02-7674.

[82] Thomas Jefferson, Letter to Samuel Adams Wells, May 12, 1819, *Founders Online*, accessed January 18, 2022, https://founders.archives.gov/documents/Jefferson/03-14-02-0281.

[83] Samuel Adams, "Letter to James Warren, July 16, 1776," in *The Writings of Samuel Adams*, ed. Harry Alonzo Cushing, Vol. 3, *Project Gutenberg,* accessed January 24, 2022, https://ia800308.us.archive.org/19/items/thewritingsofsam02093gut/3sdms10.txt.

[84] John Adams, Letter to Abigail Adams, July 3, 1776, *Founders Online,* January 24, 2022, https://founders.archives.gov/documents/Adams/04-02-02-0016.

[85] George Duffield, "A Sermon Preached on a Day of Thanksgiving," December 11, 1783, January 14, 2022, https://www.consource.org/document/a-sermon-preached-on-a-day-of-thanksgiving-by-george-duffield-1783-12-11/.

[86] Isaac Woodruff, Letter to George Washington, July 3, 1776, *Founders Online*, January 24, 2022, https://founders.archives.gov/documents/Washington/03-05-02-0125.

[87] George Washington, General Orders, July 2, 1776, *Founders Online*, January 24, 2022, https://founders.archives.gov/documents/Washington/03-05-02-0117.

[88] A British Field-Officer, "The Battle of Long Island," in *Revolution, 1753-1783 in America*, Vol. 3, 186-188 *Original Sources*, accessed January 24, 2022, http://www.originalsources.com/Document.aspx?DocID=CZGHT1HF8PXEVC9&H=1.

[89] John Marshall, *The Life of George Washington*, Vol. 2, *Project Gutenberg*, accessed January 14, 2022, https://www.gutenberg.org/files/18592/18592-h/18592-h.htm.

[90] "Copy of a letter to Mrs. ___, Newgate-Street, London, September 14," *Independent Chronicle* September 19, 1776, (Boston, Massachusetts) 2, accessed January 24, 2022, https://www.genealogybank.com/nbshare/AC01111014165929282711643159389.

[91] "Extract of a letter from an officer in New York, August 30," *Providence Gazette,* September 7, 1776, (Providence Rhode Island), 3, accessed January 22, 2022, https://www.genealogybank.com/.

[92] "Copy of a letter to Mrs. ___, Newgate-Street, London, September 14," Independent Chronicle September 19, 1776, (Boston, Massachusetts Vol. 9) 2, https://www.genealogybank.com/.

[93] "Extract of a letter from New York, Friday Morning August 30," *Pennsylvania Journal,* September 4, 1776, 3, https://www.genealogybank.com/.

[94] "Philadelphia, August 31, 1776," *Philadelphia Evening Post*, August 31, 1776, https://www.genealogybank.com/.

[95] William J. Jackman, Jacob H. Patton, and Rossiter Johnson, *History of the American Nation*, 9 vols., (Chicago: K. Gaynor, 1911) 609–31, *Original Sources*, accessed January 27, 2022, http://www.originalsources.com.

[96] Francis S. Drake, *The Life and Correspondence of Henry Knox: Major General in the American Revolutionary Army* (Boston: Samuel G. Drake, 1873), 32-33.

[97] George Washington to Samuel Washington, December 18, 1776, Founders Online, accessed April 28, 2024. https://founders.archives.gov/documents/Washington/03-07-02-0299

[98] George Washington, Letter to John Hancock, December 27, 1776, *Founders Online,* accessed January 30, 2022, https://founders.archives.gov/documents/Washington/03-07-02-0355.

[99] "New Haven," *Connecticut Journal*, January 1, 1777, 2, (New Haven: CT), *Genealogy Bank*, accessed January 22, 2022, https://www.genealogybank.com/nbshare/AC01111014165929282711643399050.

[100] "Affidavit of Reverend George Duffield," *Dunlap's Pennsylvania Packet*, April 29, 1777, 2, *Genealogy Bank,* accessed February 22, 2022, https://www.genealogybank.com/.

[101] John Rabon, "The History of Voting Rights in the United Kingdom," *Anglotopia,* accessed February 5, 2022, https://anglotopia.net/british-history/the-history-of-voting-rights-in-the-united-kingdom/.

[102] John Adams, Letter to James Sullivan, May 26, 1776, note 2 is Sullivan's May 17, 1776 letter to Eldbridge Gerry, *Founders Online,* accessed February 5, 2022, https://founders.archives.gov/documents/Adams/06-04-02-0091.

[103] Abigail Adams, Letter to John Adams, March 31, 1776, *Founders Online,* accessed February 5, 2022, https://founders.archives.gov/documents/Adams/04-01-02-0241.

[104] John Adams, Letter to James Sullivan, May 26, 1776, *Founders Online,* accessed February 5, 2022, https://founders.archives.gov/documents/Adams/06-04-02-0091.

[105] Edmond Pendleton, August 31, 1774, https://www.mountvernon.org/george-washington/martha-washington/timeline/

[106] "In Congress," *Pennsylvania Evening Post*, August 30, 1777, (Philadelphia, PA) 453, *Genealogy Bank*, accessed January 22, 2022, https://www.genealogybank.com/nbshare/AC01111014165929282711643488439

[107] "The First American Flag," *New Hampshire Sentinel*, June 16, 1870, (Keene, NH), 1, *Genealogy Bank*, accessed January 22, 2022, https://www.genealogybank.com/.

[108] "Here's the Real Betsy Ross Story from Great-Great Granddaughter," *Columbus Dispatch* (Columbus, OH), July 4, 1963, 42, *Genealogy Bank*, accessed January 22, 2022, https://www.genealogybank.com/nbshare/AC01111014165929282711643488238.

[109] Gilbert du Motier Lafayette, *Lafayette in the Age of the American Revolution: Selected Letters and Papers, 1776–1790,* Vol. 1, (Ithaca and London: Cornell University Press, 1977), 91.

[110] "The First National Thanksgiving Proclamation 1777," The Continental Congress, Pilgrim Hall Museum, First accessed January 29, 2022, https://pilgrimhall.org/pdf/TG_First_National_Thanksgiving_Proclamation_1777.pdf.

[111] General Washington, General Orders, December 17, 1777, *Founders Online*, accessed January 29, 2022, https://founders.archives.gov/documents/Washington/03-12-02-0566.

[112] General Washington, General Orders, December 17, 1777, *Founders Online*, accessed January 29, 2022, https://founders.archives.gov/documents/Washington/03-12-02-0566.

[113] Alexander Hamilton to John Hancock, September 18, 1777, *Founders Online*, accessed January 30, 2022, https://founders.archives.gov/documents/Hamilton/01-01-02-0282

[114] "Philadelphia: To the Printer," *Royal Pennsylvania Gazette*, May 26, 1778, *Genealogy Bank*, accessed January 30, 2022, https://www.genealogybank.com/.

[115] Elizabeth Drinker, *Extracts from the Journal of Mrs. Henry Drinker, September 25, 1777-July 4, 1778*, in *The Pennsylvania Magazine of History and Biography,* Vol. 13, No. 3 (October, 1889), 298-308, (Philadelphia: University of Pennsylvania Press), accessed January 30, 2022, https://www.jstor.org/stable/20083329.

[116] General Washington, General Orders, December 17, 1777, *Founders Online*, accessed January 30, 2022, https://founders.archives.gov/documents/Washington/03-12-02-0566.

[117] Dr. Albigence Waldo, "Valley Forge, 1777-1778. Diary of Surgeon Albigence Waldo, of the Connecticut Line" in *The Pennsylvania Magazine of History and Biography*, Vol. 21, 291-317.

[118] General Stirling, Letter to George Washington, November 3, 1777, *Founders Online*, accessed January 30, 2022, https://founders.archives.gov/documents/Washington/03-12-02-0098.

[119] George Washington, Letter to Thomas Conway, November 5, 1777, *Founders Online*, accessed January 30, 2022, https://founders.archives.gov/documents/Washington/03-12-02-0118.

[120] Thomas Conway, Letter to George Washington, November 5, 1777*, Founders Online*, accessed January 30, 2022, https://founders.archives.gov/documents/Washington/03-12-02-0119.

[121] Marquis de Lafayette, Letter to George Washington, December 30, 1777, *Founders Online*, accessed January 30, 2022, https://founders.archives.gov/documents/Washington/03-13-02-0063.

[122] George Washington, Letter to Horatio Gates, January 4, 1778, Founders Online, accessed January 30, 2022, https://founders.archives.gov/documents/Washington/03-13-02-0113.

[123] Alexander Hamilton, Letter to George Clinton, February 13, 1778, *Founders Online*, accessed January 30, 2022, https://founders.archives.gov/documents/Hamilton/01-01-02-0365.

[124] "Misinformation," *Dictionary.com*, accessed January 30, 2022, https://www.dictionary.com/browse/misinformation.

[125] "Printer New York, George Washington to his Lady," *Pennsylvania Ledger*, December 24, 1777, 2, *Genealogy Bank*, accessed January 30, 2022, https://www.genealogybank.com/.

[126] George Washington, Letter to Richard Henry Lee, February 15, 1778, *Genealogy Bank*, accessed January 30, 2022, https://founders.archives.gov/documents/Washington/03-13-02-0463.

[127] George Washington, General Orders, March 28, 1778, *Founders Online*, accessed January 30, 2022, https://founders.archives.gov/documents/Washington/03-14-02-0304.

[128] George Washington, General Orders, December 17, 1777, *Founders Online*, accessed January 30, 2022, https://founders.archives.gov/documents/Washington/03-12-02-0566.

[129] Ben Franklin, Letter to David Hartley, February 12, 1778, *Founders Online*, accessed January 30, 2022, https://founders.archives.gov/documents/Franklin/01-25-02-0506.

[130] Richard Henry Lee, Letter to George Washington, May 6, 1778, *Founders Online*, accessed January 22, 2022, https://founders.archives.gov/documents/Washington/03-15-02-0055.

[131] George Washington, Letter to Richard Henry Lee, May 25, 1778, *Founders Online*, accessed January 22, 2022, https://founders.archives.gov/documents/Washington/03-15-02-0220.

[132] George Washington, General Orders, May 5, 1778, *Founders Online,* accessed November 3, 2023, https://founders.archives.gov/documents/Washington/03-15-02-0039

[133] George Washington, Letter to Charles Lee, June 30, 1778, *Founders Online*, accessed January 22, 2022, https://founders.archives.gov/documents/Washington/03-15-02-0652.

[134] Richard Dale, *The Life and Character of John Paul Jones*, ed. J. H. Sherburne in *History in the First Person: Eyewitnesses of Great Events: They Saw It Happen*, ed. Louis Leo Snyder and Richard B. Morris (Harrisburg, PA: Stackpole Co., 1951), *Original Sources*, accessed January 30, 2022, http://www.originalsources.com/Document.aspx?DocID=WIMHDI1Z7IMNMI2&H=1.

[135] John Paul Jones, "A Desperate Sea-Fight (1779)," *American History Told by Contemporaries*, ed. Robert Charles Sands in *American History Told by Contemporaries*, ed. Albert Bushnell Hart (New York: The Macmillan Company, 1902), 587–90. *Original Sources*, accessed January 30, 2022, http://www.originalsources.com/Document.aspx?DocID=T8VVIGZQ4B71NEW&H=1.

[136] George Washington, General Orders, September 26, 1780, *Founders Online,* accessed January 30, 2022, https://founders.archives.gov/documents/Washington/99-01-02-03388.

[137] "Siege of Charleston, 1780," *National Park Service*, accessed January 30, 2022, https://www.nps.gov/articles/siege-of-charleston-1780.htm.

[138] Marquis de Lafayette, Letter to George Washington, August 6, 1781, August 6, 1781, *Founders Online,* accessed January 31, 2022, https://founders.archives.gov/documents/Washington/99-01-02-06609.

[139] Marquis de Lafayette, Letter to George Washington, August 11, 1781, *Founders Online,* accessed January 31, 2022, https://founders.archives.gov/documents/Washington/99-01-02-06661.

[140] George Washington, Letter to the Marquis de Lafayette, August 15, 1781, *Founders Online,* accessed January 31, 2022, https://founders.archives.gov/documents/Washington/99-01-02-06693.

[141] "A Gentleman Just Arrived," *The Royal Gazette,* August 25, 1781, New York, NY, 3, Genealogy Bank, accessed January 22, 2022, https://www.genealogybank.com/nbshare/AC0111101416592928271175650533б

[142] Thomas McKean, Letter to George Washington, October 31, 1781, *Founders Online,* accessed February 1, 2022, https://founders.archives.gov/documents/Washington/99-01-02-07335.

[143] A Proclamation by Congress, Oct. 26, 1781, https://wallbuilders.com/resource/proclamation-thanksgiving-day-1781/, accessed August 29, 2025.

[144] Journal of the Continental Congress, June 20, 1782, accessed February 5, 2022, https://memory.loc.gov/cgi-bin/query/r?ammem/hlaw:@field(DOCID+@lit(jc022113)).

[145] George Washington, Farewell Address to Army, November 2, 1783, *Founders Online,* accessed January 30, 2022, https://founders.archives.gov/documents/Washington/99-01-02-12012.

[146] Abigail Adams, Letter to John Adams, Nov. 27, 1775. Founders Online, accessed February 4, 2022, https://founders.archives.gov/documents/Adams/04-01-02-0218

[147] George Washington, Letter to John Jay, August 15, 1786, *Founders Online,* accessed February 4, 2022, https://founders.archives.gov/documents/Washington/04-04-02-0199.

[148] Alexander Hamilton, Letter to George Washington, October 30, 1783, *Founders Archives*, accessed February 7, 2022, https://founders.archives.gov/documents/Washington/04-05-02-0368.

[149] George Washington, Letter to Alexander Hamilton, November 10, 1787, *Founders Archives*, accessed February 7, 2022, https://founders.archives.gov/documents/Washington/04-05-02-0390.

[150] King George III, "Essay on the Legislative and Executive." [1746-1805] *The Royal Archives,* accessed Feb. 22, 2022, http://gpp.royalcollection.org.uk/

[151] Thomas Jefferson to William Duane, May 23, 1801, *Founders Archives*, accessed April 28, 2024, https://founders.archives.gov/documents/Jefferson/01-34-02-0130

[152] George Washington, Farewell Address, September 19, 1796, *Founders Archives*, accessed April 28, 2024, https://founders.archives.gov/documents/Washington/05-20-02-0440-0002

[153] King George III, "Essay on the Legislative and Executive." [1746-1805] http://gpp.royalcollection.org.uk/

[154] Governor Ronald Reagan, Inaugural Address January 5, 1967, https://www.reaganlibrary.gov/archives/speech/january-5-1967-inaugural-address-public-ceremony

[155] John Adams to Abigail Adams, April 13, 1777, Founders Archives, Accessed April 28, 2024, https://founders.archives.gov/documents/Adams/04-02-02-0158

[156] Museum of the American Revolution, *Virtually Tour the Tomb of the Unknown Revolutionary War Soldier,* May 25, 2020, accessed April 28, 2024, https://www.amrevmuseum.org/learn-and-explore/for-kids-and-families/digital-discovery-carts-tours-and-case-studies/virtually-tour-the-tomb-of-the-unknown-revolutionary-war-soldier

[157] George Washington, Inaugural Address, April 30, 1789, Founders Archives, access April 28, 2024, https://founders.archives.gov/documents/Washington/05-02-02-0130-0003

[158] Brandon Gillespie, "NYT, MSNBC's Mara Gay: 'Disturbing' to see 'dozens of American flags' on trucks in Long Island," June 8, 2021, *Fox News*, accessed February 7, 2022, https://www.foxnews.com/media/msnbc-analyst-disturbing-dozens-american-flags-flown-pickup-trucks-trump-supporters.

[159] "America's Wars," Department of Veterans Affairs, accessed February 7, 2022, https://www.va.gov/opa/publications/factsheets/fs_americas_wars.pdf.

[160] "William Williams," Battle of Fort McHenry, the National Park Service, accessed February 7, 2022, https://www.nps.gov/fomc/learn/historyculture/william-williams.htm.

[161] George Washington, Farewell Address, September 19, 1796, *Founders Archives,* accessed February 7, 2022, https://founders.archives.gov/documents/Washington/05-20-02-0440-0002.

[162] Melania Trump, United Nations Speech, September 9, 2017, CNN, https://www.cnn.com/videos/politics/2017/09/20/melania-trump-entire-united-nations-children-speech-sot.cnn.

[163] John Adams, Diary, Spring 1772, Founders Archives, accessed April 28, 1772, https://founders.archives.gov/documents/Adams/01-02-02-0002-0002-0001

[164] George Washington to Lafayette, April 28-May 1, 1788, *Founders Online*, access April 28, 2024, https://founders.archives.gov/documents/Washington/04-06-02-0211

[165] John Adams, Diary, Spring 1772, Founders Archives, accessed April 28, 1772, https://founders.archives.gov/documents/Adams/01-02-02-0002-0002-0001

[166] George Washington, Farewell Address, September 19, 1796, Founders Archives, accessed April 28, 2024, https://founders.archives.gov/documents/Washington/05-20-02-0440-0002

[167] John Adams, Letter to Hezekiah Niles, February 13, 1818, *Founders Online,* accessed September 7, 2021, https://founders.archives.gov/documents/Adams/99-02-02-6854.

[168] John Adams, Letter to Abigail Adams, September 16, 1774, *Founders Online,* accessed February 7, 2022, https://founders.archives.gov/documents/Adams/04-01-02-0101.

[169] John Adams, Letter to Hezekiah Niles, February 13, 1818, *Founders Online,* accessed September 7, 2022, https://founders.archives.gov/documents/Adams/99-02-02-6854.

[170] George Washington to Benedict Arnold, September 14, 1775. Benjamin Franklin to John Adams, February 3, 1790, Founders Archives, accessed June 22, 2025, https://founders.archives.gov/documents/Washington/03-01-02-0355.

[171] John McWhorter, May 24, 2020 Broadband and Liberty, accessed April 28, 2024, https://broadandliberty.com/2020/05/24/john-mcwhorter-we-cannot-allow-1619-to-dumb-down-america-in-the-name-of-a-crusade

[172] Rev. David Jones, *Defensive War in a Just Cause Sinless*, sermon, Great Valley Baptist Church, Pennsylvania, 20 July 1775. Accessed April 28, 2024, https://americainclass.org/sources/makingrevolution/crisis/crisis.htm

[173] George Washington, General Orders, July 2, 1776, Founders Archives, accessed April 28, 2024, https://founders.archives.gov/documents/Washington/03-05-02-0117

[174] John Adams, Diary, Spring 1772, Founders Archives, accessed April 28, 1772, https://founders.archives.gov/documents/Adams/01-02-02-0002-0002-0001

[175] Wilfred Reilly, "Slavery Does Not Define the Black American Experience," February 13, 2020, https://1776unites.org/essays/wilfred-reilly-2/

[176] Prince Hall, Petition to the Massachusetts Legislature, January 1777, https://constitutioncenter.org/the-constitution/historic-document-library/detail/prince-hall-petition-to-the-massachusetts-legislature

[177] Wilfred Reilly, "Slavery Does Not Define the Black American Experience," February 13, 2020, https://1776unites.org/essays/wilfred-reilly-2/

[178] Wheatley Poetry Advertisement, *Massachusetts Spy*, July 1791, accessed April 28, 2024, GenealogyBank.com

[179] Benjamin Franklin to John Adams, February 3, 1790, Founders Archives, accessed April 28, 2024, https://founders.archives.gov/documents/Adams/06-20-02-0149

[180] Robert Woodson, February 13, 2020, The Crucial Vote of 1776, accessed April 28, 2024, https://teachingamericanhistory.org/document/the-crucial-voice-of-1776/

[181] George Washington to Joh Francis Mercer, 1786, Founders Archives, accessed April 28, 2024, https://founders.archives.gov/documents/Washington/04-04-02-0232

[182] John Adams, Diary, Spring 1772, Founders Archives, accessed April 28, 1772, https://founders.archives.gov/documents/Adams/01-02-02-0002-0002-0001

[183] Ida Harper, *Life & Work Susan B. Anthony*, 1899.

[184] Ida B. Wells-Barnett, "How Enfranchisement Stops Lynching," *Original Rights,* (*NY*), June 1910.

[185] Martin Luther King, Jr. "I Have a Dream," August 1963, The Guardian, Accessed April 24, 2028, https://www.theguardian.com/theguardian/2007/apr/28/greatspeeches.

[186] Jane Austen, *Pride and Prejudice.*